Studies in Biblical Holiness

STUDIES IN BIBLICAL HOLINESS

by

DONALD S. METZ

BEACON HILL PRESS OF KANSAS CITY
Kansas City, Missouri

ISBN 083-410-1173

Printed in the
United States of America

18 17 16 15 14 13 12 11 10 9

Foreword

Here is a scholarly but readable study designed primarily for ministers and teachers who feel the need for more extensive resources to present the message of biblical holiness. While it is the product of scholarly research, the book is written in nontechnical language and is therefore a valuable mine of holiness truth for any student of this distinctive Wesleyan teaching. Teachers in colleges and seminaries may find it an excellent textbook or resource volume on this doctrine.

Dr. Metz's work is the outcome of perhaps the most extensive research on the theology of holiness to be conducted in our time. He visited the major libraries of the nation in order to examine the extant literature on the subject. He also made a careful study of outstanding theological works on sanctification, done from non-Wesleyan perspectives. Underlying all that Dr. Metz has written is a thorough scriptural examination of the idea of perfection, conducted with the aid of the best current biblical scholarship. Furthermore, as a teacher and preacher, the author has had opportunity to test these theses in the college classroom and in ministerial seminars over a period of years.

While it is impossible to gain full agreement concerning some of the areas of holiness doctrine here examined, the thoughtful reader will be seriously challenged to find solid reasons for differing with the author. All Wesleyan thinkers, however, will agree with the main line of the author's presentation and discover in these chapters new and illuminating material. The table of contents reveals the wide scope of subject matter treated.

—William M. Greathouse
President, Nazarene Theological Seminary

Contents

CHAPTER I /

Introduction

A study of an area of theology may resemble a trip through a museum or a climb up a rugged mountain. The examination of a doctrine may be similar to a tour through an ancient battlefield, with particular emphasis on historic monuments, or it may be compared to an adventure of faith. One approach is static and scholastic. The other approach is creative and experiential. In order for a doctrine to become vitalized in life, the second approach must be used.

A creative and experiential approach to the study of the doctrine of holiness is in harmony with the practice of John Wesley, founder of the modern holiness movement. Wesley was a loyal churchman and an uncompromising believer in the Bible. In an itinerant ministry of over 50 years, he made Bible truth vital and vibrant by disclosing its relevancy to life as he found it. Preaching the pessimistic doctrine of innate depravity and the optimistic doctrine of Christian perfection, Wesley made the world his parish. As a result of Wesley's work England experienced a profound social evolution, in contrast to neighboring France, which experienced an agonizing social revolution.

Later followers of the Wesleyan teaching made the doctrine of Christian perfection a worldwide force by an uninhibited and contagious presentation of soul-shattering and life-transforming gospel precepts. To these adherents, holiness was primarily a way of life—an experience which was basic and foundational. But in the final analysis, a church must rely on the content of its message as well as on its enthusiasm. For the message produces a type of experience in harmony with its inherent truth. The message of holiness is as relevant today as it was in Wesley's time, or in the decades after Wesley. However, today the problems of individual life are more complex and the problems of society are more acute. The complex nature of contemporary life makes the task of the Church much more difficult, yet much more significant. One task of the Church is to present the redemptive message to each generation. Thus the primary task of this study is to explore the doctrine of holiness. Since the doctrine of holiness is first and foremost a biblical doctrine, it is presented primarily from the biblical point of view.

I. Outline of Study

The basic principle of biblical interpretation adopted in developing the following exploration of the life and the doctrine of holiness is the concept that the Bible is the History of redemption by a holy God whose primary objective is to introduce His holy being into human life, so that man can be holy. Following this basic principle, holiness is presented as the spiritual principle which most adequately interprets biblical truth.

The discussion begins with the assumption that the only basis for man's holiness is to be found in the holiness of God. Thus man needs a vision of God, of what God is like, before he can understand what he personally should be like. This vision of God is called the necessary "prelude to holiness." With the idea of a holy God presented, the discussion moves to an analysis of sin as the ultimate spiritual antithesis. What the Bible has to say of sin is highly significant, since the Bible is the Revelation of God's effort to redeem man from sin.

The life of holiness is a primary theme of the Old Testament. In order to redeem man, God chose a people as the human instrument of divine redemption. This people became a "covenant people." The covenant of God with the chosen people, the Hebrews, was a covenant of holiness. The covenant people received directly from God a detailed program and a specific pattern of worship. Holiness was the focal point in the worship of the covenant people. This covenant people, the Hebrews, produced a wisdom literature which contains the distilled essence of their practical experience of religion. To the Hebrew mind, holiness, or perfection, or moral excellence, appears as the *summum bonum* of all wisdom.

But the greatest gift of the covenant people to the world, aside from Jesus Christ, was the prophetic order which further spiritualized and made highly ethical the concept of holiness. The prophets made it crystal-clear that God's supreme motive in all covenant relationships was to produce a holy people. However, in the prophets, the emphasis was radically shifted to the individual possibility and responsibility of reflecting God's holiness in personal living. However, this study is largely confined to New Testament teachings about holiness.

In the New Testament, the life and the doctrine of holiness became completely spiritualized and fully ethical. Holiness is thus the foundation of the kingdom of God, which is presented in the Gospels. In the Book of the Acts of the Apostles the experience of the followers of Christ on the Day of Pentecost made holiness the final residue of the spiritual dynamic of the Early Church. If one follows the Pentecostal pattern, then a second crisis is involved in Christian experience.

This second crisis is necessary because of the "carnal mind," which, according to the Bible (I Cor. 3:1-3), persists in the lives of those called Christians. This second crisis also lifts man to the New Testament norm of Christian living—Spirit-filled living and full Christian maturity. From the point of view of the New Testament, the second crisis is followed by a life of growth and service in Christian love.

II. Method of Procedure

In discussing the biblical foundations of holiness the problems related to literary biblical criticism are largely omitted, not because they are unimportant to scholarly investigation, but because they do not impinge directly on the theme involved. The attempt was also made to avoid pedantic points of semantic inferences based on exhaustive word studies which are significant only to the specialist.

In the past, three methods of presentation have been used to discuss holiness from a biblical point of view. One method was to select an array of proof texts, with the aim of persuading the listener on the basis of such texts. Another method involved the meaning of words, tenses, and other uses of grammatical analysis. A third approach involved the use of biblical characters, biblical events, or of personal testimony to exhort and to inspire the hearer to assent to and accept the doctrine of holiness. Since each of these three methods has been effective in the past, some aspects of each method are incorporated in this volume. The attempt is made, however, to explore, to expand, and to interpret the doctrine of holiness in new or fresh areas, based on biblical and historical exploration.

The method of study used here includes two areas of research —the *biblical* and the *theological.* Since the primary purpose of the investigation is to present the biblical basis of holiness, biblical exegesis and exposition naturally tend to dominate the discussion. But all biblical discussion is involved in theology in one way or another, so the theological development of some concepts is added to the biblical revelation. Since historic experience must, to some extent, become intelligible and capable of some degree of rational presentation, the logical element is also introduced on occasion to reinforce biblical and historical ideas.

The reader who is familiar with the terminology of holiness, or the reader who is anxious to bypass technical discussions, may proceed to the next chapter without any great loss. The more technically-minded probably will benefit from the discussion to follow, which is a presentation of definitions of three of the biblical terms which are basic to an understanding of the doctrine of holiness: *holiness, sanctification,* and *perfection.*

III. Defining Our Terms

A sharp comment from a contemporary writer states that "many spiritual writers suffer from the very obvious defect of not being able to define their terms, or of not being willing to do so."[1] The same writer admits, however, that "the higher a soul rises toward the heights of mystical experience in this life, the harder it becomes to describe those experiences in words."[2] But however difficult it may prove to be, the mystical experience eventuating in personal holiness should be explained in theological terms and in exact definitions wherever possible.

Since the life of holiness is the highest experience attainable, or describable, in religion, it follows that the terms used will be difficult to define adequately and satisfactorily to all. The attempt

[1]Jordan Aumann and David L. Greenstock, *The Meaning of Christian Perfection* (St. Louis: B. Herder and Company, 1956), p. 16.

[2]*Ibid.*

will be made, however, to define a few terms which are pivotal in the terminology of holiness. These terms are *holiness, sanctification,* and *perfection.* All three are biblical and essential, and do not conflict with other biblical terminology related to the life of holiness. The definitions given below are preliminary and will be expanded, along with additional terms, in later discussions.

A. Holiness

John Morley, in his essay on Voltaire, remarked that holiness is the "deepest of all words that defy description."[3] Yet "the conception of holiness, in one form or another, is necessarily almost as old as religion itself. As applied to human affairs it indicates a separation from the ordinary and the secular, a thing set apart for the sole use and enjoyment of the deity."[4] Archbishop Soderblom renders a rather extreme statement when he says: "Holiness is the great word of religion; it is even more essential than the notion of God."[5] In attempting to define *holiness,* first some general definitions are presented, followed by a selection of definitions from writers within the Wesleyan, or holiness, groups.

1. *General Definitions of Holiness*

General definitons of holiness tend to be broad and unrelated to any crisis in personal experience. St. Thomas Aquinas defines holiness in an abstract way as "that virtue by which a man's mind applies itself and all its acts to God."[6] Another general definition, which appears to present a rather odd view of holiness, is stated in these words: "Complete holiness . . . designates the state of perfect love, which exhibits itself in this, that every thought of man, every emotion and volition, hence also every deed, is determined by the will of God."[7] *Webster's Third New International Dictionary* defines holiness as "a state of moral and spiritual perfection . . . a state of sinlessness that according to some small religious groups is bestowed

[3]*Voltaire* (London: Macmillan and Co., 1923), p. 242.

[4]W. O. E. Oesterley and Theodore H. Robinson, *Hebrew Religion* (New York: The Macmillan Company, 1930), p. 240.

[5]Nathan Soderblom, "Holiness," *Encyclopedia of Religion and Ethics,* ed. James Hastings (New York: Charles Scribner's Sons, 1928), VI, 731. (Hereafter referred to as *ERE.*)

[6]Hugh Pope, "Holiness," *The Catholic Encyclopedia,* ed. Charles G. Herbermann (New York: The Encyclopedia Press, 1913), VII, 386.

[7]John M'Clintock and James Strong, *Cyclopedia of Biblical, Theological, and Ecclesiastical Literature* (New York: Harper and Brothers, 1880), IV, 297.

as a blessing on a Christian believer following conversion and is often a prerequisite to salvation."

Some writers think that "to define the modern concept of holiness, that is, to give a conventional definition, is next to impossible."[8] Such writers feel that no *one* definition would be entirely adequate and that a better plan would be to present a few general points upon which most Christians of the present age would be in more or less agreement. The following, according to Robert C. Rayle, are seven propositions regarding holiness which most Protestants would accept:

1. The holy life has its origin in a mystical, religious experience.
2. The holy life is an endowment of the Holy Spirit.
3. The holy life comes when one makes a complete surrender to God.
4. The holy life means an assurance that one belongs completely to God.
5. The holy life involves a separation from the world; yet one is not to withdraw from the world. In other words, the holy life is not to compromise with sin.
6. The holy one has assurance that God has given one a complete victory over the sins of one's past life. Whether one remains free from sin for all one's life constitutes a difference of opinion.
7. The sacrifice of Jesus Christ makes this victory possible.[9]

The definitions presented above describe the general notion of holiness. But Wesleyan terminology is much more precise in presenting a concept of holiness that is experiential and balanced.

2. *Wesleyan Definitions of Holiness*

Earlier Wesleyan scholars and contemporary Wesleyan writers agree in their definition of holiness.

a. Earlier Wesleyan writers. Richard Watson defines holiness as "conformity to the will of God, as expressed in His laws, and consists in abstinence from everything which has been comprehended under the general term of *sin,* and in the habit and practice of *righteousness.*"[10] Thomas Cook uses the term *holiness* to describe

> an experience distinct from justification—a sort of supplemental conversion, in which there is eliminated from the soul all the sinful elements which do not belong to it, everything antagonistic

[8]Robert C. Rayle, *Scriptural Holiness* (New York: Comet Press Books, 1958), p. 92.
[9]*Ibid.,* pp. 92-93.
[10]*Theological Institutes* (New York: Phillips and Hunt, 1865), I, 436.

> to the elements of holiness implanted in regeneration. It includes the full cleansing of the soul from inbred sin, so that it becomes pure or free from sinful tendency.[11]

A concise definition is given by J. A. Wood as follows: "Holiness is a state or quality of being essentially pure."[12]

b. Contemporary Wesleyan writers. Wesleyan scholars in the middle years of the twentieth century tend to agree with earlier writers in defining holiness. D. Shelby Corlett states that "holiness as spiritual wholeness means that God through His Spirit dwells in the life that is fully devoted to Him."[13] James B. Chapman defines holiness as "the grace and blessing of a pure heart filled with the love of God."[14] W. T. Purkiser writes that "the core of the meaning both in the Bible and in theology is . . . freeing from sin, purity, cleansing."[15] As it is used currently by most Wesleyan groups, the word *holiness* may be said to refer to a state of personal spiritual life resulting from the baptism with the Holy Spirit, involving freedom from voluntary sin, purity of conscious intention and motivation, the practice of personal Christian ethics, and complete devotement to God.

B. Sanctification

The term *sanctification,* like the term *holiness,* has a wide divergence of interpretation. The term *sanctification* may be defined in general terms as well as in the more specific terms which delineate its meaning in Wesleyan circles.

1. *General Definitions of Sanctification*

In general, the term *sanctification* refers to the total process of becoming and remaining a Christian. A general definition of sanctification has been given as follows: "In its wider sense, the term *sanctification* includes all those effects of God's word produced on the heart and life of man, beginning with his rebirth from spiritual death to spiritual life and culminating in spiritual perfection in life eternal."[16] Another inclusive definition states that "sanctification

[11] *New Testament Holiness* (London: Epworth Press, 1902), pp. 7-8.

[12] John A. Wood, *Mistakes Respecting Christian Holiness* (Chicago: The Christian Witness Company, 1905), p. 16.

[13] *The Meaning of Holiness* (Kansas City: Beacon Hill Press, 1944), p. 34.

[14] *Holiness Triumphant* (Kansas City: Beacon Hill Press, 1966), p. 26.

[15] *Sanctification and Its Synonyms* (Kansas City: Beacon Hill Press, 1961), p. 24.

[16] E. L. Lueker, ed., *Lutheran Cyclopedia* (St. Louis: Concordia Publishing House, 1954), p. 942.

is the work of the Holy Spirit of God, in delivering men from the guilt and power of sin, in consecrating them to the service and love of God, and in imparting to them, initially and progressively, the fruits of Christ's redemption and the graces of a holy life."[17]

2. *Theological Distinctions of Sanctification*

In technical discussions of biblical and theological concepts, the term *sanctification* is used in four different ways to convey four distinct interpretations of the term. From these four usages come the following terms: (1) positional sanctification; (2) initial sanctification; (3) progressive sanctification; (4) entire sanctification.

a. Positional sanctification. Lutheran and Calvinistic thinkers have generally sponsored the idea of positional holiness. The groups known as the Plymouth Brethren and the Keswicks also accept the idea of positional holiness. W. T. Purkiser summarizes this teaching as follows: "There is said to be a holiness which is positional, but not experiential. All redeemed souls . . . are 'saints,' and 'holy' even though they are still being 'sanctified' by the work of the Holy Spirit through the Scriptures and will never be completely sanctified until Christ comes again."[18]

According to Luther, there is no state of grace which is holier than that of the ordinary Christian. A contemporary interpreter of Luther phrases it as follows:

> Because faith receives and accepts the gift of God and thus men become saints through faith, "holy" becomes the equivalent of "believing." The saints, or holy ones, are the believers and "to make holy" means "to be made a believer." In Luther's explanation the emphasis is shifted from sanctity and sanctifying to faith and being brought to faith except that there is no real difference between the two.[19]

Another supporter of the idea of positional sanctification writes that "positional perfection is revealed to be the possession of every Christian. . . . It is, therefore, absolute perfection, which Christ wrought for us on the cross. There is no reference here to the quality of the Christian life. The issue of sinlessness is not in view. All saints (sanctified ones) are partakers of the perfection accomplished

[17] *ERE*, XI, 181.

[18] *Conflicting Concepts of Holiness* (Kansas City: Beacon Hill Press, 1953), p. 16.

[19] Herbert Girgensohn, *Teaching Luther's Catechism*, trans. John W. Doberstein (Philadelphia: Muhlenberg Press, 1959), p. 180.

by the death of Christ."[20] Thus positional perfection is synonymous with positional sanctification, which is "wrought by Christ for every believer, and which is the possession of the believer from the moment of saving faith."[21]

From the positional point of view, sanctification is "the ascription of sanctity to persons by virtue of their relationship to God. It is in this lowest sense that all Christians are said to be holy, or to be saints. The Christian Church is regarded as a separated community, the nature of which is to be holy."[22] There is no objection to the above concept, as long as it is equated with *justification* or regeneration, which denotes a change of status and a change of spiritual relationship. It is thus valid to regard all saints as called to sanctity. For those who are "sanctified in Christ Jesus" (I Cor. 1:2) are called to saintliness.

From the Wesleyan point of view, however, the concept of sanctification includes more than merely objective relationship to God and the beginning of spiritual life. John Wesley called the beginning of spiritual life initial sanctification.

b. Initial sanctification. Replying to a question regarding the time that sanctification begins, Wesley replied: "In the moment we are justified. The seed of every virtue is then sown in the soul. From that time the believer gradually dies to sin, and grows in grace. Yet sin remains in him; yea, the seed of all sin till he is sanctified throughout in spirit, soul, and body."[23] To Wesley, sanctification begins simultaneously with justification. He writes: "And at the same time that we are justified, yea, in that very moment, sanctification begins. In that instant we are born again, born from above, born of the Spirit: there is a *real* as well as a *relative* change. We are inwardly renewed by the power of God."[24] Initial sanctification is synonymous with regeneration. In this sense all truly regenerated people are sanctified.

c. Progressive sanctification. Both Calvinistic and Wesleyan stu-

[20]John F. Walvoord, *Doctrine of the Holy Spirit* (3rd ed.; Findlay, Ohio: Dunham Publishing Co., 1958), p. 208.

[21]*Ibid.*, p. 210.

[22]George Allen Turner, *The More Excellent Way* (Winona Lake, Ind.: Light and Life Press, 1952), p. 87.

[23]John Wesley, *The Works of John Wesley* (Kansas City: Nazarene Publishing House, n.d.), VIII, 285.

[24]*Ibid.*, VI, 45.

dents believe in progressive sanctfication. Dr. Hodge, noted Calvinistic theologian, writes:

> Sanctification in the Westminster Catechism is said to be "the work of God's free grace, whereby we are renewed in the whole man after the image of God, and are enabled more and more to die unto sin and live unto righteousness."[25]

Another writer states:

> Mere regeneration does not sanctify his inclination and disposition; nor is it able of itself to germinate the holy disposition. But it requires the Holy Spirit's *additional* and very *peculiar* act, whereby the *disposition* of the regenerated and converted sinner is brought gradually into harmony with the divine will; and this is the gracious gift of *sanctification.*[26]

The *Shorter Catechism,* as has been stated by Hodge, declares that "sanctification is the work of God's free grace, whereby we are renewed in the whole man after the image of God, and are enabled more and more to die unto sin, and live unto righteousness."[27] Another writes that "sanctification is the growth of the soul toward maturity."[28] And still another observes that "sanctification is thus the perfecting or the progressive cleansing of the soul."[29] To Wesleyan thinkers, initial sanctification or regeneration is the beginning of spiritual life. Growth is normal in Christian living, so there is a progression in this initial state of grace. However, initial sanctification is followed by entire sanctification.

d. Entire sanctification. Wesleyans generally believe in the progressive nature of sanctification, but add the significant idea that such progression leads to *entire* sanctification. Lindstrom offers the following explanation: "This is thought to supervene in a moment, bestowed on man by sanctifying faith. As compared with justification and new birth, complete sanctification constitutes a higher stage in the new life."[30] Wesley makes the point that when the term is used as a synonym for "*cleansed* from all sin," that "it is not prop-

[25]Charles Hodge, *Systematic Theology* (New York: Charles Scribner and Co., 1872), III, 213.

[26]Abraham Kuyper, *The Work of the Holy Spirit,* trans. Henri DeVries (New York: Funk and Wagnalls, 1900), p. 449.

[27]*The Assembly's Shorter Catechism* (Perth, Scotland, 1765), p. 222.

[28]A. A. and J. A. Hodge, *Theology of the Shorter Catechism* (New York: A. C. Armstrong and Co., 1888), p. 62.

[29]Norman W. Cox, ed., *Encyclopedia of Southern Baptists* (Nashville: Broadman Press, 1958), II, 1184.

[30]Harald Lindstrom, *Wesley and Sanctification* (London: The Epworth Press, 1950), pp. 117-18.

er to use it . . . without adding the word 'wholly, entirely,' or the like."[31] Further, Wesley makes the idea of *entire* sanctification the great distinction in the use of the word. A notable passage in Wesley's sermon "Working Out Our Own Salvation" indicates his point of view:

> By justification we are saved from the guilt of sin, and restored to the favour of God; by sanctification we are saved from the power and root of sin, and restored to the image of God. All experience, as well as Scripture, show this salvation to be both instantaneous and gradual. It begins the moment we are justified . . . It gradually increases from that moment . . . till in another instant, the heart is cleansed from all sin, and filled with pure love to God and man.[32]

H. Orton Wiley agrees substantially with Wesley in his interpretation of entire sanctification. Wiley's position is stated as follows:

> Regeneration, as we have seen, is the impartation of a life that is holy in its nature; and concomitant with it, is an initial holiness or cleansing from guilt and acquired depravity. Now this holiness already begun is to be perfected by the cleansing at a single stroke of inbred sin, and brings the soul to a constantly existing state of perfected holiness.[33]

In addition to the terms defined above, there is one additional term which should be clarified before proceeding with the biblical approach to holiness. This third term is the term *perfection.*

C. Perfection

Perhaps no term has brought more reaction and criticism to the holiness movement than the term *perfection.* Only rarely does one hear the term used in preaching today, and even more infrequently does the term appear in personal witness or testimony. Even Wesley himself, in a letter to Dr. William Dodd, in 1756, wrote: "I have no particular fondness for the term. It seldom occurs either in my preaching or writings. It is my opponents who thrust it upon me continually, and ask me what I mean by it."[34] But, as W. E. Sangster observed, Wesley "used it more frequently than he realized."[35] He claims that the reason for Wesley's use of the term

[31] *Works,* VIII, 294.

[32] *Ibid.,* VI, 509.

[33] *Christian Theology* (Kansas City: Beacon Hill Press, 1941), II, 446.

[34] John Telford, ed., *The Letters of the Rev. John Wesley* (London: The Epworth Press, 1931), III, 167.

[35] *The Path to Perfection* (New York: Abingdon-Cokesbury, 1943), p. 78.

is that it "is *scriptural* and Wesley was passionately attached to the language of Scripture."[36] And it must not be forgotten that Wesley summarized his teachings in a pamphlet-sized book entitled *A Plain Account of Christian Perfection.* Wesley's definition of perfection is as yet unimproved and still carries the essence of what is meant by the term in holiness circles. Wesley preferred to use *Christian perfection* rather than the more unqualified term *perfection.* At the end of the *Plain Account,* Wesley summarizes his teachings regarding perfection in these words: "By perfection I mean the humble, gentle, patient love of God, and our neighbour, ruling our tempers, words, and actions."[37] Wesley carefully and persistently qualified his use of perfection so that it would never carry any note of legalistic pride or Pharisaical practice. He wrote:

> There is no such perfection in this life, as implies an entire deliverance, either from ignorance, or mistake, in things not essential to salvation, or from manifold temptations, or from numberless infirmities, wherewith the corruptible body more or less presses down the soul.[38]

The branch of the Christian Church that has accepted the concept of perfection taught by Wesley has been content with his definition of the term. And while the term is not used often, except in theological explanation, the contemporary holiness movement retains the term because it is, as Sangster indicated, a scriptural term.

With this background of definition, we now turn to a discussion of the foundations of all religious ideas and particularly of the idea of holiness—man's view of God. For what man thinks of God is a necessary prelude to an understanding of perfection.

[36]*Ibid.*

[37]"A Plain Account of Christian Perfection," *The Works of John Wesley* (Kansas City: Nazarene Publishing House, n.d.), XI, 446.

[38]*Ibid.*, p. 383.

CHAPTER II /

Prelude to Perfection

The idea of holiness is possible only in relation to the idea of God. Where there is no concept of God there is no concept of holiness. However, the idea of God does not automatically produce the thought of holiness. For there have been many gods in man's march through time, but only rarely does the worship of these gods result in a concept of holiness. It is only when the holy God of biblical revelation invades history and directly confronts man that man is able to conceive of holiness. It is man's vision of God that transforms man, and leads him to the concept and the life of holiness.

I. Importance of Man's View of God

The prelude to perfection is man's vision of God. Man's most important concept is his idea of God. As Arnold Toynbee has so brilliantly written in his classic study of history, no people have ever risen above their religion and no civilization has ever survived the decay of its religion.[1] It can be added that no religion can surpass its concept of God. A. W. Tozer states the importance of a right concept of God in these words: "The history of mankind will probably show that no people has ever risen above its religion, and man's spiritual history will positively demonstrate that no religion has ever been greater than its idea of God."[2] A rich and ennobling view of God produces a rich and creative experience of religion.

[1]Toynbee's monumental study of history is a 10-volume set entitled *A Study of History*, published by Oxford University Press, London, New York, in 1948. A two-volume abridgment of Toynbee's study is D. C. Somervill's *A Study of History*, published by Oxford University Press in 1946.

[2]*The Knowledge of the Holy* (New York: Harper and Brothers, 1961), p. 9.

A. General Significance of a Right View of God

One of the gravest questions which persistently faces the Church is how it conceives of God and how it interprets man's relationship to God. Thus it is true that "the most revealing thing about the church is her idea of God. . . . She cannot escape the self-disclosure of her witness concerning God."[3] A right conception of God is essential to practical Christian living as well as to a meaningful systematic theology. A. W. Tozer adds this significant statement: "I believe there is scarcely an error in doctrine or a failure in applying Christian ethics that cannot be traced finally to imperfect and ignoble thoughts about God."[4] Man tends to become like the God he worships.

B. Holiness and Man's View of God

In regard to the doctrine of holiness it is particularly relevant to present a concept of God that lifts the doctrine and the life of holiness out of the realm of human contrivance. For the doctrine of holiness rests squarely on the existence of a God who is holy and whose highest expression of His divine nature is the impartation of His holiness to man. The perfection required of man is but a reflection of the perfection inherent in God. The holiness possible in man is simply an expression of the greatest thing that may be thought or said about God—His holiness. Thus man's view of God is a necessary prelude to the idea of perfection, or holiness. Only a perfect God can command the respect and gain the reverence of man. Only a holy God can inspire man to pursue holiness. Only a perfect and a holy God can provide for the impartation of His own nature to man. The God who imparts His holy nature to man is revealed as the living, personal God.

II. God as Living and as Personal

The existence of God is never questioned in the Old Testament. The great burden of the Old Testament is the revelation of a God of holiness and righteousness who has invaded history and who has illuminated the minds of men. Edmond Jacob says: "The fact of God is so normal that we have no trace of speculation in the Old Testament about the origin or the evolution of God: whilst neigh-

[3] *Ibid.*
[4] *Ibid.*, p. 10.

bouring religions present a theogony as the first step in the organization of chaos, the God of the Old Testament is there from the beginning."[5] Because the God of the Old Testament is "an experienced power, acting upon and through human life and the natural order . . . it is impossible to confine this God to a verbal definition or an abstract concept."[6] The subject matter which thus concerns the theologian "is simply Israel's own explicit assertions about Jahweh. The theologian must above all deal directly with the evidence, that is, with what Israel herself testified concerning Jahweh."[7]

The New Testament, following the pattern of the Old Testament, proclaims the redemptive revelation of God, with the added concept that Christ is God's ultimate Revelation. In the Old Testament and in the New Testament, the basic description of God is that He is the living, personal God.

A. The Living God

The term "living God" *(elohim, chayeem)* had profound meaning for Israel. "To say of God that he was a living God," says Jacob, "was the elementary and primordial reaction of man in the face of the experience of the power which, imposing itself on the entirety of his being, could only be envisaged as a person, that is, as a living being."[8] The most typical word for identifying the God of the Old Testament is the word "living" (Deut. 5:26; Josh. 3:10; I Sam. 17:26; Ps. 42:2; 84:2; Isa. 37:4; Jer. 10:10). The living God is "the God who acts in history, who performs mighty deeds of deliverance, and who manifests his power among men."[9]

The living God also reveals himself in words, and speaks directly to man. It is contrary to the biblical revelation to introduce an artificial distinction between the words of the Lord and the deeds of the Lord. "Thus saith the Lord" is as much a part of the fiber of Old Testament teachings as the acts of God. The living God was a God of both deeds and words. Both the deeds of God and the words of God are related to holiness in man.

[5]*Theology of the Old Testament,* trans. A. W. Heathcote and Philip J. Allcock (London: Hodder and Stoughton, 1938), pp. 37-38.

[6]Otto Baab, *The Theology of the Old Testament* (New York: Abingdon-Cokesbury Press, 1949), p. 26.

[7]Gerhard Von Rad, *Old Testament Theology,* trans. D. M. G. Stalker (New York: Harper and Brothers, 1962), I, 105.

[8]Jacob, *op. cit.,* p. 38.

[9]Baab, *op. cit.,* p. 24.

B. God Is Personal

The biblical conception of God is always strongly personal. One writer stressed the importance of the idea of the living God as follows: "Any idea of God that makes him anything other than a Person is a radical departure from biblical thought, whatever else may be said about it."[10] To make God less than personal is to remove significance from the entire conception. "While some deists have intimated that a divine-human encounter could occur, the nature of the elements in the encounter, and the fact that such encounters are rare, still leave man with the feeling that, for all practical purposes, 'God is dead.'"[11] The God of the Christian faith is not a metaphysical abstraction, but a God who is personal; who acts, speaks, and becomes involved in man's life.

1. *Metaphysical Concepts Versus Personal Concepts*

All metaphysical concepts of God, from the *Nous* of the Greeks, to the "ground of being" of Paul Tillich, inevitably pervert the biblical idea of God. As Aulén says:

> The metaphysical conceptions of God which have appeared in history may be divided into two representative groups: the deistic, which emphasizes the "transcendental," and the pantheistic, which emphasizes the "immanent" conception of God. . . . In either case, man is simply confronted with the idea of causality, and faith's living conception of God is lost.[12]

When the belief in a living God is lost, religion tends to become impersonal and non-experiential and the life of holiness is ignored.

2. *The God Who Acts*

The trend in recent theology has been to emphasize the "God who acts." Pointing to these divine activities, scholars show that God is living and is personal. Thus Walter Horton writes: "Like Judaism, the parent faith, Christianity sees the vehicle of divine revelation primarily in historical events and personages."[13] Otto J. Baab points to the God who acts, in these words:

> The nature of the God idea itself, as found in the records of

[10]Millar Burrows, *An Outline of Biblical Theology* (Philadelphia: The Westminster Press, 1946), p. 60.

[11]Donald A. Wells, *God, Man, and the Thinker* (New York: Random House, 1962), p. 73.

[12]Gustaf Aulén, *The Faith of the Christian Church*, trans. Eric H. Wahlstrom (Philadelphia: Fortress Press, 1960), p. 132.

[13]*Christian Theology: An Ecumenical Approach* (New York: Harper and Brothers, 1955), p. 46.

Israel, calls for dynamic, functional terms expressing creative power. . . . His life interacts with that of his people. He operates through and in the historical process. In his activity the phenomena of change, growth, destruction, deliverance, defeat, victory, and all other manifestations of life are present.[14]

To G. Ernest Wright, the knowledge of God is found in history. Even Christ and the Church "can be comprehended only in their relation to the purposive activity of the sovereign God."[15] However, God speaks as well as acts.

3. *The God Who Speaks*

It is true that God acts, but God also speaks. To emphasize God's activity in redemptive history and to omit God's direct communication with man is to withhold the complete biblical presentation. Of course, one might include speaking in the activities, but such is not the case with most comtemporary scholars who stress the activity of God. Events are significant, but so are ideas and concepts. And for personal, living beings, the highest type of revelation is not physical event, but personalized concept, and individualized relationship. Further, events of themselves are subject to varied subjective interpretation. Hence the conceptional truth before, or behind, the event must be communicated for two reasons: (1) to understand the ground, the source, or the motivation for the event and thus to explain the meaning of the event; (2) to enable the individual, or the group, to transmit, or to transfer, or to propagate the concept in order to reproduce the event, or its permanent residue, to those not present at the event. Wright acknowledges this aspect of God's activity:

In the Bible every historical event is always interpreted by the historian and the prophet, by those who were present at the time, and by successive generations of religious worshippers in the community of faith. Thus every event had a context of meaning attached to it.[16]

4. *The Personal God and Man*

The "personal" God is depicted in Gen. 3:8, where God came in the eventide to fellowship with Adam and Eve. Later, it was the "voice of God" which caused consternation to the guilty pair. God spoke to Noah, and the communication of this concept was the basis

[14]*Op. cit.,* p. 26.

[15]G. Ernest Wright and Reginald H. Fuller, *The Book of the Acts of God* (London: Gerald Duckworth and Co., 1960), p. 24.

[16]*Ibid.,* p. 19.

of all that followed—the building of the ark, the Flood, etc. God spoke to Moses and a nation was born. God spoke to Samuel and a prophet was called. "Thus saith the Lord" became the springboard of prophetic utterance. Many historic events in the prophetic mind are inextricably linked to the mandate issuing from the word of God.

It is on the basis of a personal God that biblical faith arises. When "the expression a 'personal God' is thus used, without reference to any plurality within the unity of the divine nature, what is really in the minds of those who so use it is, I think, always the possibility of personal relations—of worship, trust, love—between *oneself* and God."[17] Biblical religion thus rests on the acceptance of the existence of a personal God. As William Temple stated: "Religious faith does not consist in supposing that there is a God; it consists in personal trust in God rising to personal fellowship with God."[18] It is this personal fellowship with a personal God that makes the experience of holiness both possible and necessary. The experience of holiness is possible because the living God imparts His own essence and power to man. The experience of holiness is necessary because God cannot permit a sustained and progressive fellowship on any other ground than the ground of holiness. The idea of God as living and as personal culminates in the idea of the Fatherhood of God. The idea of holiness also climaxes in the teaching of the Fatherhood of God.

In relation to man the Fatherhood of God is expressed in a supreme way by His sending the Son to save mankind (John 3:16). George A. Barton expresses the thought of God's Fatherhood as follows:

> The whole work of Jesus is grounded in the Father's nature; he does nothing but what he sees the Father doing. God delights to bestow spiritual life and blessing, and he sent his Son to earth for this very purpose.[19]

The greatest blessing that God the Father can bestow upon the sons of mankind is the blessing of sharing His holy nature. The greatest expression of love and obedience that the sons of men can present

[17]C. C. J. Webb, *God and Personality* (London: George Allen and Unwin, Ltd., 1918), p. 70.

[18]*Basic Convictions* (New York: Harper and Brothers, 1936), p. 7.

[19]*Studies in New Testament Christianity* (Philadelphia: University of Pennsylvania Press, 1928), p. 51.

to the Father is to accept the highest gift God offers to man—holiness.

The God of revelation is thus the true and living God, the God who is a Person. The highest expression of God as living and as personal is found in His Fatherhood. As the Heavenly Father, He meets man to reveal His holy, redeeming love. In order to understand this more clearly it is necessary to study the divine attributes.

III. Holiness Related to the Attributes of God

Scripture is concerned with man's redemption, not with abstract truth. Abstract terms such as omnipresence, omniscience, and omnipotence are foreign to Old Testament terminology and do not exist in the Hebrew language. Instead of abstract terms the Scriptures use descriptive terms of God in action or imperative terms of God's sovereign relation to man. Thus the biblical account begins with God in action: "In the beginning God created the heaven and the earth" (Gen. 1:1). In addition to His activity, God reveals himself by word and by declaration: "Speak unto all the congregation of the children of Israel, and say unto them, Ye shall be holy: for I the Lord your God am holy" (Lev. 19:2).

While the so-called attributes do not appear as such in the Bible, yet the Scriptures do present God as having certain characteristics. It is from the revealed descriptions of God's activities and from His personal self-disclosure that it is possible to arrive at the idea of the attributes of God. All of the attributes of God are related to holiness in both God and man.

A. Preliminary Observations

God's deeds could produce awe and His words could command attention. But when God's essential being is at least partially understood, then it is possible to understand the place of holiness in the redemptive process.

1. *Defining an Attribute*

A contemporary theologian defines the attributes as "those perfections of God which are revealed in Scripture and which are exercised and demonstrated by God in His various works."[20] These divine perfections are not traits, qualities, or characteristics in the

[20]Carl F. H. Henry, ed., *Basic Christian Doctrines* (New York: Holt, Rinehart and Winston, 1962), p. 22.

sense that God *has* them, but are integral aspects of what God *is*. Nor are these divine perfections certain qualities that man ascribes to God in order to understand Him. The attributes are objective and real. The attributes are ways of describing God as He is, according to revelation. Thus God does not *have* the quality of love. God *is* love. When God loves, He is not manifesting a particular quality of His nature. When God loves, He expresses His essential being. When God is said to be holy, His essential being is again revealed.

2. *Knowledge of Attributes Is the Result of Revelation.*

The mystery of God eliminates all knowledge of God except when He makes himself known by revelation. As Emil Brunner points out, God is not an object which man can manipulate by his own reasoning.[21] Except when He chooses to reveal himself, God is a mystery dwelling in the depths of inaccessible light. And even when He reveals himself, "the believer will not even be able to fully understand all that God has revealed concerning his attributes."[22]

But man must state some sweeping and final affirmations about God's essential being or the whole idea of God becomes merely formal or academic and sterile. The modern mind seems unable or unwilling to present or to accept any ultimates about God. This confusion about the nature of God has minimized the influence of the Church. As Carl Henry writes: "The modern inability to speak literally of God's essential being, the contentment with merely relational reflections, or with only symbolical or analogical predications about God-in-himself, augur but further religious decline for the Western world."[23] Certainly the message of holiness must be based on clear-cut biblical revelation.

3. *God's Attributes Related to Holiness*

All of the attributes of God, or the divine perfections, are related to man's holiness in one way or another. However, attention will be given here to those which are most closely related. For the sake of convenience, they will be divided into two groups: (1) the *basic* attributes—those which belong to God alone and cannot be bestowed upon man; (2) the *communicable* attributes—those which may, in part, be bestowed upon man.

[21]*The Christian Doctrine of God,* trans. Olive Wyon (Philadelphia: The Westminster Press, 1950), p. 14.

[22]Henry, *op. cit.,* p. 22.

[23]Carl F. H. Henry, ed., *Christian Faith and Modern Theology* (New York: Channel Press, 1964), p. 92.

B. The Basic Attributes

1. *Self-sufficiency*

The self-sufficiency, independence, or aseity of God means that God has no origin, that He is uncreated, that He depends on nothing. When Moses trembled at the mission assigned to him, he wanted some credentials to present to the people to support the announcement of his leadership. God's answer was: "I AM THAT I AM: and he said, Thus shalt thou say unto the children of Israel, I AM hath sent me unto you" (Exod. 3:14). Brunner interprets the meaning of "I AM" as follows: "The meaning of the Sacred Name is precisely this: I am the Mysterious One and I will remain so: I am that I am. I am the Incomparable, therefore I cannot be defined nor named."[24] God's self-sufficiency signifies not only His independent existence, without beginning or end, but also characterizes His essential essence, including His decrees, His works, His providence in history, and His activity in redemption. As self-sufficient God, He has no needs. As Tozer notes, "God has a *voluntary* relation to everything He has made, but He has no *necessary* relation to anything outside of Himself."[25] God's relation to man thus benefits man, not God. God's greatest gift to man is holiness.

From the standpoint of God's self-sufficiency, or complete independence, the life of holiness is God's greatest offer to man as well as man's nearest approach to God. It has pleased the holy God to share His nature with man. When sinful man can erase his own sinful, personal "I am" to bow before the incomparable I AM of revelation, then man realizes his destiny. For God is not "worshipped with men's hands, as though he needed any thing, seeing he giveth to all life, and breath, and all things" (Acts 17:25). God works "all things after the counsel of his will" (Eph. 1:11), and "the counsel of the Lord standeth for ever" (Ps. 33:11). Man's holiness cannot add to God's stature, but God's holiness can help man to measure up to the stature of Christ.

2. *Eternality*

Scripture often refers to the "eternal God." The Psalmist paid his tribute by singing: "Before the mountains were brought forth, or ever thou hadst formed the earth and the world, even from ever-

[24] *Op. cit.*, p. 120.
[25] *Op. cit.*, p. 39.

lasting to everlasting, thou art God" (Ps. 90:2). When Abraham planted a grove in Beersheba, he called "on the name of the Lord, the everlasting God" (Gen. 21:33). Isaiah had a lofty concept of a God, "that inhabiteth eternity, whose name is Holy" (Isa. 57:15). Paul paid tribute to the "King eternal" (I Tim. 1:17). Peter expressed the idea of God's transcendence over time by writing that "one day is with the Lord as a thousand years, and a thousand years as one day" (II Pet. 3:8). John the Revelator showed that time dwells in God, but God dwells in eternity by describing God as "Alpha and Omega" (Rev. 1:8).

God's design in redemption is to make man a partaker of His eternality. Thus God's love is extended to man so that man might believe and "have everlasting life" (John 3:16). The end result of God's mercy and love should be personal holiness in man. For if man is to take up his residence in an eternal abode, holiness is the one supreme requirement for receiving as well as sustaining eternal life. A holy God could permit man to be a partaker of everlasting life only if man became holy. Otherwise God would bring about a situation in which unholy beings would share the eternal essence of God himself. This would be a contradiction and an absurdity. Only the holy can enter into God's eternal day.

3. *Immutability*

A perfect being cannot increase or decrease in any respect. Thus immutability refers to the unchanging nature of God. God does not change in regard to His being, in relation to His decrees, nor in respect to His works. In speaking to Malachi, God said: "For I am the Lord, I change not" (Mal. 3:6). The writer of the Hebrew letter states that, in order to offer consolation to His people, God was "willing more abundantly to shew unto the heirs of promise the immutability of his counsel" (Heb. 6:17). James describes God as "the Father of lights, with whom is no variableness, neither shadow of turning" (Jas. 1:17).

God can never be more or less holy than He is now. God can never be more or less just than He always has been. God's love will not increase or diminish. God does not change in His love of righteousness and His hatred of sin. God remains the same in His insistence on holiness in man, and the call is still, "Be ye holy; for I am holy" (Lev. 19:2; I Pet. 1:16).

Man has a legitimate duty to make the biblical message of redemption relevant to the contemporary mind. But man usurps the truth when he modifies his concept of God in any way which changes His essential being. To mold God to conform to changing values is to make God in man's image. Since God is unchanging, His requirement of personal holiness is also unchanged. The call to holiness is as basic to spiritual life today as it was at Sinai or in the pages of the New Testament.

4. *Omnipresence*

When God is stated to be superior to space, or transcendent over space, or unlimited by space, this perfection is called *immensity*. When God is said to be present everywhere in creation, this perfection is named *omnipresence*. In describing God as present everywhere the Psalmist wrote:

> *If I ascend up into heaven, thou art there:*
> *If I make my bed in hell, behold, thou art there.*
> *If I take the wings of the morning, and dwell*
> *in the uttermost parts of the sea;*
> *Even there shall thy hand lead me,*
> *and thy right hand shall hold me* (Ps. 139:8-10).

Jeremiah also declares the presence of God everywhere, when he speaks for God: "Can any hide himself in secret places that I shall not see him? saith the Lord. Do not I fill heaven and earth? saith the Lord" (Jer. 23:24). John's Gospel also teaches the universal presence of God, for God is spirit (John 4:24).

Because God as spirit is present everywhere, His power and love are also present everywhere. No man is too remote, no sin is too strong to be out of the boundaries of God's presence and power. Thus the life of holiness is possible anywhere because God is everywhere. Since God's presence knows no limits, holiness is as universal as the presence of God.

5. *Omnipotence*

Some contemporary scholars, such as Emil Brunner, reject the term "omnipotence" as an intrusion of Greek philosophy into biblical thought.[26] Brunner prefers to use the term "almighty" instead of "omnipotent." But, for all practical purposes, the distinction he makes is forced, and few would disagree with his idea of Almighty:

> God is Free and Sovereign Lord, whose power cannot be limited by anything or anyone. In His unrestricted freedom He created the All, over which He, because He is its Creator, has com-

[26] *Op. cit.*, p. 248.

> plete authority. . . . The fact that God is absolute Lord over His own creation is an integral part of His nature, as the Living God.[27]

God as almighty is thus free to deal with the universe He has created when and how He wills. This means that "no difference exists between what God *wills* and what He can *do*, that His will already contains its realization."[28]

Isaiah associates the power of God with creation when he writes, "Lift up your eyes on high, and behold who has created these things, that bringeth out their hosts by number: he calleth them all by names by the greatness of his might, for tnat he is strong in power" (Isa. 40:26). The Psalmist said: "Power belongeth unto God" (Ps. 62:11). Jesus said: "All power is given unto me in heaven and in earth" (Matt. 28:18). Paul declares that nature itself gives evidence of the eternal power of the Godhead (Rom. 1:20). God's power indicates His sovereignty. "He doeth according to his will . . . and none can stay his hand" (Dan. 4:35). Tozer points out that the word *Almighty* "occurs fifty-six times in our English Bible and is never used of anyone but God. He alone is *Almighty*."[29]

In relation to holiness, God's sovereign power means two things: first, that He is free to require holiness of man, since man is a created being and God can deal with man in harmony with His own holy nature; second, that God's power would be sufficient to impart adequate power to man to live the life of holiness. If God's power could not overcome sin, then God would not be almighty. In this sense, the life of holiness is the greatest testimony possible to the creating and redeeming power of God.

6. *Omniscience*

God's perfect knowledge is called omniscience. God knows all that is knowable. God knows himself comprehensively and absolutely. "The things of God knoweth no man, but the Spirit of God" (I Cor. 2:11). Only the Infinite can fully understand and know the Infinite. In addition, God knows all that exists outside of himself. God not only knows all that is knowable up to the present, but also knows all that is possible potentially. The Creator has perfect knowledge of all creation and of every creature. The Psalmist was aware of God's perfect knowledge: "Thou knowest my

[27] *Ibid.*, p. 250.
[28] *Ibid.*, p. 253.
[29] *Op. cit.*, p. 71.

downsitting and mine uprising, thou understandest my thought afar off" (Ps. 139:2). And the Psalmist was aware that nothing could be hidden from God:

> *If I say, Surely the darkness shall cover me;*
> *Even the night shall be light about me.*
> *Yea, the darkness hideth not from thee; but the night shineth as the day: the darkness and the light are both alike to thee* (Ps. 139:11-12).

John said: "God is light, and in him is no darkness at all" (I John 1:5). Even the Word of God is "a discerner of the thoughts and intents of the heart" (Heb. 4:12). Perhaps the most significant statement regarding God's knowledge is found in these words: "Neither is there any creature that is not manifest in his sight: but all things are naked and opened unto the eyes of him with whom we have to do" (Heb. 4:13).

If God's knowledge is perfect, then several ideas follow. First, it follows that God knows man better than man knows himself. The finite cannot understand the Infinite, but the Infinite can comprehend the finite. Thus every weakness, every bit of subterfuge, every shred of self-seeking, every act of pride, every impulse to evil, are known to God. Second, man's only hope in the face of such awful knowledge is the love, mercy, and grace of God. Third, if God knows man so thoroughly and indicates that man should be holy, then holiness must be a possibility. To regard God as omniscient and to state that God expects the impossible of man is a contradiction. So when the biblical revelation presents God as perfect in knowledge and also presents man as a candidate for personal holiness, the only possible response is to accept the life of holiness as God's will.

Summary

Man's concept of God is supremely important. Man's relationship to God is both the source and the outcome of his view of God. Further, man's idea of himself is largely dependent upon his concept of God.

The Bible presents God as living and as personal.

Man's understanding of God is expressed technically by a discussion of His attributes. Some of these attributes are basic—that is, they are perfections of God that cannot be transferred to any other personality. Other attributes of God are communicable—they may be imparted to man when certain conditions are met.

CHAPTER III /

The Holiness of God

A student of the Hebrew religious background writes that "the most frequent name for God in the Rabbinic literature is 'The Holy One.'"[1] Old Testament writers, such as Isaiah, also called God "The Holy One." Aulén states that "holiness is the foundation on which the whole conception of God rests."[2] He continues:

> In addition, it gives specific tone to each of the various elements in the idea of God and makes them part of a fuller conception of *God*. Every statement about God, whether in reference to his love, power, righteousness . . . ceases to be affirmation about God when it is not projected against the background of his holiness.[3]

The significance of the term *holy* as a description of God's nature is indicated by "the fact that it has been found possible to characterize the whole religion of the Old Testament as a 'religion of holiness.'"[4]

In the introduction, a definition of holiness was given. But as it relates to God, the term *holiness* needs a more comprehensive analysis. According to A. B. Davidson, "in modern usage the term 'holy' has drifted away from its proper sense and lost its original comprehensive meaning."[5] Although the original content of the

[1]Solomon Schechter, *Some Aspects of Rabbinic Theology* (New York: The Macmillan Co., 1910), p. 199.

[2]*Op. cit.*, p. 103.

[3]*Ibid.*

[4]Walter Eichrodt, *Theology of the Old Testament*, trans. J. A. Baker (Philadelphia: Westminster Press, 1961), I, 270.

[5]*Ezekiel* (Cambridge University Press, 1892), p. xli.

idea "is not now recoverable,"[6] attempts have been made to explain the origin and the meaning of the term *holy.* Two of the most prominent explanations of the significance of the term are the evolutionary or naturalistic and the mystical. Holiness groups generally reject both the naturalistic and the mystical approaches, preferring an explanation based on biblical revelation.

I. The Evolutionary Concept of Holiness

Some scholars, applying the scientific assumption of biological evolution to the development of religion, have associated the concept of holiness with the idea of tabu, or taboo, or with primitive expressions of religion. W. Robertson Smith asserts that "holiness is essentially a restriction on the license of man in the free use of natural things."[7] He suggests that because primitive people generally adopt a system of restrictions on man's arbitrary use of natural things which involves a dread of supernatural penalties, the idea of holiness is associated with the idea of taboo. Smith continues:

> The fact that all the Semites have rules of uncleanness as well as rules of holiness, that the boundary between the two is often vague, and that the former as well as the latter present the most startling agreement in point of detail with savage taboos, leaves no reasonable doubt as to the origin and ultimate relations of the idea of holiness.[8]

The naturalistic interpretation of holiness is also presented by J. G. Frazer. In contrasting the idea of holiness in more advanced groups with the concept of holiness in primitive groups, Frazer concludes that "the savage makes no such moral distinction between them, the conception of holiness and pollution are not yet differentiated in his mind."[9]

From the biblical point of view this attempt to explain the origin of holiness is unacceptable, for it completely ignores the concept of God's redemptive revelation. Also, it is as plausible to explain the idea of taboo as a regression from original holiness as it is to accept it as a development toward an ethical concept of holiness.

[6] *Ibid.*

[7] *Religion of the Semites* (London: Adamond Charles Black, 1907), p. 150.

[8] *Ibid.*, p. 153.

[9] *The Golden Bough* (New York: St. Martin's Press, 1966 [reprint]), II, 224.

II. The Mystical Interpretation of Holiness

Rudolph Otto has popularized the mystical interpretation of the idea of holiness. He writes that "'holiness'—'the holy'—is a category of interpretation and valuation peculiar to the sphere of religion."[10] According to him, all religion has a clear "overplus" of meaning. This "overplus," this unanswered "Something," this "wholly other" is universal in religion. Otto writes:

> There is no religion in which it does not live as the real innermost core, and without it no religion would be worthy of the name. It is pre-eminently a living force in the Semitic religions, and of these again in none has it such vigour as in that of the Bible. Here, too, it has a name of its own, viz. the Hebrew *qādôsh,* to which the Greek *hagios* and the Latin *sanctus,* and more accurately still, *sacer* are corresponding terms.[11]

Otto attempts to recapture the "overplus" in the original meaning of *holy* by coining a new word from the Latin, *numen—numinous.*[12] C. Ryder Smith points out that three other terms are used by Otto to analyze the "numinous."[13] The first term is *mysterium,* which means a sense of the unknown. With the sense of the unknown there went a creature-feeling, a sense of helplessness and of fear. The *mysterium* was a *mysterium tremendum.* While there was fear, there was also an eerie fascination as well, if only *as a snake fascinates a bird.* The mysterium was thus *fascionoscum* as well as *tremendum.* Here lies the paradox of the word *holy.* Though God is separate and awesome, yet man desires some kind of relationship to God.

Otto's idea of "the holy" gained wide acceptance in theological thought. Typical of the influence of Otto's idea is the following statement: "Basically, 'the holy' and the 'numinous' are identical. In Hebrew thought the notion has assumed a uniquely dominant place, identifying the numinous with the personal God."[14] Another writer praised Otto in these words: "Otto's *Idea of the Holy* as definitely as Barth's *Commentary on Romans* provided a reorientation of life upon a distinctly religious basis, emphasizing a 'dimension of

[10] *The Idea of the Holy,* trans. John W. Harvey (New York: Oxford University Press, 1958), p. 5.

[11] *Ibid.,* p. 6.

[12] *Ibid.,* p. 7.

[13] *Bible Doctrine of Man* (London: Epworth Press, 1954), p. 38.

[14] Melancthon W. Jacobus, *A New Standard Bible Dictionary* (New York: Funk and Wagnalls Co., 1936), p. 356.

depth' in experience which 'liberal' Protestant theology had too largely lost from view."[15]

Holiness theology may express serious reservations to Otto's attempt to explain the origin of the idea of holiness. The God of the Bible, the great "I AM," is radically different from the "wholly other" of Otto. The God of the Bible is a living, personal Being who enters into covenant relationship with man. Otto's *numinous* appears to be more in harmony with Oriental mysticism than with the personal God of biblical revelation. Oriental mysticism presents God as an impersonal, transcendent being who is hidden from man. Biblical revelation presents God as personally involved in man's history. Others have also expressed criticisms of Otto's position.[16]

III. The Biblical Revelation of Holiness

Wesleyan scholars prefer to use biblical terminology and biblical experience in discussing the meaning of the term "holiness." According to James B. Chapman, this interest in Bible terminology for holiness serves a twofold purpose. In the first place it is important to know what terms men of the past used in expressing the truths they held and propagated. Chapman writes:

> We want to know these words both for the assurance such knowledge will give us that their users did indeed hold the views we have heard they held, and then we want to know that we may include them in our own list of words for the sake of variety and fullness.[17]

In the second place, a meaningful terminology serves a practical purpose, for "we want to tell others of the treasure we have found in language that is both accurate and adequate."[18]

[15]Robert F. Davidson, *Rudolf Otto's Interpretation of Religion* (Princeton, N.J.: Princeton University Press, 1947), p. 2.

[16]Some doubt is reflected on Otto's ideas by psychologists. L. W. Grensted writes: "This interpretation of the holy has had a considerable influence, but by its very nature remains a conjecture, incapable of clear statement or proof . . . All that really emerges from Otto's discussion is that religion is concerned with the Other and that Other is greater than ourselves" (L. W. Grensted, *The Psychology of Religion*, New York: Oxford University Press, 1912, p. 158).

Another psychologist, while finding Otto's theory appealing, is not certain that it is psychologically acceptable, for his theory is "almost wholly intuitive; since to establish his hypothesis of the numinous, he must postulate a kind of sixth sense which enables man to come into contact with the divine" (Walter H. Clark, *The Psychology of Religion*, New York: The Macmillan Co., 1958, p. 59).

[17]James B. Chapman, *The Terminology of Holiness* (Kansas City: Beacon Hill Press, 1947), p. 16.

[18]*Ibid.*

A. Old Testament Meaning of Holiness

An understanding of the term *holiness* is gained from a study of the meaning of the term in the biblical text. One of the largest family of words in the Old Testament is the word *kodesh* and its cognates, which appear more than 830 times.[19] These terms suggest several meanings of the basic term. In the term *kodesh (qadosh)* there is the attempt to express both ontological and moral transcendence. Three meanings are embedded in the term *qadosh*, which primarily denotes "set aside," "separate."[20] First, it means separate or unapproachable because of danger, as in the case of Mount Sinai (Exod. 19:12) or the ark (I Sam. 6:20). Second, the term means to set aside for moral excellence and divine worship, as in Exod. 19:6. Third, *qadosh* means unapproachable, because of ontological and ethical excellence.

Israel's God was never an abstraction, not an aloof and unknown God. The God of Israel was interested in man, and He revealed himself to man. "For the self-manifestation of divinity, we have the Biblical term *kabod*."[21] A study of the term indicates other meanings in addition to separateness. Among the significant meanings of *kabod* are

> the ethical nature of God; his self-manifestation in history; radiance, a variety of physical phenomena accompanying a theophany, such as fire and cloud; his self-revelation in the beauty and harmony of the cosmos: "the heavens declare the glory of God and the earth showeth his handiwork."[22]

From the above discussion it appears that three ideas are derived from the word *kodesh* and its cognates, so that it means brilliance, separation, or moral purity.

1. *Holiness as Brilliance*

According to its usage, one meaning of the word holiness *(kodesh)* is "to break forth with splendor."[23] The adjective *kuddusa* (in Accadian) is used in parallelism with *ellu* and *ebbu*, and consequently seems to mean "bright, shining, pure."[24] Brightness seems to have

[19]Turner, *op. cit.*, pp. 21-22.

[20]Israel Efros, "Holiness and Glory in the Bible," *Jewish Quarterly Review*, XLI, 364.

[21]*Ibid.*, p. 366.

[22]*Ibid.*, pp. 367-68.

[23]Helmer Ringgren, "The Prophetical Concept of Holiness," *Uppsala Ludequistska Bokhanjeln* (Leipzig: Otto Harrassowitz, 1948), II, 6.

[24]*Ibid.*

been a constitutive idea in the Accadian conception of holiness as well as an integral aspect of the Hebrew concept of the term.

The idea of brilliance is indicated in Lev. 10:3 and in Exod. 29: 43, where it is stated that God will meet with the children of Israel at the door of the Tabernacle, and "it shall be sanctified by my glory." In the lofty vision of Isaiah (6:3) the description reads: "Holy, holy, holy, is the Lord of hosts; the whole earth is filled with his glory" (holiness). "The word *holiness* is used to describe the brilliance of the presence of the Lord seventeen times in Ezekiel, who represents the divine glory as a physical phenomenon, a bright and fiery presence."[25] Another outstanding example of holiness as brilliance is found in Exod. 15:11, which reads: "Who is like thee, glorious in holiness?" In these instances the Hebrew word *kabod,* a synonym for *kodesh,* is used. Both appear to convey the meaning of holiness as brilliance.

In all the cases cited above, the content of the word *holiness* is clear. It is thus not adequate to say that the word stands only for a relationship, nor even to say that it stands for the separation between God and man. One scholar summarized the meaning of *holiness* as follows: "It comes also to stand for the positive activity and resplendent presence of that Personal Other, whom the Hebrews recognized as Jehovah."[26] He shines forth positively and radiantly as shown at flaming Sinai (Exod. 19:18). Even after Moses descended to his people, he reflected from his presence sufficient divine brilliance to bedazzle the eyes of those who looked at him. The Psalmist writes that the mighty God, even the Lord, "hath shined" out of Zion (Ps. 50:2). The prophet Isaiah describes the power of God by saying, "The light of Israel shall be for a fire, and his Holy One for a flame" (Isa. 10:17). In a like manner, at the dedication of Solomon's Temple "the cloud filled the house of the Lord, so that the priests could not stand to minister because of the cloud: for the glory of the Lord filled the house of the Lord" (I Kings 8:10-11). The memory of this experience and the development of a figure of speech to describe it is indicated in the Shekinah of later Jewish tradition. One meaning of the word *kodesh,* "holiness," is brilliance, or radiance, which frequently represents the unique nature and the awesome presence of God.

[25] *Ibid.*

[26] Norman Snaith, *The Distinctive Ideas of the Old Testament* (London: The Epworth Press, 1950), p. 49.

2. *Holiness as Separation*

Perhaps the most commonly held view among scholars is that *kodesh* originally carried the meaning of "separation," or "cutting off." In this sense the ark was set aside, or separated, as a sacred object to which holiness had been imparted because of its use in the worship of God. This quality of holiness had tragic and dreadful potency in incidents of accidental and unallowed contact with it. The well-known incident of the death of Uzzah, who stretched out his hand to steady the ark as it was being hauled by oxen to Jerusalem, is an example of the sacredness of that which is set apart for divine use. When applied to things, *holiness* as a term is "never used in the general sense of separate, or lying apart; it always signifies separated for deity, or belonging to the sphere of deity."[27]

The term *kodesh* (holiness) was also applied to the people of Israel in the sense of separation. When holiness is ascribed to the covenant people and to covenant ordinances, it implies two things: first, being taken out of the world; second, being appropriated by God. Whenever this character of holiness pertains to a person or object, it never rests on a natural quality. The idea of natural purity and impurity does not coincide with that of holiness. "The holiness of the creature always goes back to an act of the divine will."[28] It is always a state in which the creature is regarded as holy because of his relationship with God. Examples of holiness as separation are abundant, especially in the Old Testament. Moses was instructed to inaugurate Aaron and his sons as priests with the command: ". . . and shalt anoint them, and consecrate them, and sanctify them, that they may minister unto me in the priest's office" (Exod. 28:41). When the Passover was first observed in Egypt, God commanded Moses to separate the firstborn: "Sanctify unto me all the firstborn . . . among the children of Israel, both of man and of beast; it is mine" (Exod. 13:2).

Where *kodesh* (holiness) is a designation of a divine attribute, it carries a negative element, by which it designates a state of apartness, or separation, of God raising himself above others. So the Lord, as the Holy One, stands apart and in opposition to other, imaginary

[27] A. B. Davidson, *The Theology of the Old Testament* (New York: Charles Scribner's Sons, 1928), p. 152.

[28] Gustav Oehler, *Theology of the Old Testament* (rev. ed.; Grand Rapids, Mich.: Zondervan Publishing House, n.d.), p. 106.

gods, as stated in Exod. 15:11: "Who is like unto thee . . . among the gods? who is like thee, glorious in holiness?" The complete separation of God also stands in contrast to all that is unholy or secular or to all that is not He himself. This divine elevation is aptly described by Isaiah in these words: "To whom then will ye liken me, or shall I be equal? saith the Holy One" (Isa. 40:25). Accordingly this divine elevation is God's absolute uniqueness, for "there is none holy as the Lord: for there is none beside thee" (I Sam. 2:2). The positive expression for God's absolute elevation and transcendence would be that, in His transcendence over the world, and in His apartness from the creature, "God is He who ever preserves His own proper character, maintaining Himself in that being which is distinct from everything created."[29] Baab says that "the basic idea of holiness never changes in Hebrew thought. . . . The idea always suggests transcendence, divine power, the awful otherness of God, which nonetheless makes possible the nearness of his redemption."[30] Eichrodt adds this thought: "'Holy' describes the character of God as it has been made known to his people; and, as understood in the priestly conception of God, this means *him who is unapproachable because of his complete 'otherness' and perfection when compared with all created things.*"[31] Revere F. Weidmer softens the idea of separateness somewhat in his idea of "holy." He writes:

> Two things lie in the divine holiness. (1) God stands apart and in opposition to the world, and (2) He removes this opposition by a redemptive offer of communion with Himself. All the demonstrations of the divine covenant are issues of the divine holiness.[32]

In every one of the more than 800 places where the root word for holiness, *kodesh*, is used, the meaning of separation is permissible; in many places it is demanded.[33] Some scholars state that the meanings of holiness as "radiance" and holiness as "separation" are mutually exclusive and that the word must signify either one or the other. But substantial evidence has been presented to indicate that both meanings are correct, that both brilliance and separation are two facets of the central idea of holiness.

A third meaning, that of purity, is also a most significant inter-

[29] *Ibid.*

[30] *Op. cit.*, p. 38.

[31] *Op. cit.*, I, 273.

[32] *Biblical Theology of the Old Testament* (Minneapolis: Augustana Book Co., n.d.), p. 72.

[33] Turner, *op. cit.*, p. 22.

pretation of the word. Some scholars oppose any exposition that stresses the ethical and moral nature of the term. But to omit the ethical aspect is to negate the total trend of biblical writing as well as to deny the dynamic experience of the people of Israel.

3. *Holiness as Purity*

It has been the custom among modern scholars to describe the moralization of the idea of holiness in the Old Testament and to make a distinction between ritualistic and ethical holiness. There is actually little contextual support for this approach. The reason for this recent interpretation seems to be due largely to the modern view that the development of religion must be traced from below and not from above. The conclusion of such scholars is ultimately dependent on the view that religion is a movement from man to God rather than a revelation of God to man. "This is the leading *motif* in the modern study of the history of religion, being a product of the application to the study of religion of the New Scientific Method with its rigid evolutionary hypothesis."[34]

According to Ringgren, "The Arabic use of the root seems to speak in favour of the meaning 'to be pure.'"[35] This writer further states that in the use of the term "the idea of withdrawal or separation is not always very prominent; the meaning of 'pure' also deserves attention."[36] To ignore the idea of purity in relation to the root term *kodesh* is to explain away a vital part of the religious experience of Israel. To relate the idea of purity to the word *kodesh* is to interpret the religious experience of Israel more adequately.

The Biblical text indicates that the ethical ideal of holiness was apparent in the earliest acts of worship and sacrifice which occured in Israel. "The actions of worship fall under the general notion of *offerings. The essential nature of an offering in general is the devotion of man to God, expressed in an outward act.*"[37] Man feels impelled to express, in actions which he directs exclusively to God, both his dependence on God in general and the special relationship in which he is placed toward God. In connection with the offerings, the sprinkling of the altar does not merely signify God's acceptance of the blood, but at the same time serves to consecrate the place where the offering is made.

[34]Snaith, *op. cit.*, p. 29.
[35]*Op. cit.*, p. 6.
[36]*Ibid.*
[37]Oehler, *op. cit.*, p. 261.

But when a portion of the blood accepted by God is further applied to the people by an act of sprinkling, this is meant to signify that the same life that is offered up in the atonement for the people themselves binds the people to covenant fellowship with God. "The act of consecration thus becomes an act of renewal of life,—a translation of Israel into the kingdom of God, in which it is filled with divine vital energy, and is sanctified to be a kingdom of priests, a holy people."[38] The literary and historical "evidence of this pervasive and overwhelming religious consciousness cannot be lightly dismissed as scribal glosses or corruption of the text."[39] The central text of the covenant is Lev. 19:2: "Ye shall be holy: for I the Lord your God am holy." In referring to this covenant text, Eichrodt declares: "The injunctions that follow make it clear that this holiness which is required of the people because of the holy nature of Yahweh implies moral purity and blamelessness."[40]

The ethical concept of holiness is especially prominent in the prophetic movement. Isaiah represents the "Holy One of Israel" as morally perfect. In chapter 6, he reveals a God who induced within the prophet a consciousness, not only of creaturely infirmity, but also of moral unworthiness, an unworthiness that belonged both to himself and to the nation. Compared with the Holy One, he and the people among whom he dwelt were morally unclean. It is Isaiah's general teaching that Israel's sin is rebellion against God and that the divine holiness has manifested itself and will continue to manifest itself in righteous judgment on his people.[41]

The conception of holiness as purity appears to some extent in Ezekiel (43:7-9) and is especially prominent in the Levitical legislation. Cleanness, outwardly and inwardly, was a condition of holiness. "Only clean objects could become holy. Hence cleanness and holiness came to be used almost synonymously. Both formed an antithesis to uncleanness. Holiness in this sense as applied to God expressed a sensitiveness on His part to everything impure.[42]

Summarizing the Old Testament idea of holiness as an attribute of God, it may be said that the term holiness is the nearest to

[38]*Ibid.*, p. 264.
[39]Baab, *op. cit.*, p. 21.
[40]*Op. cit.*, I, 278.
[41]*Ibid.*, pp. 278-79.
[42]Albert C. Knudson, *The Religious Teaching of the Old Testament* (New York: Abingdon-Cokesbury Press, 1918), p. 149.

an adequate definition of God found in its pages. One scholar phrases the thought as follows:

> It is the biblical word which most clearly distinguishes the God concept from all other concepts of human thought. Yet it cannot be understood in complete isolation from all other ideas associated with God. The holy God is a living God at work in the world with righteous and intelligent purpose. He is a personal Being calling men to seek and serve Him. His holiness stamps His life and personal character with the quality of deity. It declares to the world that He is God.[43]

B. New Testament Meaning of Holiness

In the New Testament the word *hagiadzo* is the parent of a family of words used to denote holiness. It carries four meanings: (1) of things—to set aside or to make suitable for ritual purposes (Exod. 29:27; Matt. 23:19); (2) of persons—to consecrate, to dedicate, to include in the inner circle of what is holy (Exod. 28:41); (3) to treat as holy, to reverence (I Pet. 3:15; Isa. 8:13); (4) to purify (Rom. 15:16; I Cor. 1:12; I Thess. 5:23).[44]

In the Vulgate of the New Testament, *holiness (sanctias)* is the rendering of two distinct words, *hagiosune* (I Thess. 3:13) and *hosiotes* (Luke 1:75; Eph. 4:24*b*). "These two Greek words express respectively the two ideas connotated by *holiness*, viz.: that of *separation* as seen in *hagios*, which denotes any matter of religious awe (the Latin *sacer)*, and that of *sanctioned (sanctitus)*, that which is *hosios*, has received God's seal."[45]

From a study of the biblical vocabulary and the use of the word "holiness" three distinct meanings have emerged. These basic meanings are "radiance," "separation," and "purity." These concepts are not contradictory nor mutually exclusive, but are complementary. The idea of holiness as related to God may be summarized as follows:

> Holiness is, first, the distinctive property of deity; second, that it is communicable to creatures, and hence involves a relationship to the divine; third, that in man it is either a formal or personal moral quality, or both; and fourth, that the moral content of the term is based on the moral character of God and is coextensive therewith.[46]

[43]Baab, *op. cit.*, p. 39.

[44]William F. Arndt and Wilbur Gingrich, eds., *A Greek-English Lexicon of the New Testament* (Chicago: University of Chicago Press, 1957), p. 9.

[45]*The Catholic Encyclopedia*, VII, 386.

[46]Turner, *op. cit.*, p. 28.

Holiness is thus the unique and exclusive quality of Deity, but is capable, under proper conditions, of being imparted to persons, places, and things.

IV. Holiness and Related Attributes

Among the attributes which God may impart to man when man enters into a vital relationship with God are righteousness, justice, love, grace, and faithfulness.

A. Righteousness

Righteousness, as an attribute, is the conformity of God to the moral and spiritual law which He himself has established. To put it another way, righteousness is the consistent and unvarying expression of God's nature in complete harmony with His holiness. Holiness represents God's essential nature, while righteousness represents holiness in action. Because God cannot act contrary to His own nature, His actions are dependable and become a law—the law of righteousness.

Many contemporary scholars stress the righteousness of God. To Brunner the righteousness of God means "the constancy of God's Will in view of His Purpose and Plan for Israel."[47] Thus righteousness "is simply the Holiness of God as it is expressed when confronted with the created world."[48] Brunner identifies righteousness with mercy and justification.[49] Karl Barth divides God's attributes into "The Perfections of the Divine Loving" and "The Perfections of the Divine Freedom." To Barth the righteousness of God means that in founding and maintaining fellowship with His creation God "wills and expresses and establishes what corresponds to His own worth."[50] These expressions of the righteousness of God appear to agree in general with the definition of H. Orton Wiley: "The term *holiness* refers to the nature or essence of God as such while *righteousness* is His standard of activity in conformity with that nature."[51]

The Bible clearly presents the teaching that God reveals himself

[47] *Op. cit.*, p. 275.

[48] *Ibid.*, p. 278.

[49] *Ibid.*, pp. 300ff.

[50] *Church Dogmatics, The Doctrine of God*, trans. T. H. L. Parker, *et al.* (Edinburgh: T. and T. Clark, 1957), II, Part I, 377.

[51] H. Orton Wiley and Paul T. Culbertson, *Introduction to Christian Theology* (Kansas City: Beacon Hill Press, 1949), p. 107.

and acts in harmony with His holy nature. The Psalmist frequently sang of the righteousness of God. "The judgments of God are true and righteous altogether" (Ps. 19:9); "The heavens . . . declare his righteousness" (Ps. 50:6). Isaiah looked to a time when God's rule would be supreme, for "righteousness shall be the girdle of his loins" (Isa. 11:5). Paul thrilled to the glory of the gospel, "For therein is the righteoueness of God revealed" (Rom. 1:17). According to the Book of the Revelation, even angels testify to God's righteousness: "Thou art righteous, O Lord, which art, and wast, and shalt be" (Rev. 16:5).

The righteousness of God has a direct bearing on the doctrine of holiness. Since righteousness is God's conformity to His own standard, it would follow that those whom God calls sons and daughters would be required to conform to a similar standard. For God to enter into a paternal relationship with man on any other grounds than holiness would destroy or deny His essential nature. A relationship on non-holy grounds would contradict His righteousness, for God would then be acting *out* of conformity to His holiness. Thus the righteousness of God points directly to the holiness of man.

According to William Temple, "The first great illumination to be found in the Old Testament is the interpretation of holiness as first and foremost righteousness."[52] This righteousness[53] is primarily regarded as justice. In Hebrew thinking there was no such thing as abstract concepts divorced from practical relationships. Thus righteousness is "a concept of relation referring to an actual relationship between two persons, and implying behaviour which corresponds to, or is true to, the claims arising out of such a relationship."[54] Von Rad adds a significant quotation regarding righteousness from the German biblicist, H. Cremer: "'Every relationship brings with it certain claims upon conduct, and the satisfaction of these claims, which issue from the relationship and in which alone the relationship can persist, is described by our term

[52]*Op. cit.*, p. 10.

[53]The Hebrew words for "righteousness" are TSEDEQ (masculine) and TSEDAQAH (feminine). Closely associated with TSEDEQ (righteousness) is the word (MISHPAT) (judgment). Some regard the original meaning of TSDQ to have been "to be straight," hence the meanings of "that which is, or ought to be firmly established, enduring."

[54]Eichrodt, *op. cit.*, I, 240.

[righteousness].'"[55] Jacob also presents a clear summary of the relation of righteousness and holiness when he states that righteousness is attributed to both God and man. He says:

> Righteousness is attributed to the holy God who commits no iniquity; it is attributed to the holy God who cannot leave wickedness unpunished nor the good unrecognized; it is attributed to the God who is merciful and slow to anger who, according to Ezekiel's phrase, does not desire the death of a sinner but that he should repent and live. It is attributed to the God of love who pursues after the salvation of his people; and finally it is attributed to the God of love who communicates his righteousness to the sinner and justifies him.[56]

B. Justice

Wiley suggests that the attribute of justice is commonly divided into four categories.[57] First comes *legislative* justice, which determines the moral duty of man and defines the consequences of man's response in rewards and penalties. Second there is *judicial* justice, or distributive justice, according to which God grants rewards or imposes penalties to man according to his works. More technically, the justice by which God rewards the obedient is sometimes called *remunerative justice.* Finally, the justice by which He punishes the guilty is labeled *retributive* or *vindictive* justice.

The idea of divine justice is not an isolated biblical theme, but appears persistently from the initial events of the Garden of Eden to the final events of Revelation. The theme of divine justice is particularly prominent in the writings of Paul, who is the apostle of faith, grace, liberty, and justice. Paul writes of justice in Rom. 2:6-10:

> Who will render to every man according to his deeds: to them who by patient continuance in well doing seek for glory and honour and immortality, eternal life: but unto them that are contentious, and do not obey the truth, but obey unrighteousness, indignation and wrath, tribulation and anguish, upon every soul of man that doeth evil, of the Jew first, and also of the Gentile.

Liberalism rejects the idea of retributive justice almost entirely. Barth accepts the necessity of retributive justice,[58] but proceeds to state that God's retributive or punitive righteousness is

[55] *Op. cit.,* I, 371.
[56] *Op. cit.,* p. 96.
[57] Wiley and Culbertson, *op. cit.,* p. 107.
[58] *Op. cit.,* II, Part I, 382ff.

wholly satisfied by the crucifixion of Christ.[59] This idea of Christ dying for all leads Barth to a universal election, where all men are saved. Brunner rejects the idea of universal salvation, stating that the New Testament points to a final judgment.[60] Yet Brunner has reservations about eternal punishment, saying that it is impossible to indicate the ultimate fate of the unbeliever.[61] But in later writing, Brunner suggests that to die without Christ is equivalent to being annihilated.[62] Nels Ferré rejects the idea of everlasting punishment,[63] but L. Harold DeWolf is reluctant to discard the concept. DeWolf thinks that there should be a reformulation of the entire concept, but believes that God's judgment will be expressed in our experience after death in some manner hidden to us at the present.[64]

The attributes of divine justice, like the other attributes, is directly related to the concept of holiness. Justice is the administration of the laws and principles of righteousness. To regard God as holy in His essential being and as righteous in every expression of His nature leads inevitably to the idea of justice. For a holy God could not reverse His pattern of response in conformity with His nature, even when dealing with man. Thus holiness in man is necessary, for it permits God to govern and to redeem man in harmony with His own nature. Further, the holiness of God requires Him to act in harmony with himself in dealing with free human agency. To violate human freedom and impose holiness on man would be a violation of God's holiness, for thus God would withdraw something which he originally granted to man as good. To sanction human freedom and permit an ultimate rejection of His holiness would also be a violation of God's justice, for then God would permit a perversion of something which He originally granted to man as good. Divine justice operates as a necessity in requiring man's holiness. Man's holiness operates as a necessity in sustaining God's justice.

[59] *Ibid.*, pp. 395-406.

[60] *Op. cit.*, p. 349.

[61] *Ibid.*, p. 353.

[62] Emil Brunner, *Faith, Hope, and Love* (Philadelphia: The Westminster Press, 1956), p. 56.

[63] *The Christian Understanding of God* (New York: Harper and Brothers, 1957), pp. 217ff.

[64] *A Theology of the Living Church* (rev. ed.; New York: Harper and Brothers, 1960), pp. 280ff.

C. Love

The holiness of God emphasizes His moral excellence, His transcendence, His "otherness." But "God is love"—Holy Love. It is God's love that makes the transcendent God also the immanent God. "God is love; and he that dwelleth in love dwelleth in God, and God in him" (I John 4:16). Wiley writes that "the love of God is in fact the desire to impart holiness and this desire is satisfied only when the beings whom it seeks are rendered holy."[65] When Barth gives a definition of God's love, he extends love to include all men and all of creation: "God is He who in His Son Jesus Christ loves all His children, in His children all men, and in men His whole creation."[66] Emil Brunner sustains the idea of Luther and quotes with approval Luther's assertion that God is "an abyss of eternal love."[67] Anders Nygren has drawn a valid distinction between *agape* and *eros*. *Agape* represents God's love, while *eros* suggests human love. *Agape* is "spontaneous and unactuated, uncalculating, unlimited and unconditional."[68] The divine *agape* has nothing to do with the concept of love that depends upon the recognition of a valuable quality in its object. "The man who is loved by God has no value in himself; what gives him value is precisely the fact that God loves him."[69]

God is love, that is, God is a holy Being who desires and provides for the impartation of His nature to man. "Holiness creates distance, but love creates communion. Holiness erects barriers, love breaks through them."[70] The holiness of God demands that He always acts out of pure love. The love of God requires that man, as the object of love, be won to share in the holiness of God. If God loves man, He must seek to make man holy. If man loves God, then man must seek to share the divine nature—to be holy. Holiness in man is in harmony with God's love. Such holiness in man transcends a mere relation, or a formal confrontation, or a divine-human encounter. Holiness in man is, because of God's love, an experience in which man enjoys the highest privilege possible to a created being—sharing in the nature of the holy Creator.

[65]Wiley and Culbertson, *op. cit.*, p. 105.
[66]*Op. cit.*, II, 1, 351.
[67]*Christian Doctrine of God*, p. 168.
[68]*Agape and Eros*, trans. Philip S. Watson (Philadelphia: The Westminster Press, 1953), p. 9.
[69]*Ibid.*, p. 78.
[70]Brunner, *Christian Doctrine of God*, p. 188.

D. Grace

Closely associated with God's love are grace and mercy. Grace is the meeting point of holy love and human sin. "What the righteousness is to the holiness of God, that His grace is to His love."[71] Grace is the love of God communicated to man through the Holy Spirit. William B. Pope discusses various aspects of grace.[72] The grace of God that seeks the well-being of the entire human race is the divine *philanthropy* or kindness to humankind. The grace that sees man in his sin and waits to be accepted in redeeming relationship is *compassion* and *pity*. The grace that withholds judgment and justice while waiting the sinner's repentance is *forbearance* or *long-suffering*. The grace which readily and freely forgives the repentant sinner is *mercy*.

Paul made grace the hub of personal redemption when he wrote: "For by grace are ye saved through faith, and that not of yourselves; it is the gift of God" (Eph. 2:8). Perhaps Paul was thinking of his own deliverance when he wrote: "Being justified freely by his grace through the redemption that is in Christ Jesus" (Rom. 3:24).

If grace represents the love of God exercised toward man, then grace should lead to personal holiness. For God's love compels Him to desire and to provide for man's holiness. And if grace is an expression of divine love, then grace begins and ends with the holiness of God which may be shared by man. Such grace is truly overwhelming and shattering. That God would deign to share himself with an unworthy sinner should be sufficient inspiration to cause one to sing of the "marvelous, infinite, matchless grace of our loving Lord." Such knowledge should also provide adequate motivation to seek to respond to God's proposal by joyously sharing God's personal presence in holiness of heart and life.

E. Veracity and Faithfulness

God is the Source of all truth because Holy Love is true to itself. God's truth is the correspondence of His revelation with His essence. Truth as an attribute means that God can never be capricious, whimsical, indulgent, or misleading. Any act or any word of revela-

[71] William Burt Pope, *A Compendium of Christian Theology* (New York: Phillips and Hunt, 1881), I, 346.

[72] *Ibid.*, p. 347.

tion by God must be an expression of holy love. Truth as an attribute means that God's analysis of man must be based on the Creator's knowledge of what man is, and what man can be. Thus, when the Scripture describes man as a sinner, this description is true. When God promises to share His holiness with man and requires and provides for this sharing, it is also in fact true.

God is true and faithful. His knowledge is perfect and His wisdom is beyond understanding. Paul wrote to the wavering Corinthians that "God is faithful" (I Cor. 1:9). To these same Corinthians Paul wrote a word of encouragement about God's faithfulness in temptation, for "God is faithful, who will not suffer you to be tempted above that ye are able" (I Cor. 10:13). In the first letter to the Thessalonian Christians, Paul continually exhorted these Christians to go on to holiness. He prayed that "the very God of peace sanctify you wholly" (I Thess. 5:23). Then Paul ended his exhortation and his prayer with a ringing affirmation: "Faithful is he that calleth you, who also will do it" (I Thess. 5:24). God's great truth is that man can be sanctified, that man can live a Spirit-filled life called the life of holiness.

Summary

The prelude to perfection is man's view of God. When man sees God as sovereign, free, and holy, then he identifies holiness with the essential nature of God. And if God is Holy Love, then every aspect of the divine nature is a reflection of His holiness. This holy God has revealed himself in a redemptive fashion to man. The history of redemption is the history of God's endeavor to impart His own nature, His holiness, to man. The biblical revelation leaves no doubt that holiness is the focal point of redemptive history.

An adequate view of God is essential to a proper understanding of holiness. If man accepts the biblical revelation of God, then man also accepts the biblical teaching of man's sinfulness. To understand the nature of redemption it is necessary to understand the nature of sin. The next chapter presents a biblical view of sin as the ultimate source of opposition between God and man. Sin is the ultimate spiritual antithesis of holiness.

CHAPTER IV /

Sin Versus Holiness

The ultimate spiritual antithesis is the opposition between holiness and sin. Man was designed for holiness, created in holiness, and destined for holiness. But sin marred the original design, ruined the state of innocent holiness, and now threatens man's destiny.

One of the highest tributes ever paid to man is found in Shakespeare's *Hamlet*. Musing upon the nobility of man, Hamlet says:

> What a piece of work is a man! How noble in reason! How infinite in faculty! In form and moving how express and admirable! In action how like an angel! In apprehension how like a god.[1]

Even though Hamlet expresses such a lofty ideal, the plot reveals Claudius, the king, involved in intrigue, immorality, and murder, with the consequent guilt, shame, and tragedy.

Such is the tragic situation of man. With Godlike qualities and unlimited potential, he finds himself living far below his possibilities. With holiness as his original destiny, man finds himself groveling in the slime of depraved living. The great human tragedy is the reality of sin. The grand human hope is the possibility of holiness. Holiness and sin represent the basic and permanent clash of opposites. Holiness represents the essential nature of God. Sin stands for the denial of holiness and opposition to God's very existence. Since sin stands in direct opposition to holiness, it is necessary to analyze the entire problem of sin, and to show its relation to holiness.

It is possible to understand the nature of holiness only to the

[1] Act II, Scene ii.

extent that we understand the nature of sin. Among the great focal themes of the biblical revelation—God, man, sin, and redemption—sin is seen as the ugly intruder. The nature of sin must be discerned if it is to be treated properly. H. Orton Wiley states that the great doctrinal truths are so related that the basic views held concerning any one of them profoundly influence the others. In connection with the relation of sin to the other great doctrines, Wiley writes:

> Since Christianity is a religion of redemption, it is greatly influenced by the various views concerning the nature of sin. Any tendency to minimize sin has its consequences in a less exalted view of the person and work of the Redeemer.[2]

In his book entitled *A Right Conception of Sin,* Richard S. Taylor writes: "The doctrines relating to sin form the center around which we build our entire theological system."[3]

A pioneer leader of the modern holiness movement, James B. Chapman, states that "men's conception of sin is fundamental to all their thinking and speaking on soteriology in all its various phases."[4] An outstanding contemporary theologian, not known for conservative doctrines, writes that one reason for the triumph of early Christianity over such popular religions as Mithraism and Manichaeism was that "it took evil more realistically than any other religion and presented a hope that was invincible because it grew out of the heart of starkest tragedy."[5] The history of the Church reveals that great revivals of spiritual activity have been preceded by a serious and profound concept of sin.

I. Non-biblical Ideas of Sin

To a great extent non-biblical theories have attempted to account for the nature of evil from a rationalistic point of view. Rejecting the biblical explanation of the origin of sin as mythology or allegory, these views attempt to account for the existence of moral evil from within the framework of a humanistic or a naturalistic philosophy. The following discussion presents several such explanations, and presents the objections to them as stated by conservative theology.

[2]*Christian Theology,* II, 51.

[3](Kansas City: Nazarene Publishing House, 1939), p. 9.

[4]*The Terminology of Holiness,* p. 24.

[5]Walter M. Horton, *Realistic Theology* (New York: Harper and Brothers, 1934), p. 54.

A. Sin as the Limitation of Finite Being

A current interpretation of sin, based on existential philosophy, regards sin as rising from man's finitude. Paul Tillich and Reinhold Niebuhr are representative of this approach. For Tillich, man's "creation and fall coincide."[6] Man's "estrangement from God, the flight from Him, the rebellion against Him,"[7] are inherent in his creation. This condition of estrangement "underlines all human history and makes history what it is."[8]

Reinhold Niebuhr views sin as rising from man's finiteness, although finitude itself is not evil. The core of man's sin is his effort to make himself God.[9] Man seeks to make himself God because of anxiety. Anxiety is said to be "the inevitable spiritual state of man, standing in the paradoxical situation of freedom and finiteness."[10] Thus anxiety is the "internal precondition of sin," according to Niebuhr. When man's finitude is asserted he becomes corrupt and sensual, attempting to "escape from his unlimited possibilities of freedom . . . by immersing himself into a 'mutable good.'"[11] When man expresses his freedom by refusing to accept his finitude, the result is pride, injustice, and sensuality. Sin then becomes both religious and moral. Niebuhr concludes that "the religious dimension of sin is man's rebellion against God, his effort to usurp the place of God. The moral and social dimension of sin is injustice."[12]

Man's sinfulness may also be expressed in his pride of virtue. The ultimate sin, in Niebuhr's thinking, is spiritual pride, when one parades his self-righteousness to all or when one masks selfish aims behind spiritual pretense.

B. Sin as Ignorance

Many scholars, from Socrates in ancient Athens to John Dewey in New York City in the twentieth century, have equated sin with ignorance. From this point of view the good life can be achieved by inner, rational self-development. In this approach, knowledge equals

[6]*Systematic Theology* (Chicago: University of Chicago Press, 1957), II, 44.

[7]Paul Tillich, *Biblical Religion and the Search for Ultimate Reality* (Chicago: University of Chicago Press, 1955), p. 55.

[8]Paul Tillich, *The Protestant Era* (Chicago: University of Chicago Press, 1948), p. 166.

[9]*The Nature and Destiny of Man* (New York: Charles Scribner's Sons, 1943), I, 180.

[10]*Ibid.*, p. 182.

[11]*Ibid.*, p. 186.

[12]*Ibid.*, p. 179.

virtue, for "he who knows will be good; he who is habitually good knows." It follows also that no man errs or sins except through ignorance. Ignorance is thus the essence of sin, while knowledge is the essence of virtue. This idea was dominant in the *Liberalism* of theology and the *Progressivism* of education in the first half of the twentieth century.[13]

C. The Evolutionary-Lag Theory

Many who accept the evolutionary theory of man's origin state that what is called sin[14] is actually a carry-over of animal qualities from lower stages of existence. This theory regards man as the consummation of the development of physical nature. However, the process of man's evolvement is not symmetrical, with every aspect of personality advancing evenly. Rather, the pattern of ascent is jerky and irregular, with gaps existing in certain periods. Thus man has developed to a greater extent in physical and mental abilities than he has in moral and spiritual capacities, with a resulting "gap" or "lag." Man is thought to be an organism in which the human has not yet escaped from the animal, and sin is primarily the brute inheritance which every man carries with him. One writer describes this view of sin as "a relic of the animal not yet outgrown, a resultant of the mechanism of appetite and impulse and reflex action for which the proper inhibitions are not yet developed, and only slowly does it grow into a consciousness of itself as evil."[15]

D. Other Views of Sin

Among other views of the nature of sin are: (1) the social theories represented by Jean Jacques Rousseau and Karl Marx; (2) the view coming from Platonic and Gnostic teachings that sin is related to man's sensuous nature; (3) the view that all life, both material and spiritual, is governed by the law of opposites or of necessary antagonism; (4) the concept that sin has its source in a principle of evil which has existed eternally in the universe.

[13]See A. C. Knudson, *Principles of Christian Ethics* (New York: Abingdon-Cokesbury Press, 1943), pp. 90-95; and John Dewey, *Democracy and Education* (New York: The Macmillan Co., 1939), pp. 412ff.

[14]For a discussion of the evolutionary theory of sin's origin, where historian John Fiske is considered its spokesman, see N. W. Stroup and Walter Rauschenbusch, *Christianity and the Social Order* (New York: Macmillan Press, 1919), pp. 124ff.

[15]Borden Parker Bowne, *Studies in Christianity* (Boston: Houghton Mifflin Co., 1909), p. 145.

All of the non-biblical interpretations of sin, or evil, have weaknesses which make them unacceptable to those who find the best explanation of sin in the Bible.

E. Reasons for Rejecting Non-biblical Views

Among the reasons for rejecting the non-biblical ideas of sin are the following:

1. They eliminate personal responsibility. The Bible makes sin intensely personal.
2. They deny both the religious and the moral aspects of sin. The religious aspect of sin is rebellion against God. The moral aspect of sin is voluntary breaking of the laws of both God and man.
3. They ignore the basic spiritual nature of sin, which is related to man's inherent sinfulness.
4. They limit the power of God and of His redemptive work as revealed in Jesus Christ.
5. There are many sins of the spirit, so sin cannot be equated with man's sensuous nature.
6. Knowledge does not appear to be virtue, for human history as well as contemporary experience point to the fact that not only the ignorant, but the highly educated, are involved in the deepest sins.
7. All non-biblical theories reject the authenticity of the full biblical revelation. It would follow that these non-biblical views attempt to explain sin in a way which is antithetical to the biblical description. Non-biblical concepts of human sin, or wrongdoing, make no provision for personal holiness as the result of an experiential relationship to God. All such concepts regard man's deliverance from evil as the result of human endeavor or as the result of a formal relationship to God.

II. Biblical Terminology of Sin

Since the doctrine of holiness is primarily a biblical doctrine, the doctrine of sin should be considered first from the biblical, religious point of view rather than from a strictly moral or ethical point of view. Sin thus has a theocentric orientation rather than an anthropological background. The terms used in the Bible to describe sin are significant, even though it is admitted that etymology as such cannot provide conclusive data for the formation of a doctrine. Yet the insights gained by a study of biblical terms are significant. Both the Old Testament and the New Testament are vivid and descriptive in the terminology related to sin.

A. Old Testament Terminology

In the Old Testament sin is not an abstract idea nor a theoretical problem. Here it is "the attitude of rebellion against God that is displayed by living historical man."[16] The language of the Old Testament points to historical acts and states of rebellion which separate man from his Creator. Old Testament terminology also indicates that man's disobedience resulted in a state of spiritual and moral decay. The basic Old Testament terms for sin are discussed below.

1. *Sin as "Missing the Mark"*

The most common word for sin, "both with respect to its linguistic use and its content, is *chet,* or *chattath,* derived from a root meaning 'to miss,' so that it denotes sin as an *error.*"[17] The word and its cognates appears more than 400 times in the Old Testament.[18] *Chet* first appears in Gen. 4:7: "If thou doest well, shalt thou not be accepted? and if thou doest not well, sin lieth at the door."

In its technical sense *chet* means "to miss the mark or target, in shooting" (Judg. 20:16). A variation of the use in a nontechnical sense, where failure means *overlooking,* is found in Job. 5:24*b*: "And thou shalt visit thy habitation, and shalt not sin" (miss nothing). Thus *chet* "means sin in the sense of failure, i.e., that sin which is recognized as a clear violation of a given command or prohibition. It corresponds exactly even in etymology to the Greek *hamartia.*"[19] The significance of the word to the Hebrews was that their God was a holy God and that the individual needed to aim to conform to the standard set by God, and that every departure from this aim and purpose was a missing of the mark by one's actions.

However, the "missing of the mark," or sin, was not always deliberate and willful, but frequently referred to wrongs committed

[16]George A. F. Knight, *A Christian Theology of the Old Testament* (Richmond, Va.: John Knox Press, 1959), p. 199.

[17]T. C. Vriezen, *An Outline of Old Testament Theology* (Newton, Mass.: Charles T. Branford Co., 1960), p. 211.

[18]Cf. Ludwig Köhler, *Old Testament Theology,* trans. A. S. Todd (Philadelphia: The Westminster Press, 1957), p. 169.

[19]*Ibid.*

through negligence or ignorance, as indicated by the following words:

> *And if the whole congregation of Israel sin through ignorance, and the thing be hid from the eyes of the assembly, and they have done somewhat against any of the commandments of the Lord concerning things which should not be done, and are guilty; when the sin, which they have sinned against it, is known, then the congregation shall offer a young bullock for the sin, and bring him before the tabernacle of the congregation* (Lev. 4:13-14).

These sins of ignorance were to be recognized and a sin offering made for them (Lev. 4:21). Rulers and common people could also sin through ignorance (Lev. 4:22 and 4:27). In each case a sin offering was required to atone for the sin of ignorance (Lev. 4:24 and 4:29).

An awareness of sins of ignorance is also found in the laws of the offerings in the Book of Numbers: "And if any should sin through ignorance, then he shall bring a she goat . . . for a sin offering" (Num. 15:27). But even when making provision for the sins of ignorance, Moses is quick to warn against willful sins, for he declares:

> *But the soul that doeth ought presumptously . . . the same reproacheth the Lord; and that soul shall be cut off from among his people. Because he hath despised the word of the Lord, and hath broken his commandment, that soul shall utterly be cut off; his iniquity shall be upon him* (Num. 15:30-31).

In this drastic warning, following so closely to the assurance of forgiveness for sins of ignorance, the idea of personal, individual responsibility for "missing the mark" is sharp and unmistakable.[20]

2. *Sin as Crookedness or Perversion*

The word *awon (avah)* is used in the Old Testament to suggest crookedness or perversion. The idea of crookedness is suggested in Lam. 3:9*b*: ". . . he hath made my paths crooked"; and in Gen. 15:16*b*: ". . . for the iniquity of the Amorites is not yet full." "The *awon* is thus what twists away from God's straightness; and it goes further than *chattath* in that it indicates wrong intention."[21] Another shade

[20]In addition to the two ideas given above, *chattah* is sometimes translated in the King James Version by some word other than sin. Thus it is rendered "fault" in Gen. 41:9 and Exod. 5:16; "trespass" in I Kings 8:31; "harm" in Lev. 5:16; "blame" in Gen. 43:9 and 44:32; "offend" in Gen. 29:9 and 40:1 as well as in the following: I Kings 1:21; II Kings 18:14; Eccles. 4:10; Isa. 29:21; Jer. 37:18.

[21]J. Barton Payne, *The Theology of the Old Testament* (Grand Rapids, Mich.: Zondervan Publishing House, 1962), p. 196.

of meaning is that "*awon* is to turn aside or to become lost, shown not only in act but in thought."[22] It is used 231 times (e.g., in Ezekiel 44; Leviticus 18; Numbers 12; Jeremiah 24; Hosea 11). Its meanings are: "crime or iniquity, 55 times; guilt, 159 times; and punishment, 6 times. Its origin shows that it indicates an action or omission which is not straight, or not right."[23]

Referring to the two terms used thus far, *chattath* and *awon (avah)*, A. B. Davidson writes:

> It may be admitted that something is gained by these terms. Sin is of the nature of what is crooked compared with what is straight; uneven as contrasted with what is smooth; of the nature of what is unclean compared with what is clean, and so on. The physical ideas are transferred to the moral sphere. There underlies all such transferences . . . also the idea that that which hits the mark and does not fail is straight and not crooked, is clean and not unclean, is in that outer physical sphere "good" and its opposite "bad."[24]

This comment of Davidson points to an important practice of the Hebrew vocabulary in its application of common expressions to the area of the religious and the ethical. The basic reason for the utilization of certain expressions in showing the different aspects of sin is a practical, pedagogical reason. For these expressions transfer familiar physical ideas into the moral sphere and drive home the idea of human sin in relation to divine holiness. Jesus used a similar method in His teachings.

3. *Sin as Rebellion*

Pasha refers to deliberate transgression, to a revolt or a refusal to be subject to rightful authority (Gen. 50:17), and is derived from a root meaning "to rebel": "So Israel rebelled against the house of David unto this day" (I Kings 12:19). In many places *pasha* is used to indicate transgression or deliberate violation. The Psalmist writes: "Then will I teach transgressors thy ways" (Ps. 51:13*a*). In Proverbs the idea of deliberate transgression is again presented: "For a piece of bread that man will transgress" (Prov. 28:21*b*). The prophet Isaiah levels a serious charge at Israel in these words: "Thy first father hath sinned, and thy teachers have transgressed against me" (Isa. 43:27). The idea of revolt and rebellion is conveyed in the description of the revolt of Edom and Libnah (II Kings 8).

[22]Jacob, *op. cit.*, p. 281.
[23]Köhler, *op. cit.*, p. 169.
[24]*Theology of the Old Testament*, p. 207.

Pasha occurs 86 times and is "the Old Testament's most profound word for sin."[25] The depth of meaning in the term is clear and precise. "Since *pésha* is deliberate and premeditated transgression, it becomes more serious than the earlier terms for sin. Job 34:37 therefore speaks of adding *pésha* to *chattath*."[26] A summary of the idea of sin as rebellion is given in the following significant statement:

> Essentially and in the last resort in the Old Testament revelation sin is not the violation of objective commandments and prohibitions and not the iniquities which demonstrate their weakness and folly (I Chron. 21:8!) and perversity. *Sin is revolt of the human will against the divine will:* men are *theóstuges* (haters of God) (Rom. 1:30).[27]

4. *Sin as Wickedness*

Rasha, a word appearing in patriarchal times, is usually translated "wickedness." According to Payne, "the adjectival form of *résha* occurs in Gen. 18:23 and comes from the idea of 'loose' or 'ill-regulated.' The noun thus signifies a raging against God (Job 3: 17)."[28] From the context in which it is found, *rasha* seems to suggest the activity of the wicked which results in confusion and perpetual agitation for the wrongdoer and others who come under his influence. Isaiah appears to have this idea in mind when he writes: "But the wicked are like the troubled sea, when it cannot rest, whose waters cast up mire and dirt. There is no peace, saith my God, to the wicked" (Isa. 57:20-21).

This same idea of wickedness as a restless, confused agitation against God is found in Job's use of *rasha:*

> *For now should I have lain still and been quiet, I should have slept: then had I been at rest,*
>
> *With Kings and counsellors of the earth, which built desolate places for themselves;*
>
> *Or with princes that had gold, who filled their houses with silver:*
>
> *Or as an hidden untimely birth I had not been; as infants which never saw light.*
>
> *There the wicked cease from troubling; and there the weary be at rest* (Job. 3:13-17).

Ezekiel regards wickedness as a more direct and deliberate agi-

[25]Köhler, *op. cit.,* p. 170.
[26]Payne, *op. cit.,* p. 196.
[27]Köhler, *op. cit.,* p. 170.
[28]*Op. cit.,* p. 196.

tation against God, as he contrasts the conscious activities of the righteous with those of the wicked:

> *The soul that sinneth, it shall die. The son shall not bear the iniquity of the father, neither shall the father bear the iniquity of the son: the righteousness of the righteous shall be upon him, and the wickedness of the wicked shall be upon him.*
>
> *But if the wicked will turn from all his sins that he hath committed, and keep all my statutes, and do that which is lawful and right, he shall surely live, he shall not die* (Ezek. 18:20-21).

The idea of personal responsibility for continued wickedness is shown in another statement of Ezekiel: "Again, when the wicked man turneth away from the wickedness which he hath committed, and doeth that which is lawful and right, he shall save his soul alive" (Ezek. 18:27).

Not only is the wicked man responsible for his agitation against God, but also the prophet is under personal obligation to warn the wicked.

> *When I say unto the wicked, O wicked man, thou shalt surely die; if thou dost not speak to warn the wicked from his way, that wicked man shall die in his iniquity; but his blood will I require at thine hand.*
>
> *Nevertheless, if thou warn the wicked of his way to turn from it; if he do not turn from his way, he shall die in his iniquity; but thou hast delivered thy soul* (Ezek. 33:8-9).

From the preceding discussion it is possible to regard *rasha* in a fourfold perspective: (1) the confusion and strife of the wicked; (2) the undue agitation caused to others by the wicked; (3) the contrast of the righteous and wicked; (4) the responsibility to warn the wicked of his way.

Köhler points out that *rasha,* "the wicked," is the most common word for sinner in the Old Testament, appearing 261 times.[29] The word has an individual, particular meaning, describing a wrong that has been committed. "Mostly, however, the word has a more general sense, describing character rather than individual action. . . . The word means one who is seen to be a sinner by his conduct and character both."[30] In all cases the sin, or the sinner, are regarded as hostile to God.

5. *Sin as Unfaithfulness*

Maal is introduced by Moses in Lev. 5:15 as a "trespass." Later, in Num. 5:12, the verb form is used to indicate infidelity in mar-

[29]*Op. cit.,* p. 171.
[30]*Ibid.*

riage. Thus *maal* suggests betrayal or faithlessness and points to the treachery of sin, in that it implies breach of trust. More particularly, the word means a breach of faith in regard to the covenant relationship. The idea of a breach of trust is presented in Prov. 16:10, in regard to the integrity of a king in dealing with his subjects: "A divine sentence is in the lips of the king: his mouth transgresseth not in judgment."

In many instances, persons guilty of "unfaithfulness" were persons in authority. In addition, the nation Israel was regarded as enjoying a special covenant relationship *(b'rith)* with God. Thus when the people betrayed the trust placed in them by God, their act was described by this word suggesting unfaithfulness. The idea of sin as unfaithfulness is shown in three passages from Ezekiel. In 14:13 he says: "Son of man, when the land sinneth against me by trespassing grievously, then will I stretch out mine hand upon it, and will break the staff of the bread thereof, and will send famine upon it." In the next chapter Ezekiel issues a solemn judgment: "And I will make the land desolate, because they have committed a trespass, saith the Lord God" (Ezek. 15:8). And the final outcome of their unfaithfulness is found in these words: "And the heathen shall know that the house of Israel went into captivity for their iniquity: because they trespassed against me, therefore hid I my face from them, and gave them into the hand of their enemies: so fell they all by the sword" (Ezek. 39:23).

6. *Sin as Evil*

Ra is a general term for *bad* as contrasted to *good.* It is used in reference to bad fruit (Jer. 24:2) and in relation to unpleasant experiences (Gen. 49:7). Its original meaning is uncertain, although some scholars indicate it may have been associated with a loud noise. "*Ra* would thus suggest a physical calamity or a violent breaking (of God's orders)."[31] The Hebrew word *ra* thus carries with it an inference which is near the English word *evil.* It implies both the nature and the consequences of the deed. In almost every instance where the words *mischief, harm,* and *ill* are found, *ra* is the word from which they are derived.

Variations of the word are rendered as *calamity* in Ps. 141:5; *affliction* in Num. 11:11; *trouble* in Ps. 41:1; *sore* in Deut. 6:22; *hurt* in Gen. 26:29; *sorrow* in Gen. 44:29; *sad* in Gen. 40:7; *grief* in Neh. 2:10;

[31]Payne, *op. cit.,* p. 196.

misery in Eccles. 8:6; *distress* in Neh. 2:17; *noisome* in Ezek. 14:15, 21; and *vex* in II Sam. 12:18. Despite the many variations of the term, yet the general context indicates a consistent reference to evil. *Ra* usually seems to imply the adverse nature and circumstances as well as the results of a misdeed. It depicts the prominent characteristics of the ungodly man; that is, his course of injury to himself resulting from his own evil deeds.

7. *Sin as Iniquity*

It is difficult to arrive at an entirely consistent interpretation of the Hebrew *avel.* The most prevalent meaning seems to be *iniquity.* Even though there are various other renderings—such as *unjust* in Ps. 43:1; 82:2; Prov. 29:27; Isa. 26:10; and Zeph. 3:5; *unrighteous* in Lev. 19:15; Deut. 25:16; Job 27:7; Ps. 71:4; *ungodly* in Job 16:11; *perverse* in Isa. 59:3; and *wicked* in Ps. 89:22 and other psalms—yet in the approximately 30 instances where *avel* is used the idea of iniquity seems to suggest the most consistent and suitable meaning.

The Hebrew word *aven* is also used frequently to express iniquity and is often connected with idolatry. This association seems to be made because it has a technical reference to vanity and nothingness, which in the Hebrew mind was often connected with idols and idol worship. The idea of *iniquity* is seen in the use of the word *aven* in the following passages: Num. 23:21; I Sam. 15:23; Ps. 5:5; Isa. 1:13; and Mic. 2:1. The word is translated *unjust* in Prov. 11:7; *false* in Prov. 17:4; *mischief* in Ps. 36:4; *affliction* in Job. 5:6; and *evil* in Ps. 140:11.

In summarizing the meaning of Old Testament terms for sin, A. B. Davidson states that the terms suggest two lines of thought. "In the one case it was failure to hit, or to correspond to any objective standard; in the other it was an attitude taken by a person toward one who was his superior."[32] The general Old Testament idea is that of rebellion, of the assertion of self-authority, for "sin has reference to God the Person, not to His will or His law as formulated externally."[33] In the Old Testament sin may be regarded primarily as rebellion, as a stubborn self-assertion of the individual, race, or nation against the authority of the person of God. It is also regarded as a state or condition which is evil or corrupt.

[32]*The Theology of the Old Testament,* pp. 210-11.
[33]*Ibid.,* p. 213.

B. New Testament Terminology

The New Testament uses a vast variety of words for sin. The ethical vocabulary of the New Testament borrows many terms from the Old Testament, especially the psalms, but also uses many terms common to current religious-philosophical language in the Graeco-Roman world. Frederick C. Grant shows the variety of terms used by analyzing 20 passages in which a total of 115 terms[34] are used—and the list is not presented as exhaustive. One need not examine all the terms involved, for a study of many of the primary terms will cover the total volume of terms. Some of the basic New Testament terms for sin are presented in the following discussion.

1. *Sin as Transgression*

Hamartia is the most common New Testament term for sin. The verb equivalent of the noun *hamartia* means "to do wrong," "to trespass," "to sin against God." "The older idea of 'missing the mark' is not adequate to translate its New Testament meaning. It is failure, but it is more."[35] Henry Alford says the word stands for "the practice of sin, in its most pregnant sense."[36] According to Vincent, "Sin, regarded both as principle and act, is designated by John as *hamartia*."[37] The context of *hamartia* supports the statement that sin includes more than simply "missing the mark"—that it contains the element of personal responsibility.

The concept of sin as an act or as acts carrying personal responsibility is presented in Mark 2:5*b*, where Jesus said, "Son, thy sins be forgiven thee." In Heb. 9:14, sins require cleansing. In the city of Nain a woman "which was a sinner" washed the feet of Jesus with her tears. Jesus, in a parable of forgiveness, explains her actions and climaxes the occasion with the words, "Thy sins are forgiven" (Luke 7:48). In John 8:24, Jesus bluntly tells the Pharisees that because of unbelief "ye shall die in your sins." In John 9:41, *hamartia* is more than mere failure or error—it is a responsible condition or attitude involving guilt: "Jesus said unto them, If ye were blind, ye should have no sin *[hamartian]*: but now ye say, We see; therefore your sin *[hamartia]* remaineth."

[34]*Op. cit.*, pp. 176-77.

[35]Frank Stagg, *New Testament Theology* (Nashville, Tenn.: Broadman Press, 1962), p. 15.

[36]*The Greek Testament* (Cambridge: Deighton, Bell, and Co., 1868), I, 7.

[37]Marvin R. Vincent, *Word Studies in the New Testament* (Grand Rapids, Mich.: Wm. B. Eerdmans Pub. Co., 1940), II, 322.

Paul refers to *hamartia* in terms of personal responsibility in Rom. 6:1: "Shall we continue in sin *[hamartia]?*" and again in I. Tim. 5:22: "Neither be ye partakers of other men's sins *[hamartia]:* keep thyself pure." James writes: "But if ye have respect of persons, ye commit sin *[hamartian],* and are convinced of the law as transgressors" (Jas. 2:9). "Clearly, then, *hamartia* in the New Testament implies more than 'missing the mark.'"[38] It indicates that sin includes attitudes and inner responses.

2. *Sin as Unrighteousness*

The term *adikia* indicates unrighteousness, wrongdoing, wickedness, or injustice. I John 5:17 states that all *adikia* is *hamartia* (sin). Thayer writes that *adikia* refers to "unrighteousness of heart and life."[39] When referring to a person, *adikos* means "one who breaks God's laws, *unrighteous, sinful.*"[40] Paul speaks of the wrath of God being revealed against the unrighteousness *(adikian)* of men (Rom. 1:18). In the catalogue of sins listed as characteristic of the reprobate mind, in Rom. 1:29-32, unrighteousness *(adikia)* heads the blanket indictment of mankind. In I John 1:9 the promise is made, "If we confess our sins, he is faithful and just to forgive us our sins, and to cleanse us from all unrighteousness *[adikia].*"

3. *Sin as Lawlessness*

The term *anomia* refers to "acts or manifestations of lawlessness."[41] It also refers to "lawless men, those who despise the law."[42] Thus the term may mean a lawless act or a lawless man, but in both uses it denotes defiance of the law rather than ignorance of it. In the English the term is frequently rendered as "iniquity."

In Matt. 7:23*b,* Jesus says: "Depart from me, ye that work iniquity" *(anomian).* Again in 24:12, Matthew quotes Christ as saying: "And because iniquity *[anomian]* shall abound, the love of many shall wax cold." In Rom. 6:19*b* this lawlessness is contrasted with righteousness and holiness: "For as ye have yielded your members servants to uncleanness and to iniquity unto iniquity *[anomia];* even so now yield your members servants to righteousness unto holiness."

[38]Stagg, *op. cit.,* p. 15.

[39]Jospeh H. Thayer, *Greek-English Lexicon* (New York: American Book Co., 1886), p. 12.

[40]*Ibid.*

[41]G. Abbott-Smith, *A Manual Greek Lexicon of the New Testament* (3rd. ed.; New York: Charles Scribner's Sons, 1936), p. 39.

[42]Arndt and Gingrich, *op. cit.,* p. 71.

Sin as lawlessness is a pattern of conduct, a state of continuous rebellion against God.

4. *Sin as Unfaithfulness*

Apistia denotes unfaithfulness, unbelief, lack of belief. Referring to an individual, *apistos* signifies faithless or unbelieving. In Mark 6:6 we read that Jesus "marvelled because of their unbelief." In Rom. 3:3 unbelief is regarded as the enemy of faith. Heb. 3:12 speaks of the "evil heart of unbelief" *(apistias)* as the cause of departing from God. Referring to those whose "carcases fell in the wilderness," Heb. 3:19 states that "they could not enter in because of unbelief" *(apistian).* In the great eschatological scene in Revelation 21, those that overcome shall inherit all things. But among the doomed are "the fearful and unbelieving" *(apistois)* (Rev. 21:8*a*). Unbelief is a state of mind, or a condition or attitude toward God.

5. *Sin as Debauchery*

The term *aselgeia* is a general term denoting "*unbridled lust, excess, licentiousness, lasciviousness, wantonness, outrageousness, shamelessness, insolence.*" [43] Eph. 4:19 contrasts the mature Christian with the depraved worldling who has given himself over to debauchery *(aselgeia).* Mark 7:21-22 presents a vivid list of sins which arise out of the depraved, sinful man, such as "evil thoughts, adulteries, fornication, murders, thefts, covetousness, wickedness, deceit, lasciviousness *[aselgeia].*" In II Pet. 2:7 the term means "wanton *acts* or *manners,* as filthy words, indecent bodily movements, unchaste handling of males and females, etc."[44]

Kittel interprets the word as follows:

> In the New Testament only the older and sensual sense of "voluptuousness" or "debauchery" is relevant (Mt. 7:22). Man necessarily falls victim to this when cut off from God. It characterizes Sodom and Gomorrah (II Pet. 2:7) and the pagan world generally (Eph. 4:19), also heresy and apostasy (Jd. 4; II Pet. 2:2, 18). The special sense of sexual excess is probably in Gal. 5:19 and certain in Rev. 13:13; I Cor. 12:21; II Pet. 2:2, 18.[45]

Here again the idea is that of a state, or condition, which permeates the entire personality.

[43]Thayer, *op. cit.,* p. 79.

[44]*Ibid.*

[45]Gerhard Kittel, *Theological Dictionary of the New Testament,* trans. by G. W. Bromily (Grand Rapids, Mich.: Wm. B. Eerdmans Pub. Co., 1964), I, 490.

6. *Sin as Perverted Desire*

Epithumia is a term denoting strong desire. The moral character of the desire, good or bad, is determined by the setting of the word. "Matters of motive, intention, direction, and relationship to other concerns give to *epithumia* its moral character."[46] Jesus used the term in a morally valid sense when He said: "With desire I have desired to eat this passover with you you" (Luke 22:15). The Epistle of James uses the term in the sense of perverted or invalid desire, which becomes the springboard for sin: "But every man is tempted, when he is drawn away of his own lust, and enticed" (Jas. 1:14). The idea of the relation of the law to improper desire (lust) is presented by Paul in Rom. 7:7, where the law evaluates slumbering desire and regards it as sin. Commenting on Paul's reference to perverted desire as sin, Kittel remarks:

> Desire *(epithumia)* is not to be limited to the sensual or sexual sphere, but must be understood in a comprehensive sense as the mania for self-assertion over against the claim of God, which bursts into flame when challenged by the commandment. Here is the nerve of every kind of sin, from the primal flouting of God (Rom. 1:21) to the sexual perversions and the anti-social crimes and all that further sinning which Paul sees as the divine punishment of sin.[47]

7. *Sin as Irreverence*

A deliberate pattern of irreverence, *asebeia*, is another New Tesment term for sin. It is sometimes translated "ungodliness," as in II Tim. 2:16: "But shun profane and vain babblings; for they will increase unto more ungodliness" *(asebeias)*. The term may also be translated as "godlessness, impiety, in thought and act."[48] Lenski states that ungodliness and unrighteousness are the two sides of sin:

> All ungodliness is also unrighteousness and vice versa. Irreligion manifests in immorality (violation of the norm of right), and immorality is the evidence of irreligion (contrariness to God). God sees these two in every sin.[49]

8. *Sin as Enmity*

Hostile feelings or active hatred towards God are conveyed by

[46]Stagg, *op. cit.*, p. 16.

[47]Gerhard Kittel, *Bible Key Words from Theologisches Worterbuch Zum Nuen Testament*, trans. J. R. Coates (New York: Harper and Bros., 1951), I, 79.

[48]Arndt and Gingrich, *op. cit.*, p. 114.

[49]R. C. H. Lenski, *St. Paul's Epistle to the Romans* (Columbus, Ohio: Wartburg Press, 1945), p. 92.

the term *echthra.* Enmity, or *echthra,* is a strong term used by both Paul and James to describe a set of the feelings in a particular direction. To Paul, enmity is "active hatred towards God, hostile opposition to his will, on the part of man in his determination to live for himself and manage by himself. This thought of hatred becomes the constitutive element in the Pauline conception of sin."[50] Paul thus says that "the carnal mind is enmity against God" (Rom. 8:7). In another sense the idea is that of a feud existing between two people, as between Pilate and Herod (Luke 23:12).[51] In an extremely powerful statement James shows the antagonism or hostility involved in *enmity (echthra):* "Ye adulterers and adulteresses, know ye not that the friendship of the world is enmity *[echthra]* with God?" (Jas. 4:4)

9. *Sin as Depravity*

A comprehensive term for wickedness as opposed to virtue and as an evil disposition is the word *kakia.* Thayer translates it by giving two shades of meaning.[52] First, it means *malignity, malice, ill will, desire to injure* (Rom. 1:29; Eph. 4:31; Col. 3:8; Titus 3:3; Jas. 1:21; I Pet. 2:1). Second, it means *wickedness, depravity,* as in I Cor. 5:8 and 14: 20; Acts 8:22. In I Pet. 2:16 it means "wickedness that is not ashamed to break the laws."[53] According to some writers *kakia* denotes a vicious disposition. Thus *kakia* is a negative term describing a condition or disposition that is useless, unsuitable, bad, improper, "that which in its nature and purpose ought to be different."[54] Sin is thus seen to be a state as well as an act.

10. *Sin as Active Evil*

Where *kakia* refers to a state or condition, *poneros* denotes the positive expression of evil—that which is "dangerous, destructive, injurious, evil."[55] In the natural sense it may mean unfit for use or worthless, as in Matt. 7:17, where "a corrupt tree bringeth forth evil fruit." But in the moral sense, "*poneros* is the concrete embodiment of a *kakos;* and while *kakos* denotes the nature of character, *poneros* refers to the behavior."[56] Thayer interprets the term to mean "evil

[50]Kittel, *Bible Key Words,* I, 76.

[51]*The Analytical Greek Lexicon* (New York: Harper and Bros., n.d.), p. 779.

[52]*Op. cit.,* p. 320.

[53]*Ibid.*

[54]Hermann Cremer, *Biblio-Theological Lexicon of New Testament Greek,* trans. William Urick (Edinburgh: T. and T. Clark, 1962), p. 320.

[55]*Ibid.*

[56]*Ibid.,* p. 512.

purposes and desires," as in Mark 7:22, or as "a soul conscious of wickedness,"[57] as in Luke 6:45, where the evil act is permitted deliberately because of the essential corruptness of the person.

11. *Sin as a Violation*

As a result of a state of evil or corruption, *(kakia)* a pattern of evil purposes and desires *(poneros)* become part of the person living in sin. Mere evil purposes and desires become overt acts and deliberate deeds. Thus sin is a transgression. The word "transgression," *parabasis,* is from the root word *para-baino* and means to cross the line, to transgress, also to depart or desert (Acts 1:25). Thus the term *parabasis* means a disregarding, a violation. In connection with Adam's sin, as discussed by Paul in Rom. 5:14, the term means "the breach of a definite, promulgated, ratified law."[58]

The purpose of the law, according to Paul, is to bring an awareness of transgression (Rom. 4:15; 5:20; Gal. 3:19). The purpose of the law was "that sins might take on the character of transgressions, and thereby the consciousness of sin be intensified and the desire for redemption be aroused."[59] In Heb. 2:2, *parabasis* is linked with disobedience. In I Tim. 2:14 it is stated that Eve was led into transgression *(parabasis)* by being deceived. In summary, *parabasis* "denotes sin, objectively viewed, as a violation of a known rule of life."[60]

12. *Sin as an Offense*

The term *paraptoma* is another strong word denoting sin. The word may be used as an offense in two senses. The first meaning of the word corresponds generally to *hamartia,* as suggested in Gal. 6:1. Here the idea is of unknown or unintentional failure. But there is a stronger meaning in the term, for "it may . . . be regarded as synonymous with *parabasis,* which designates sin as the transgression of a known rule of life, and as involving guilt."[61] It is used of transgressions against men (Matt. 6:14) but means "as a rule of sins against God."[62] Hence *paraptoma* means "a lapse or deviation from truth and uprightness; a sin, misdeed."[63]

[57]*Op. cit.,* p. 530.
[58]*Ibid.,* p. 478.
[59]*Ibid.,* p. 479.
[60]Cremer, *op. cit.,* p. 499.
[61]*Ibid.,* p. 498.
[62]Arndt and Gingrich, *op. cit.,* p. 627.
[63]Thayer, *op. cit.,* p. 485.

Summary

From a study of the biblical terms it may be stated that in its comprehensive use the word *sin* means two things. First, it refers to external acts which fail to conform to a recognized standard or an accepted law. This failure to conform may be deliberate or involuntary, but the idea of deliberate, willful violation is dominant. Second, sin is also a subjective state, or condition, which involves rebellion, antagonism, evil desire, and deliberate preference of evil. From the preceding study of biblical terms, it is possible to formulate a biblical definition of sin.

CHAPTER V /

A Biblical Definition of Sin

The Bible presents no formal definition of sin, although James states that sin is the neglect of the good (Jas. 4:17). The nearest statement giving a definition of sin is I John 3:4, where the writer states that "sin is the transgression of the law." The Bible deals with sin as a reality in man's existence, with the redemptive power of God in dealing with sin, and with God's love for the sinner. While the Bible does not present a formal definition of sin, it does present the raw materials for a workable definition.

This attempt to formulate a definition of sin is not merely semantic hairsplitting nor academic gamesmanship. To have a workable definition is essential to the practical preaching of the gospel and is equally essential to honest and sincere personal Christian living.

I. The Importance of a Definition of Sin

In discussing the importance of arriving at a definition of sin, James B. Chapman wrote: "We are driven to the necessity of arriving at definitions for sin that we may intelligently consider terms for describing the cure for sin."[1] H. V. Miller, in his book, *The Sin*

[1]*The Terminology of Holiness*, p. 24.

Problem, emphasizes the importance of a definition of sin as follows: "The sin question is the pivotal question. Anything taught or preached which obscures the cruciality of sin becomes an enemy of the cross of Christ."[2] Richard S. Taylor says that "we need to know exactly what sin is, of what kinds, how it acts, its effects, its relation to man, how it must be dealt with, and God's provision for it."[3] W. T. Purkiser renders a significant comment in the following statement:

> One of the most important issues emerging in modern evangelical circles is concerned with the definition of sin. It is more than a theological argument over the proper usage of terms. It goes directly to the heart of Christian life and experience. It has bearings on every branch of the doctrine of salvation. Our conception of the whole plan of redemption is radically affected thereby.[4]

A number of significant reasons can be presented which show the necessity and the importance of arriving at a right conception of sin.

A. A Wrong Concept of Sin Produces Wrong Results.

First, a wrong concept of sin may make preaching a path to hypocrisy, an avenue to despair, or a road to presumption. Preaching may lead to hypocrisy when it tends to make sin exclusively legal or objective. Such preaching tends to encourage Pharisaism, for it ignores the inner area of motive and desire. Preaching may lead to despair when it makes that sin which is not sin and the sensitive soul lives under a continual cloud of condemnation. Preaching may lead to presumption when sin is committed freely and continually because of false notions about the inability of divine power to free one from those moral and spiritual aberrations which need to be eliminated.

B. A Wrong Concept of Sin May Lead to Sin.

H. Orton Wiley has pointed out: "Calling that sin which is not sin, opens the door to actual sinning."[5] For if there are no recognizable distinctions between sin and non-sin, man operates under a double hazard. He neither knows when he is sinning, nor is he able

[2](Kansas City: Beacon Hill Press, 1947), p. 23.
[3]*Op. cit.,* p. 10.
[4]*Conflicting Concepts of Holiness,* p. 45.
[5]*Christian Theology,* II, 508.

to ever be freed from the bondage of sin. Thus it is true that "to make everything sin, is, in effect, to make nothing sin."[6] On the other hand, to make everything sin, including mistakes, is to make it impossible to be free from sin. If a person believes it is impossible to be free from sin, he may become careless and commit sins of an open and voluntary nature.

C. A Wrong Concept of Sin Eliminates Personal Responsibility.

Only a moral being, with consciousness and conscience, is able to make moral distinctions and feel moral obligations. A tree feels no compunction if a coconut drops on a man's head, knocking him unconscious. A dog feels no guilt when he snatches a piece of hamburger from the table. But man is a being with a capacity for moral distinctions, and sin, in the ethical sense, becomes meaningful only in the light of moral responsibility. As James Orr suggests, there are several elements in the constitution of the moral agent:

> (1) Capacity of moral knowledge—perception of moral distinctions of right and wrong, good and evil, with recognition of the obligation which the perception of the right imposes on the will.
>
> (2) Capacity of moral affections (approval and disapproval, etc.).
>
> (3) Possession of a measure of self-determining freedom. Moral law prescribes to the agent at once what he ought to *be* and what he ought to *do;* and sin arises from shortcoming or disobedience in either respect.[7]

D. A Wrong Concept of Sin Misinterprets the Bible.

While the Old Testament teaches that certain things, mostly ceremonial, done in ignorance were to be atoned for by sin offerings and trespass offerings, yet the major emphasis is upon personal responsibility and individual obedience to a holy God. The New Testament even more sharply distinguishes mistakes and infirmities from sins. For instance, Jesus was so named because "he shall save his people from their sins" (Matt. 1:21). More important than the name of Jesus is His redemptive work, for "Christ loved the church, and gave himself for it; that he might sanctify and cleanse it" (Eph. 5:25*b*-26*a*). Christ forgives sins and cleanses the carnal nature (I John 1:7), but His compassion is shown in the fact that He is fully sympathetic with our infirmities (Heb. 4:15). There is a vast differ-

[6]Purkiser, *Conflicting Concepts of Holiness*, p. 57.
[7]*Op. cit.*, pp. 31-32.

ence between sympathy for infirmities and forgiveness and cleansing from sin. Sympathy cannot eliminate the infirmity, nor does an infirmity involve guilt.

E. A Wrong Concept of Sin Misrepresents Sanctification.

One who does *not* accept the Wesleyan idea of sanctification writes:

> The theory of entire sanctification rests on the false premises that only conscious sins are truly sins; that God requires only a relative holiness; i.e., a holiness according to the individual's ability; and that God would not command holiness if He did not also enable man to be holy.[8]

A similar sentiment is expressed in the statement of another scholar: "Practically all heresies characterizing the holiness movement and false doctrines of sanctification, eradication or perfectionism have their origin in a failure to comprehend the scriptural teaching regarding the sin nature."[9]

John Wesley, on the other hand, taught that the Bible regarded only voluntary transgressions as sins, for he wrote: "Nothing is sin, strictly speaking, but a voluntary transgression of a known law of God. Therefore, every voluntary breach of the law of love is sin; and nothing else, if we speak properly."[10] Wesley acknowledged that a mistake was "a transgression of the perfect law."[11] But he adds "This is not sin, if love is the sole principle of action."[12] But both voluntary sins and involuntary mistakes need the atonement, according to Wesley. He writes:

> Not only sin, properly so called, (that is voluntary transgression of a known law,) but sin, improperly so-called (that is, an involuntary transgressing of a divine law, known or unknown,) needs the atoning blood.[13]

The correct understanding of the Wesleyan view of sanctification can thus be understood only if the nature of sin is properly defined. Many critics of the holiness movement and of sanctification present their objections in a context completely different from Wesley's idea of sin. The critics of perfectionism are often

[8]*Lutheran Cyclopedia*, p. 479.
[9]Walvoord, *op. cit.*, p. 234.
[10]*Works*, XII, 394.
[11]*Ibid.*, XI, 395.
[12]*Ibid.*
[13]*Ibid.*, p. 396.

more perfectionistic than the perfectionists themselves. Wesley wrote:

> I believe there is no such perfection in this life as excludes these involuntary transgressions which I apprehend to be naturally consequent on the ignorance and mistakes inseparable from mortality. . . . Therefore, *sinless perfection* is a phrase I never use, lest I should seem to contradict myself.[14]

However, Wesley refused to call such involuntary transgressions sins. It is only in the background of his definition of sin as "a voluntary breach of the law of love" that Wesley could say that "a Christian could be perfect so as not to commit sin." The entire concept of personal holiness is valid only if the nature of sin is understood in a framework such as Wesley gave it. Otherwise the entire structure of holiness points either to proud legalism or to absurd fanaticism. But within the context of Wesleyan interpretation the experience of holiness is both experientially possible and logically sound.

F. A Proper Definition of Sin Necessary.

The nature of the religious experience called "holiness," or deliverance from sin, needs to be described for the benefit of those within the group as well as those without.

For those within the group, an adequate definition will save from legalism on the one hand and from self-condemnation on the other. It will save from legalism in that the only perfection claimed is that the grace of Christ is sufficient to deliver from external transgression and from internal pride. It will save from self-condemnation by admitting the presence of human frailities and infirmities. To those on the outside it will state the position clearly and adequately.

A misleading interpretation of sin and perfection is seen in the following statements:

> The New Testament knows no short cut to sinless perfection by some special blessing or endowment of the Spirit. This idea is a false "holiness" doctrine which evades the hard demands of salvation. One "being sanctified" is a person brought into a covenant relation with God and thus brought under the corrective discipline of his zealous love. At Pentecost, as already stated, the disciples were endowed with power, not with perfection.
>
> The first epistle of John is appealed to by those who seek

[14] *Ibid.*

> support for the claim to sinless perfection. Ironically, this epistle was a refutation of just such claims made by self-styled spirituals. There were those who claimed to be "in the light" and to be above sin. Claiming that they were above sin, they ignored the contrary evidence of their own practices.
>
> First, John rejects outright the theory of sinless perfection, saying: "If we say that we have no sin, we deceive ourselves, and the truth is not in us" (1:8); and again, "If we say that we have not sinned, we make him a liar, and his word is not in us" (1:10).[15]

A proper biblical definition of sin will indeed indicate that sinless perfection is not possible. Since a biblical theology of holiness makes no claims to such perfection, the allegation of the above statement is directed against a straw man. It might be added that the holiness movement exalts Christ as the Source of holiness. Thus the holiness people can in no way be associated with those to whom John was speaking in his First Epistle, for these people denied the Incarnation and the atonement. It might also be added that, in I John 2:1, John gently reminds his readers of the purpose of the Epistle: "My little children, these things write I unto you, that ye sin not."

II. A Biblical Definition of Sin

Since Wesley's definition of sin is the basic one in the contemporary holiness movement, his definition is again stated, along with some criticisms of it. Then a definition of sin which is built on Wesley's thought is presented and evaluated by the rules and principles already stated.

A. Wesley's Definition of Sin

John Wesley, as already suggested, presented a clear, concise definition of sin from which he never varied. The definition is repeated here for the sake of emphasis: "Nothing is sin, strictly speaking, but a voluntary transgression of a known law of God. Therefore, every voluntary breach of the law of love is sin, and nothing else, if we speak properly."[16] Most men, in criticizing Wesley's definition, fail to note that Wesley includes in his proposition the phrase *law of love*. By including the subjective idea of the "law of love," Wesley avoided making his concept of sin completely external, moral, or legal, as is often claimed.

[15]Stagg, *op. cit.*, pp. 108-9.
[16]*Works*, XII, 394.

1. *Objections to Wesley's Definition*

In a classic work, *The Idea of Perfection in Christian Theology,* R. N. Flew suggests that the most serious defects in Wesley's idea of perfection "spring from an inadequate analysis of the nature of sin."[17] Flew's objection arises from Wesley's stress on the *volitional* and the *known,* for he says:

> Our worst sins are often those of which we are unconscious. The stress on the consciousness and deliberate intention of the agent is the most formidable defect in Wesley's doctrine of the ideal. If only those transgressions are overcome which are recognized to be transgressions by the agent, the degree of sanctification attained by him will depend on his previous moral development, on his own insight into his motive, and on his knowledge of himself.[18]

Olin A. Curtis, one of the most sympathetic among students of Wesley's doctrine, who taught within Methodism, also pointed out what appeared to be a weakness in Wesley: "I have found no way of harmonizing all of Wesley's statements at this point; and I am inclined to think that he never entirely cleared up his own thinking concerning the nature and scope of sin."[19]

2. *The Validity of Wesley's Definition*

No one can read Wesley's sermons, with their concern for perfect love and with their sharp condemnation for everything contrary to perfect love, without realizing his deep concern for the subjective aspect of sin. And those class meetings! The various groups of Methodists agreed to meet each week, under the direction of a leader, who would "speak on his own state first, and then to ask the rest, in order, as many and as searching questions as may be, concerning their state, sins, and temptations."[20] Wesley was concerned with a practical, workable, biblical concept of sin that would be simple in presentation and powerful in application. He may have oversimplified the definition but he was nearer to the heart of biblical truth than other definitions have been.

Let us consider briefly several popular definitions of sin which meet neither biblical interpretations nor existential requirements.

[17](London: Oxford University Press, 1934), p. 332.

[18]*Ibid.,* p. 333.

[19]Olin A. Curtis, *The Christian Faith* (New York: Eaton and Mains, 1905), p. 378.

[20]Wesley, *Works,* VIII, 258.

B. Non-Wesleyan Definitions

Two common non-Wesleyan definitions are the moral and legal definitions.

1. *Moral Definition*

According to F. R. Tennant, "Sin will be imperfect compliance . . . with the moral ideal in so far as this is, in the sight of God, capable of apprehension by an agent at the moment of the activity in question."[21] At this point it is evident that Tennant is not far from Wesley. His reasons for identifying sin with personal responsibility are three: (1) this usage accords best with Christian tradition; (2) it is demanded by our ethical sense; (3) there is no real alternative in any case, because perfect human nature cannot be defined.

The weaknesses of Tennant's definition are twofold. First, he makes "sin" exclusively moral and ethical, rather than religious and personal. A second weakness is that the nature of the definition "is to reduce sin to one among the many evils which plague human existence."[22] While an acceptable definition of sin would include Tennant's ideas of moral and ethical responsibility, the definition must go beyond to include the biblical ideas of original sin and the religious idea of sin as rebellion against God.

2. *Legal Definition*

A classic definition of sin is stated in the *Westminster Catechism.*[23] The famous definition of sin rendered in the *Shorter Catechism* stated that sin was "any want of conformity to or transgression of the law of God."[24] Commenting on this definition, T. W. Manson writes:

> This definition is too narrow to cover the different ways in which Jesus regards sin. Moreover . . . sin is not primarily a matter of omissions and commissions, but a condition of the soul,

[21]*The Concept of Sin* (Cambridge: University Press, 1912), p. 245.

[22]Mary Thelan, *Man as Sinner* (New York: King's Crown Press, 1946), p. 21.

[23]The Westminster Assembly of Divines met on July 1, 1643, being summoned by the two Houses of Parliament for the purpose of effecting a more perfect reformation of the liturgy, discipline, and government of the Church of England. The preparation of a catechism was put by the assembly in December, 1643, into the hands of Herbert Palmer, master of Queens College, Cambridge, who was known as the best catechist in England. It was five years later, in 1648, that the 13 pages in the catechism were presented, adopted, and readied for printing.

[24]S. W. Carruthers, *Three Hundred Years of the Westminster Shorter Catechism* (New Brunswick: University of New Brunswick, 1957), p. 5.

> analogous to disease in the body. This analogy is implied in the saying: "They that are whole have no need of a physician, but they that are sick. I came not to call the righteous, but sinners" (Mark 2:17). . . . This is the fundamental point, and the explanation why, in the ministry of Jesus, so much stress is laid on repentance (*metanoeo,* change of character) rather than on reformation of behaviour. The attempt by rules and regulations to mend the manners of mankind is to treat symptoms instead of disease.[25]

A contemporary amplification of the Westminster definition of sin is given in the following statement: "The slightest outward or inward departure from absolute mathematical parallelism with God's revealed will and character constitute a sin, and at once makes us guilty in God's sight."[26] This definition will not stand up under biblical analysis. By examining the 41 verses in which the verb "to sin," *hamartano,* appears in the New Testament, W. T. Purkiser has shown that the legal definition of sin is inadmissible, for the definition cannot be substituted for the verb "to sin" without completely warping the scriptural meaning involved.[27] The following example is presented by Purkiser:

> First, let us take an illustration from the Gospels. In John 5:14, we read: "Afterward Jesus findeth him in the temple, and said unto him, Behold, thou art made whole: sin no more, lest a worse thing come unto thee." Let us substitute the legal definition. Then we would read: "Behold, thou art made whole: *deviate* no more *in any manner from an absolute standard of perfect behavior,* lest a worse thing come unto thee." This would certainly place the poor fellow in a terrible spot! How could he avoid all deviations from a perfect standard, known or unknown, voluntary or involuntary?[28]

C. A Biblical, Religious Definition of Sin

Sin may be defined as *a voluntary transgression of a known law of God by a morally responsible agent,* or as *any state or attitude which is contrary to Christian love.* From a study of the terminology of sin it has been shown that the word *sin* means two things: (1) external acts which fail to conform to a given standard, and (2) a subjective state contrary to love. It is possible to test this definition according

[25]*The Teaching of Jesus* (Cambridge: The University Press, 1931), p. 308.
[26]J. C. Ryle, *Holiness* (Westwood, N.J.: Fleming H. Revell Co., n.d.), p. 2.
[27]*Conflicting Concepts of Holiness,* pp. 45 ff.
[28]*Ibid.,* p. 51.

to the rules and principles of definition generally accepted, as follows:

a. Defining sin as both act and as state presents fully the essence of sin. To regard sin as *voluntary act* and as *subjective state,* both of which are contrary to God's revealed and known will, is to clearly define the essence of sin.

b. The above definition is not circular. It does not contain the term to be defined, nor does it circle back on itself. It proceeds in a direct path toward the presentation of the concept defined.

c. It is positive rather than negative. It is an affirmative proposition involving direct activity or realistic self-awareness.

d. It is expressed in understandable terms rather than in vague, abstract language.

e. The definition has the quality of universality. It can be applied to all men equally.

f. The definition also has the characteristic of particularity. It can be related to each individual in his specific existential situation.

g. It is anthropologically oriented, in that it is directed to the understanding, needs, and ideals of man. Because of its concerns for the needs of man, the definition incorporates the essential human aspects of freedom, love, and justice.

h. Finally, the definition is biblical. It contains the basic idea of sin as revealed in a study of Old Testament terminology. It also reflects the fundamental idea of sin which is expressed in New Testament terminology. Further, it is possible to substitute the definition for the term defined, as suggested by Purkiser.[29] If this substitution was made, the words of Jesus to the woman accused of adultery in John 8:3-11 would read as follows: "Neither do I condemn thee: go, and do not voluntarily transgress any known law of God, and no longer permit any attitude or state of mind contrary to Christian love to be part of your day-to-day living."

Now that a definition of sin has been presented, it is possible to discuss the nature of sin.

III. The Nature of Sin

The nature of sin may be discovered by describing its activity, or expression, as well as by attempting a final definition of its es-

[29]Cf. Purkiser, *Conflicting Concepts of Holiness,* pp. 50-51.

sential nature. Positively, sin involves the substitution of self for God as the ultimate end of life. Negatively, sin is a transgression of the law. Both the negative and positive aspects of sin spring from a state of spiritual corruption. Theologians have described sin as selfishness,[30] as a want of conformity to the divine law or standard of excellence,[31] as rebellion,[32] and as estrangement.[33] From these definitions and from the Wesleyan definition stated above, it is possible to state that sin is both an act and a state. Sin is an overt act; but by legitimate extension, sin also includes those attitudes, dispositions, and propensities which are at the core of the voluntary act.

A. Sin as an Act

Sin, as we have defined it, is a voluntary transgression of a known law of God by a morally responsible agent. To accept this definition of sin is to accept the biblical teaching of the personal, volitional nature of sin. Accepting this definition of sin also involves the rejection of non-biblical ideas of sin.

1. *Sin as Personal, Volitional Act*

Since the sin of the original pair in the Garden of Eden is the prime example of all acts of sin, this first sin may be used to suggest the elements involved in every act of sin. These necessary elements are: (1) an objective Being or standard; (2) free, self-aware personality; (3) a live option; (4) a deed which is committed or an attitude which is sanctioned.

a. God as the objective Being, or Standard. Sins are possible only if there is a holy God. If there is no God, there is no sin. Crimes are transgressions of human laws, although a crime might be also a sin. Sins are transgressions of divine laws. When God created man, He made man in His own image. By creation, then, man was to be subordinate to God. God was God and man was man. By creation man was given a perfect personality and a perfect environment, which included person-to-person fellowship with God. But God made it emphatically clear that man was a steward who was under

[30]A. H. Strong, *Systematic Theology* (Philadelphia: Griffith and Roland Press, 1907), II, 567.

[31]Charles Hodge, *op. cit.*, II, 187.

[32]Niebuhr, *op. cit.*, II, 179.

[33]Tillich, *Systematic Theology*, II, 46.

obligation to obey and to live in harmony with divine commands (Gen. 2:15-17).

b. Man as free, self-aware personality. The essence of personality is self-awareness to which are added rational powers of choice. Man is thus able to recognize himself as a distinct, unique being. Man also is able to transcend himself, to reflect or think beyond himself. Man is conscious of values, can make moral judgments, and can choose. Further, man is aware that his choices are not imposed from without, but find their sanction and motivation from within.

c. A live option. Sin, to be an act of sin, involves a live option—a choice between two alternatives of moral and spiritual significance which are in competition and which are recognized. The sin of Adam and Eve was not the result of ignorance, weakness, nor blunder. They came to a crucial point in their existence. It is true that the temptation came through a subtle personality which was evil. But the first pair knew the limitations placed upon them. They also knew God as no other human beings have known God. They faced the live option—and they failed. The alternatives presented to Eve centered upon physical craving, intellectual desire, the drive for self-expression or for success, and social influence.

d. A deed committed. The overwhelming evidence of biblical and historical evidence regards sin as a deed which is deliberately committed in defiance of or in indifference to God's revealed law. When Cain became angry because his offering was rejected, the Lord suggested that there was no mystery attached to the rejection. Then came the incisive judgment: "If thou doest well, shalt thou not be accepted? and if thou doest not well, sin lieth at the door" (Gen. 4:7). When Moses had finished his valedictory address to his people, he reminded them of their obligation in these words: "I call heaven and earth to record this day against you, that I have set before you life and death, blessing and cursing: therefore choose life, that both thou and thy seed may live" (Deut. 30:19).

It was a deliberate deed which wrung the agonized cry from David: "For I acknowledge my transgressions: and my sin is ever before me" (Ps. 51:3). When Isaiah warned Israel of the coming judgments of God, his warning was directed to the "rebellious children" who added "sin to sin" (Isa. 30:1). When Jeremiah attempted to comfort his bereaved people, he assured them that God had not forsaken them, even "though their land was filled with sin against the Holy One of Israel" (Jer. 51:5). The sins that Jeremiah referred to were deeds of evil—idolatry, immorality, dishonesty, etc. When the prodigal son came home, his brokenhearted cry, "Father, I have sinned against heaven" (Luke 15:21), was an admission of wrong deeds. Finally, both Paul and John issued persistent calls to the Christians to cease from all deliberate wrongdoing (Rom. 6:1; I Cor. 15:34; I John 3:9).

From the biblical point of view a sin is an act or a deed which is deliberately committed, or willfully purposed, in the face of a knowledge that God's will does not permit it. To accept this biblical description of sin is to reject all non-biblical ideas of sin. But sin is not confined to an act or deed which is deliberately committed. The Bible broadens the reality of sin to include attitudes and motives and the whole range of inner responses (Matt. 5:21 ff).

B. Sin as a State

The Bible teaches that sin is a state as well as an act. As a state, sin consists of those attitudes, dispositions, and propensities which lead to voluntary transgression. The most direct way to discuss sin as a state or condition is to look to the Bible for direction. In addition to the Bible, however, the voice of theology has generally accepted the reality of sin as a state of the human personality. This state is usually called original sin.

1. *Biblical Teaching of Original Sin*

The idea of original sin revolves around the universal hereditary sin of mankind as related to the original sin of Adam. Both the Old Testament and the New Testament present the universal nature of original sin.

a. Old Testament teachings about original sin. After the Fall, the human race became depraved, except for a few who sustained a saving relationship to God. This depravation was the result of freedom deprived of fellowship with God. After Cain killed Abel he was exiled and his lament is significant: "Behold, thou hast driven me out this day from the face of the earth; and from thy face shall I be hid" (Gen. 4:14). Cain then built a culture completely separated from God. Thus *deprivation* led to *depravation,* for when God passed judgment on the world prior to the Flood, He did so because He "saw that the wickedness of man was great in the earth, and that every imagination of the thoughts of his heart was only evil continually" (Gen. 6:5). In referring to the state of man before the Flood a theologian wrote:

> This was not an occasional or even a frequent lapse into pollution, but it was the constant and uninterrupted state, not of a portion of the human family, but of "man," the general mass of the race of *Adam.*[34]

After the Flood, in the midst of Noah's sacrificial thanksgiving, the Lord again stated that "the imagination of man's heart is evil from his youth" (Gen. 8:21). Three things are expressed forcibly in the statement. First, it refers to the depravity of man in general—to the entire race. Second, the statement was made when only Noah and his family were living upon the earth. Third, the depravity of man is presented as characteristic of human nature throughout his life ("from his youth," that is, his infancy or earliest stage of personal accountability).

Job indicated man's natural sinfulness when he said: "Who can bring a clean thing out of an unclean? not one" (Job 14:4). Following up on this, Eliphaz asks: "What is man, that he should be clean? and he which is born of a woman, that he should be righteous?" (Job 15:14) The reading of the Septuagint here is, "Who shall be clean from filth? not one, even though his life on earth be a single day." Here is pinpointed the natural state of man.

That there is an inborn, corrupt state, from which sinful acts and dispositions flow, is evident from David's confession: "Behold, I was shapen in iniquity, and in sin did my mother conceive me" (Ps. 51:5). This passage is not to be interpreted as meaning that the act of conception, or procreation, is an act of sin. Neither does it indicate that the process of birth is impure. It does recognize that the Psalmist and his parents were part of the human race, and as such they carried the taint or stain of sin in the race. Again the Psalmist makes his penetrating assertion: "The wicked are estranged from the womb: they go astray as soon as they be born, speaking lies" (Ps. 58:3). Here the words *estranged* (alienated from the divine image) and *speaking lies* (actual sin) describe a state of sin which is not acquired, but which is evident from birth.

A prophetic verdict on man's corruption was rendered by Jeremiah in these words: "The heart is deceitful above all things, and desperately wicked; who can know it?" (Jer. 17:9) Here is a blanket indictment of the human race. The race is not partially bad nor

[34]Thomas N. Ralston, *Elements of Divinity* (New York: Abingdon-Cokesbury Press, 1924), p. 130.

occasionally truant—it is "desperately wicked." In the Old Testament, man's spiritual picture is painted in tragic and realistic colors. Man—all men—is by nature corrupt and separated from God. The New Testament paints man's spiritual portrait with the same unmistakable colors.

b. New Testament teachings about original sin. Paul teaches that through one man sin entered the world (Rom. 5:12-21), bringing with it the twin disasters of universal sin and the condemnation of universal death. In Paul's writings it is clearly seen that neither human sin nor death existed before the sin of Adam. After Adam's fall, both sin and death became realities in human existence, and are regarded as the direct consequence of Adam's sin. The apostle also states that death as a consequence of sin was passed upon all men. Thus original sin and inherited depravity are identical. Further, in I Corinthians 15, Paul directly associates the coming of death on the human race as due to the sin of Adam. Again in his letter to the church at Ephesus, Paul declares that all men are "by nature the children of wrath" (Eph. 2:3). Here "nature" signifies something inborn and original, as distinguished from that which is subsequently acquired.

While depravity is primarily a biblical doctrine, it is not exclusively such. For history reflects the influence of depravity, literature portrays its agonies, existential philosophy expresses its despair. And contemporary depth psychology, although using a different terminology, sets forth views strangely akin to the biblical idea of depravity. Original sin, or inherent depravity, according to the Bible, is a quality, predisposition, bias, twist, or state of the human personality from which arise all actual transgressions and all unchristian attitudes such as pride, selfishness, self-will, and enmity against God.

Summary

This chapter has attempted to show the relevance of the doctrine of sin to the life of holiness. From a study of basic biblical terms it has been shown that sin is both an act and a state, or condition, which involves attitudes, disposition, etc. Then a definition was presented based on the study of biblical terminology and incorporating the general rules and principles governing the formation of definitions. With sin adequately defined, it was then possible to show that sin is both an act and a state.

CHAPTER VI /

Holiness: The Foundation of the Kingdom

The Old Testament presented cultic and personal holiness as the essence of the religion of Israel. However, it was not until Christ came to earth that man could understand the true nature of holiness.

The Gospels present the reality of divine truth embodied in sinless humanity. The foundational truth of the gospel message is simply that a holy, divine-human Being revealed the redemptive truth of a holy God. In the Gospels, holiness became the ultimate objective of the redemption and the foundation of the kingdom of God.

Holiness is one of the focal points for understanding the Gospels. The Gospels are composed of principles which are to be proclaimed, teachings which are to be interpreted, and ethics which are to be applied. Although not without ritual and not averse to ceremony, Christianity is not a mystical religion with hidden meanings and obscure values. Its doctrines do not lie completely outside the limits of intelligible expression or of rational apprehension. Its ethical concepts are profound and personal, but Christianity is the combination of ceremony, doctrine, and ethics in an experience of dynamic spiritual power. Such an experience is called the experience of holiness.

Each of the four Gospels revolves around the life of holiness as presented by Christ. The life of holiness is always expressed in relation to the Kingdom. In Matthew, holiness is the basis of ideal citizenship in the Kingdom. In Mark and in Luke, holiness is the springboard to active service in the Kingdom, while John's Gospel presents holiness as the basis of continued fellowship in the Kingdom on earth and of eternal life in the kingdom of Heaven.

I. Importance and Nature of the Kingdom of God

The entire ministry of Christ centered around the announcement of the kingdom of God and the invitation to all men to become part of God's people. The Kingdom concept thus fulfilled and embraced the nationalistic emphasis of Judaism and the personal covenant replaced the covenant with Israel. In order to understand the vital place of holiness in the new covenantal relationship, it is essential to first recognize the importance and the nature of the kingdom of God.

A. Importance of the Kingdom Concept

The teaching regarding the kingdom of God is one of the basic New Testament ideas. As one writer states it: "The student of the New Testament cannot but realize that the idea which is everywhere fundamental is that of the Kingdom of God. It was primary with Jesus himself, and when we look beneath the surface it was no less so with Paul and the later teachers."[1] The Kingdom concept was closely related to the Messianic consciousness of Jesus. Relating the Messianic work of Jesus to the Kingdom concept, one author commented: "It is now generally recognized by New Testament scholars that during His ministry our Lord thought of Himself as the expected Messiah come on earth to establish the promised Kingdom of God."[2] His main work was "to preach the advent of the Kingdom of God, and to summon men to be citizens of that Kingdom."[3] Millar Burrows writes that "the concept of God's kingdom is most important in the teaching of Jesus."[4] Jesus proclaimed the kingdom of God as a Kingdom of redeemed and regenerated persons, a spiritual Kingdom working and expanding amid the temporal, mundane world.

[1]E. K. Scott, *The Kingdom of God* (New York: The Macmillan Co., 1931), p. 3.

[2]Leonard Hodgson, *The Doctrine of the Atonement* (New York: Charles Scribner's Sons, 1951), p. 71.

[3]*Ibid.*

[4]*Op. cit.*, p. 66.

B. Nature and Meaning of the Kingdom of God

The Greek word *basileia* was used in a dual sense. It was used concretely to signify a "kingdom," that is, the territory and people and general political unit over which a king rules. Abstractly, the term meant "kingship," or the rule of a king. Both meanings are involved in the New Testament usage of the term. The phrase "kingdom of God" thus meant the sovereign rulership of God and the community of those forgiven, regenerated, and obedient to the rule of the Holy Spirit. In Matthew the rulership of God is expressed by means of a spiritual constitution.

C. The Constitution of the Kingdom

The significance of holiness as related to the kingdom of God was proclaimed by Zacharias and John the Baptist before Christ appeared. When Christ came, one of His first acts was to set forth the constitution of the Kingdom. In setting forth the constitution of the Kingdom, Christ indicated the following principles: the requirements of citizenship in the Kingdom; the ideal of character desired in citizens of the Kingdom; the nature of acceptable service in the Kingdom; and finally, the doctrine of eternal life as part of the Kingdom life. Each of these principles revolves around the concept of holiness.

II. Holiness: The Basis of Citizenship in the Kingdom

Holiness is required for full citizenship in the Kingdom. The term "full citizenship" does not imply that there are first-grade citizens and second-grade citizens in the Kingdom. Nor does the idea of "full citizenship" imply that there are secular citizens and saintly citizens. The term does indicate that man's spiritual status is determined by his response to spiritual principles, and that full citizenship is of necessity possible only to those who make the kingdom of Heaven their ultimate object of loyalty and their final object of love. The loyalty and love of those in God's kingdom are expressed in holy living.

A. Heralds of Citizenship in the Kingdom

The experience of holiness as a requisite for full citizenship was seen by Zacharias and John the Baptist even before Christ appeared. When Christ did appear, the nature of the Kingdom as well as the direct teachings of Christ revealed that holiness, or perfection, was the supreme qualification of heavenly citizenship.

1. *Zacharias—Witness to Holy Citizenship*

Zacharias was privileged to share in the miraculous events which preceded the birth of Christ. One of the preparatory events for the coming of Christ was the birth of John the Baptist. Zacharias, the father of John the Baptist, through the inspiration of the Holy Spirit, realized that the ancient covenant made with Abraham (Gen. 17:1-8; 22:16-17) was about to be completed in the person of the Messiah. And while the words of Zacharias were colored with a traditional nationalistic emphasis of deliverance from enemies, "yet his prayers and aspirations in this song rose above the height of mere victory over national foes, even to a peaceful reign of truth, righteousness and purity, through all their days."[5]

More specifically, Zacharias gave witness to the possibility of holy living as a direct outcome of the birth of Christ. "God's promises and the fulfillment of those promises in the redeeming work of Christ include personal holiness and righteousness for His children."[6] The possibility of holy living is presented in the following words:

> That he would grant unto us, that we being delivered out of the hand of our enemies might serve him without fear, in holiness *[hosiotes]* and righteousness before him, all the days of our life (Luke 1:74-75).

This witness to holy citizenship in God's kingdom was to be a contemporary possibility, for the witness of Zacharias refers to "all the days of our life." A clear and precise comment on the potential for present holiness is given in the following comment:

> *All the days of our life.* Here is the answer to any quibble over the divine timetable for holy living. These are not only future heavenly blessings in store for God's people, but privileges which we may enjoy now. Nor does this inward grace need to be spasmodic; it is intended to be an established mode of life.[7]

2. *John the Baptist—Herald of Holy Citizenship*

After four centuries of silence in the prophetic order, John the Baptist appeared with dramatic suddenness in the wilderness of

[5]Henry Cowles, *Luke: General History and Acts of the Apostles* (New York: D. Appleton and Co., 1881), p. 18.

[6]Charles L. Childers, "The Gospel According to Luke," *Beacon Bible Commentary* (Kansas City: Beacon Hill Press, 1964), VI, 443.

[7]*Ibid.*

Judea. The message of John was direct and challenging: "Repent ye: for the kingdom of heaven is at hand" (Matt. 3:2). The way into the kingdom of Heaven was repentance.

Looking beyond initial acceptance into the Kingdom by faith and repentance, John anticipated the nature of full citizenship in the Kingdom when he said:

> *I indeed baptize you with water unto repentance: but he that cometh after me is mightier than I, whose shoes I am not worthy to bear: he shall baptize you with the Holy Ghost, and with fire: whose fan is in his hand, and he will throughly purge his floor, and gather his wheat into the garner; but he will burn up the chaff with unquenchable fire* (Matt. 3:11-12).

The important truth here is that when Christ comes to establish His kingdom in the hearts of men, His main objective is the baptism, the purging of His followers. Fire is used as the instrument of purging, for fire illuminates and invigorates the soul and would "*penetrate* every part, and *assimilate* the whole to the image of the God of glory."[8] Another writer states that "fire will purify that which can stand it . . . but will burn away all that is unworthy (Mal. iv.1; Mk. ix.49; I Cor. iii.13-15)."[9] In Wesleyan terminology "the baptism with the Spirit and the purging of the floor are coterminous acts—they go together."[10] Both Zacharias and John the Baptist declared that the coming of Christ would mark the beginning of a new concept—the spiritual kingdom of God on earth. Both of these Spirit-filled men stated that holiness would be the distinguishing feature of citizenship in the Kingdom.

B. Requirements of Citizenship in the Kingdom

The requirements for citizenship in the kingdom of God were presented without apology and without confusion.

1. *The Necessity of Repentance*

Without question repentance was the basic human qualification (Matt. 3:1; 4:7; Mark 1:15; Luke 13:3; Acts 2:38). Such repentance is identified with faith and with the new birth (John 3:3; I Pet. 1:23; I John 2:29; Rom. 3:28). Not because these experiences are unimportant or incidental, but because the purpose of this book is to discuss the doctrine of holiness, the acts of repentance and re-

[8]Adam Clarke, *Commentary*, V, 53.

[9]Alan Hugh M'Neile, *The Gospel According to Matthew* (London: Macmillan and Co., 1961), p. 29.

[10]Purkiser, *Conflicting Concepts of Holiness*, p. 22.

generation are not discussed here. Following repentance, faith, and regeneration there comes the experience of holiness, through sanctification, which is the supreme quality of the citizen of the Kingdom.

2. *Perfection—the Essence of Citizenship*

The biblical terms "holiness," "perfect love," and "perfection" are used synonymously in Wesleyan theology, because they all point to the same state of grace. Holiness is the presence of all spiritual graces, unhindered by the presence of personal, volitional sin and unhampered by inner carnality. Perfect love is expressive of the spirit and temper, or the moral atmosphere in which the entirely sanctified Christian lives. Perfection "signifies that spiritual completeness or wholeness into which the soul enters when the last inward foe is conquered, and the last distracting force harmonized with the mighty love of Christ, every crevice of the nature filled with love, and every energy employed in the . . . service of the . . . Savior."[11] Such perfection implies not only complete deliverance from all spiritual pollution, but the possession of the unmixed graces of faith, humility, resignation, patience, meekness, self-denial, and all other graces of the Holy Spirit.

In his conversation with the young man who was anxiously inquiring about eternal life, Christ stated the fundamental principle of complete surrender as the basic requirement of citizenship in the Kingdom. Christ pointed out that there can be no divided loyalties in the highest spiritual state when He said, "If thou wilt be perfect, go and sell that thou hast, and give to the poor" (Matt. 19:21). Divided loyalties render the life of holiness impossible, for "no man can serve two masters" (Matt. 6:24). Even earthly nations require complete and undivided loyalty as a basis for full citizenship. An example of the complete loyalty required of those about to become citizens of a voluntarily chosen nation is found in the oath taken by those becoming citizens of the United States.

> I hereby declare, on oath, that I absolutely and entirely renounce and abjure all allegiance and fidelity to foreign prince, potentate, state, or sovereignty, of whom or of which I have heretofore been a subject or citizen. That I will support and defend the constitution and laws of the United States against all enemies, foreign and domestic . . . and that I take this obligation freely without any mental reservation or purpose of evasion.

Full citizenship requires full surrender and complete dedica-

[11]Cook, *op. cit.*, p. 57.

tion. Jesus taught that in the realm of the kingdom of Heaven the only workable concept of full spiritual realization is found in the life and the experience of holiness, or perfection.

3. *The Meaning of Perfection*

Few words have caused so much confusion and controversy among Christians as the word "perfect." Many feel that the term reflects spiritual pride or, at best, spiritual presumption. Yet the term is a biblical one and is used more frequently in the Bible than any other single term to indicate the essential nature of Christian experience. It occurs 138 times in the Scriptures, and in more than 50 of these instances it refers to human character under the operation of grace.[12] In the teachings of Christ and in the writings of Paul the word *perfect* is used 17 times describing fitness for the kingdom of Heaven, while the cognate noun *perfection* is used twice and the verb *to perfect* 14 times.

4. *Evangelical Perfection*

New Testament Greek contains the words which are translated *perfect—teleios* and *artios.*

a. Perfection as completeness. Thayer, in his *Greek-English Lexicon of the New Testament,* suggests the following meaning of *teleios*: "brought to its end, finished; wanting nothing necessary to completeness; perfect."[13] When used substantively, as *to teleion, "that which is perfect:* consummate human integrity and virtue, Ro. xii.2."[14] According to Thayer the verb form of this word, *teleioo,* means, among other things, "to complete (perfect), i.e., add what is yet wanting to render a thing full . . . to bring one's character to perfection."[15] One of the meanings of *teleios* suggested by Arndt and Gingrich is "persons who are fully up to standard in a certain respect . . . perfect, fully developed in a moral sense . . . Js. 3:2."[16]

b. Perfection as fitness, or adequacy. In II Tim. 3:17, the word *artios* is used to refer to being "in fit shape or condition." As Lenski puts it: "There is nothing wanting in the Christian's outfit for work, in his equipment for what God expects him to do."[17] However,

[12] *Ibid.*

[13] P. 618

[14] *Ibid.*

[15] *Ibid*

[16] *Op. cit.,* p. 817.

[17] R. C. H. Lenski, *The Interpretation of St. Paul's Epistles to the Colossians, to the Thessalonians, to Timothy, to Titus, and to Philemon* (Columbus, Ohio: The Wartburg Press, 1956), p. 848.

Lenski rejects the translations of both the Authorized Version, where *artios* is interpreted as *perfect*, and the Revised Version, where it is translated *complete*. Vincent translates *artios* as the "harmonious combination of different qualities and powers,"[18] while rendering the word *katartisai* (Heb. 13:21) as making perfect, or "to bring into complete adjustment."[19]

The evangelical conception of perfection is inherent in another rendition of *artios* as follows: "complete, capable, proficient . . . able to meet all demands."[20] In commenting on the verse where *artios* appears (II Tim. 3:17), Godbey makes a definite Wesleyan application: "Christian perfection removes everything out of the heart impedimental to our full efficiency in the work of the Lord."[21]

When taken in its context, *artios* can be said to refer to spiritual fitness, spiritual harmony, spiritual adequacy, or spiritual maturity. In a general sense, the above terms could be used as synonymous with the term *evangelical perfection*. Those who are perfect in this sense of the word are fully prepared and adequately equipped for service in the kingdom of God and possess the spiritual graces which it is possible, by the gift of divine grace, to receive.

c. Perfection as love. To John Wesley, Christian perfection meant simply "that love of God and our neighbour, which implies deliverance from all sin."[22] In a more inclusive definition, Wesley remarks that Christian perfection is

> the loving God with all our heart, mind, soul, and strength. This implies, that no wrong temper, none contrary to love, remains in the soul; and that all the thoughts, words, and actions, are governed by pure love.[23]

According to Thomas Cook, evangelical perfection embraces two things:

> (1) A perfection of love proportioned to the powers of each individual;
> (2) A steady progress in love harmonizing with our circumstances and increasing our capacities and abilities.[24]

In Wesleyan theology there is no claim to or sense of absolute

[18]*Op. cit.*, IV, 318.

[19]*Ibid.*

[20]Arndt and Gingrich, *op. cit.*, p. 110.

[21]W. B. Godbey, *Commentary on the New Testament* (Cincinnati, Ohio: M. W. Knapp, 1898), III, 319.

[22]*Works*, XI, 393.

[23]*Ibid.*, p. 394.

[24]*Op. cit.*, p. 61.

perfection, which is the essence of God alone. Nor is there in it any compulsion to strive for a perfection beyond the limit of spiritual attainment. Evangelical perfection is a fulfillment of the New Testament commandment: "And thou shalt love the Lord thy God with all thy heart, and with all thy soul, and with all thy mind, and with all thy strength" (Mark 12:30). There is no command or statute in the Bible which sets up or requires any other standard, for "love is the fulfilling of the law" (Rom. 13:10). Love is to be complete to the extent of the present capacity of the person possessing it.

Full citizenship in the kingdom of Heaven is established on the basis of holiness. The Bible stresses a vital religion which climaxes in holiness. It logically follows that the Lord Jesus Christ knows nothing of a holiness that does not manifest itself in inner and outward obedience to God and service to man.

When John, and Jesus, and Peter, and Paul said, "Repent ye," they meant now, immediately, not at some vague point in the distant future. Similarly, the possibility of experiential holiness here and now is reflected in the commands, "Be ye perfect," and, "Be ye holy." The dependable, sacrificial, and loyal citizen of the kingdom of God is one who has responded and does respond to the call of holiness, to perfection. But holiness, or perfection, is not only the basis of full citizenship in the Kingdom. Holiness is also the ideal of Christian character in the Kingdom.

C. Holiness: The Ideal of Christian Character

The kingdom of God, like every other kingdom, presents an ideal of character which is desirable, or acceptable, in the Kingdom. Both the ideal and the reality of holy character in the Kingdom are described in the Sermon on the Mount. "The Sermon on the Mount is in truth the very constitution of this Kingdom."[25] The Beatitudes in particular present the qualities of holiness which the Kingdom requires. John Wesley describes the approach of Christ with penetrating insight. Wesley said that Christ, when He delivered the Sermon on the Mount, seemed to "lay aside His supreme authority as our Legislator, that He may better act the part of our Friend and Saviour. Instead of using lofty style, in positive commands, He, in a more gentle and engaging way . . . pronounces those happy

[25]Chester K. Lehman, *The Holy Spirit and the Holy Life* (Scottdale, Pa.: Herald Press, 1959), p. 46.

who comply with it."[26] To Wesley the Beatitudes were a "sweet invitation to true holiness and happiness." An examination of the eight beatitudes indicates that only a person living in a vital relationship to Christ, in holiness, could ever find happiness by the spiritual ideal presented by the Christ of the Mount.

1. *A Sense of Need*

One of the strongest motivations to the development of holy character is a sense of need. "Blessed are the poor in spirit: for theirs is the kingdom of heaven" (Matt. 5:3). Since there is nothing ethical, let alone blessed, in economic poverty as such, the first beatitude cannot refer to one's economic situation. It states that the primary quality leading to a holy character is a sense of *spiritual* poverty. One of the greatest of all principles in regard to man's behavior is the principle that nothing can be done for a person, or for a group, until there is a sense of need. Since pride is frequently man's greatest sin, "poverty of spirit is essentially the dethronement of pride."[27] The poor in spirit "are those who recognize . . . that they can do no good thing without divine assistance, and that they have no power in themselves to . . . do what God requires them to do."[28]

To be poor in spirit does not mean an attitude of emptiness or of supineness. To be poor in spirit means to have emptied oneself of all desire to exercise personal self-will. To be poor in spirit means a willingness to set aside present habits of thought, contrary views, and prejudices, to "jettison, in fact, anything and everything that can stand in the way of your finding God."[29] Such an attitude is possible only in a state of true holiness.

2. *Spiritual Sensitivity*

Mature Christian character is sensitive to personal and social evils. "Blessed are they that mourn: for they shall be comforted" (Matt. 5:4). The mourners are not those who lament their fate nor those who "sigh for the touch of a vanished hand and the sound of a voice that is still," although such mourners do receive the com-

[26]*Explanatory Notes upon the New Testament* (London: Epworth Press, 1941 [reprint]), p. 28.

[27]William Fitch, *The Beatitudes of Jesus* (Grand Rapids, Mich.: Wm. B. Eerdmans Pub. Co., 1961), p. 24.

[28]R. V. G. Tasker, *The Gospel According to St. Matthew* (London: The Tyndale Press, 1961), p. 61.

[29]Emmet Fox, *The Sermon on the Mount* (New York: Grosset and Dunlap, 1934), p. 22.

fort of God. The mourners are those who express genuine sorrow over their sins and sincerely repent. The mourners are also those to whom the evil that is in the world is a continual grief, those who are grieved at the apparent eclipse of God's cause, and those who suffer at the indifference to righteousness of a depraved race. Holiness is the great "sensitizer"—it makes people aware of wrong to an unusual degree.

3. *Spiritual Perspective*

Meekness is as rare as it is essential. Strong, confident Christian character is meek. "Blessed are the meek: for they shall inherit the earth" (Matt. 5:5). To a generation which has made a cult of social and physical self-assertion, the term "meek" suggests a person of servile and apologetic spirit, devoid alike of courage and self-respect, a kind of blundering creature like Charles Dickens' Uriah Heep.

The English writer Emmet Fox regards this beatitude among the half dozen most important verses in the Bible, for in this text lies the "Secret of Dominion, the secret of overcoming every kind of difficulty."[30] Meekness is a state of mind which reflects a perfect willingness to accept God's will in every situation and a state of grace which evaluates everything, including oneself, in the light of spiritual values. Meekness is self-acceptance, without shame and without pride. More important, meekness is that perspective which views life from a stance of submission to God. "It is that temper of spirit in which we accept his dealings with us as good, and therefore without disputing or resisting."[31]

4. *Spiritual Appetite*

A developing character is a character reaching out for God's best. "Blessed are they which do hunger and thirst after righteousness: for they shall be filled" (Matt. 5:6). The Christian life is a life which includes crises and development. The experience of holiness, in particular, is a life that must be fed upon righteousness. To hunger and thirst after righteousness means to have a genuine desire to know the truth. It means holding a challenging concept of right and wrong. Martin Luther felt that he was a really blessed man who perseveringly and assiduously attempted to promote the general welfare and the right conduct of everyone, and one who helped to

[30]*Ibid.*, p. 28.

[31]Richard C. Trench, *Synonyms of the New Testament* (Grand Rapids, Mich.: Wm. B. Eerdmans Pub. Co., 1958, [reprint]), p. 152.

maintain and carry this out with word and deed, with counsel and act.[32]

5. *Discriminating Compassion*

Holy character never adjusts to sin or injustice. It always feels the impact of suffering. "Blessed are the merciful: for they shall obtain mercy" (Matt. 5:7). There is a type of naive and indulgent mercy that feeds the ego of the offender by making it appear that "he has gotten away" with something. To ignore wrong or to disregard the results of misdeeds is to encourage lawlessness. In the experience of holiness there is an open-eyed, realistic appraisal of wrong action that is neither gullible nor harsh. It is the expression of mercy. To be merciful is the holy way of doing things. The mercy described in this beatitude is the spirit of forgiveness in a situation "in which, through wrongdoing or failure of some other kind, another human being is in our power."[33] In such a situation the "happy man" does what is right.

6. *The Vision Splendid*

Holy character has a long-range perspective. It looks beyond the horizons to another world. "Blessed are the pure in heart: for they sall see God" (Matt. 5:8). Jesus did not say blessed are the pure in wisdom, or knowledge, or judgment, but the pure in heart. The term *heart* signifies the will and the affections. A pure heart is a heart which contains nothing contrary to the will of God. Purity of heart also stands for single-mindedness, or sincerity. The pure in heart have a dominating purpose to serve in God's kingdom and to contribute to His kingdom.

This beatitude of the pure heart, like its companions, is presented as characteristic of people in this present world. Certainly there is no mourning in heaven (Matt. 5:3), and the peacemakers are not engaged in patching up quarrels in heaven (Matt. 5:9), nor are those in heaven persecuted for righteousness' sake (Matt. 5:10). These beatitudes represent experiences in this life. In the center of these beatitudes which refer unmistakably to this life Jesus says, "Blessed are the pure in heart." A noted holiness writer describes purity of heart in these words: "In the pure heart all the Christian virtues exist to the exclusion of their opposite vices; as love without hatred, submission without rebellion, faith without unbelief, humility with-

[32]Martin Luther, *Commentary on the Sermon on the Mount*, trans. Charles A. Hay (Philadelphia: Lutheran Publication Society, 1892), p. 46.

[33]Eric Baker, *The Neglected Factor* (New York: Abingdon Press, 1963), p. 59.

out pride, meekness without anger, patience without impatience, and peace with no strife."[34] Purity of heart opens the eyes of the soul to visions of God.

7. *Benevolent Arbitration*

The Christian personality should be like healing oil in the body of mankind. "Blessed are the peacemakers: for they shall be called the children of God" (Matt. 5:9). Warfare, rather than peace, is the natural state of man. In a little more than 6,000 years of recorded history there has not been a single year in which the whole world was at peace.[35] Since peace is not the natural state of man, peace must come as the result of direct effort or as a result of the grace of God. The peacemaker is thus one who attempts to resolve the conflicts within, between, and among men.

The blessed men Christ referred to are not those who purchase peace at any price, but those who actively and courageously reconcile and enlarge the area of human goodwill. By so doing they indicate their moral relationship to the God of peace (Rom. 15:33). Holiness is the key to peace and to peacemaking, for in holiness the seeds of rebellion and corruption are removed, to be replaced by love and mercy. The only enduring peace is the peace built upon holiness.

8. *Holy Courage*

There is a courage which is greater than physical bravery or social concern. It is the courage of the pure heart. "Blessed are they which are persecuted for righteousness' sake: for theirs is the kingdom of heaven" (Matt. 5:10). Up to this time Jesus had been describing the idea of character acceptable in the Kingdom. In this final beatitude He tells of the reception that the genuine Christian will meet in the world.

Because the citizen of the Kingdom is listening to the beat of a different drummer than the world hears, he is met with indifference or even with open antagonism. Holiness is not acceptable in a depraved race, for holiness stands as a rebuke to sin. Jesus lived out the Beatitudes to the point of perfection, and the response of sinful humanity was a cross against the sky. Paul was willing to spend and be spent for the healing of the wounds of a bleeding humanity—and

[34] J. A. Wood, *Purity and Maturity* (Chicago: The Christian Witness Company, 1913), p. 49.

[35] D. R. Davies, *Secular Illusion or Christian Realism* (London: Latimer House, Ltd., 1942), p. 19.

his reward was the blade of the executioner. Paul's summary of the reception of holiness in an ungodly world is: "Yea, and all that will live godly in Christ Jesus shall suffer persecution" (II Tim. 3:12).

Jesus did not indicate that suffering *qua* suffering was blessed, but He did mean that when persecution arises because of holy living, then the Christian has an opportunity to display holy courage. Not only does the Christian exhibit holy courage; he adds to this courage a new note—joy.

The ideal of character in the Kingdom is possible only in the experience of holiness. For only in such an experience can the Christian develop the qualities of a profound sense of continual need, spiritual sensitivity, spiritual perspective, spiritual appetite, discriminating compassion, the vision splendid, benevolent arbitration, and holy courage.

Christian character cannot be expressed in a vacuum. Holy character must step into the arena of life with supreme confidence in the power and grace of Christ to meet issues head on and to demonstrate the nature of acceptable conduct in the Kingdom. Holiness is best demonstrated in man's day-by-day activities, attitudes, and decisions.

D. Holiness: a Revolution Within Personality

In the Bible there is no false tension between theory and practice, between principles of conduct and the expression of these principles in life. Acceptable conduct in the Kingdom is the outgrowth of holy character, which in turn is the result of an inner renovation coming from the presence of the Holy Spirit. As the expression of holy character, this inner revolution includes purified intention, spiritual motivation, self-discipline, dedicated affections, open allegiance, generous allowance, and absolute commitment. These qualities should exist in the regenerate, but the experience of regeneration is often weak and spasmodic. The Spirit-filled life, the life of holiness, on the other hand, is marked by the strong and consistent expression of Christian graces.

1. *Purified Intention*

Jesus said: "Except your righteousness shall exceed the righteousness of the scribes and Pharisees, ye shall in no case enter into the kingdom of heaven" (Matt. 5:20). Jesus did not intend to lessen the demands of the law. "Rather, it is his wish to sharpen these and to indicate how very deeply they cut into the pattern of daily living."[36] Righteousness, or holiness, is considered to be a personal morality. But it must be more than observance of external law. The righteousness of the Pharisees failed because it was an outward performance only, with little regard for subjective intention. It is the addition of purified intention to outer observance that elevates personal holiness above Pharisaical righteousness. By presenting a series of six contrasts between legal observance and purified intention Jesus revealed the starting point of spiritual living in the Kingdom.

a. Anger versus murder (Matt. 5:21-26). Whedon comments on the passage as follows: "Not merely bodily killing, but the mental impulse and purpose, which are the root of all murder—whether it be mental murder of the body, of the intellectual reputation *[raca]*, or of the moral honour *[moron]*—are to be punished according to their aggravations in the High Court of heaven."[37] Anger is thus equated with murder, for the desire to kill a man physically, intellectually, or morally is labeled sin. Only a holy heart, in which perfect love dwells, can eliminate hate from the heart. Hate, while it is not as heinous as actual murder, is harmful enough to consign one to hell.

b. Lust versus adultery (Matt. 5:27-30). Holiness does not dehumanize a person so that he is exempt from temptation in the area of sex, nor does it remove an awareness or an appreciation of normal and natural sex urges. Holiness does make it possible to be free from lust, which is awareness of sexual attraction to which is added an openly admitted or nurtured desire. Lust is volition added to imagination. The absence of opportunity may prevent the overt act and restrain one from actual sin, but if in intention the act is committed or if in imagination the deed is fancied, then guilt is present. Jesus did not condemn normal and legitimate sexual desire. What He condemns is the regarding of a woman simply as a means for the gratification of desire—to regard her as an object and not a person.[38]

c. Valid and invalid divorce (Matt. 5:31-32). The law of Moses had allowed divorce as a concession to unenlightened humanity. The

[36]John Wick Bowman and Roland W. Lapp, *The Gospel from the Mount* (Philadelphia: The Westminster Press, 1957), p. 63.

[37]D. D. Whedon, *Commentary on the Gospels, Matthew—Mark* (New York: Carlton and Porter, 1860), p. 80.

[38]A. D. Lindsay, *The Moral Teaching of Jesus* (New York: Harper and Brothers, 1937), p. 145.

inner life of holiness regards marriage as a divinely established institution, having for its aim the lifelong union of a man and a woman. Luther commented that Christians are not to be divorced, but "each to retain his or her spouse, and bear and experience good and evil with the same, although he or she may be strange, peculiar, or faulty; or if there be a divorce, that the parties remain unmarried; and that it will not do to make a free thing out of marriage."[39]

d. Integrity versus cleverness (Matt. 5:33-37). Having struck at three of the most devastating sins of society—murder, adultery, and divorce—Jesus strikes out against the sin of excessively clever, profane, idle talk. The holy man is simple and unaffected in his speech. The whole "mechanics of swearing" was simply a clever method of confusing issues. Holy integrity does not need the reinforcement of an oath for the simple reason that real truth is a matter of intention as well as of words. A plain "yes" or a plain "no" should serve the purpose of integrity.

e. Forbearance versus retaliation (Matt. 5:38-42). Jesus presented a principle which lifted personal revenge out of the hands of the offended party. The old law was "an eye for an eye" (Exod. 21:23-25; Lev. 24:17-21; Deut. 19:16-21). The new life of holiness was the principle of forbearance in cases of personal wrong. Jesus was talking to disciples and of personal relations between the disciples. If this principle of forbearance is applied indiscriminately to depraved humanity, it would result in violence, anarchy, and slavery.

All cases of personal assault, of unfair suit at law, official imposition of burdens or unofficial exploitation of talents, and requests for assistance should be met with forbearance rather than retaliation. Jesus nowhere disallows a desire for justice and nowhere sanctions brutal exploitation. Jesus was saying only that holiness does not seek revenge. "We can never know," remarks Montefiore, "how much hot anger has been quelled, how much lust for vengeance has been suppressed, how much self-sacrifice has been evoked, by the paradoxical stimulating and picturesque doctrine of *the other cheek* and of *the coat* and the cloak."[40]

f. Inclusive love versus exclusive affection (Matt. 5:43-38). To render evil for evil is animallike; to render good for good is humanlike; to render good for evil is Godlike. By love *(agape)* Jesus did not

[39] *Op. cit.*, p. 169.

[40] C. J. Montefiore, *The Synoptic Gospels* (London: The Macmillan Co., Ltd., 1924), p. 82.

mean an emotion or an affection *(eros, phileo).* Jesus was not referring to romantic love, brotherly love, parental love, filial love, patriotic love, or comradely love.

Divine love, as it is reflected in human conduct, is a principle of action, a purity of intention, a persistent goodwill towards all men. Divine love is the God-given desire to see every human being attain to his highest degree of self-realization under God, plus a willingness to make whatever contribution possible to such attainment.

2. *Proper Motivation*

Christian character and true spirituality depend upon true motivation. "Take heed that ye do not your alms [righteousness] before men" (Matt. 6:1). Only an omniscient God knows all the motives that prompt human activity. Certainly one's fellow citizens are not able to scrutinize one's motives, and often the individual himself is unaware of his true motives. It is in the area of intention and motivation that the experience of holiness makes the greatest difference. Acceptable motivation before God is expressed in three ways: unobtrusive giving, reverential prayer, and undeclared self-discipline.

a. Holiness provides proper motivation in giving. Jesus taught that there was a wrong way and a right way to give offerings and to help others (Matt. 6:1-4). The wrong way was to announce the act or the gift, to publicize the act of piety in order to gain goodwill or prestige among men. Such motivation for giving one's means for good purposes is hypocritical; it is acting a part; it is using a mask of piety to cover selfish motives. The right way to give is to dispense the gift so unobtrusively and so casually that it is unnoticed by others and and unrehearsed to ourselves. It is done and forgotten, without hope of human plaudits or divine reward.

b. Holiness produces proper motivation in prayer. Another area of spiritual activity where proper motivation is important is in the act of praying (Matt. 6:5-8). Holiness results in reverential prayer. As there are acceptable and non-acceptable ways to give offerings, so there are acceptable and non-acceptable methods of praying. The wrong way to pray is to concentrate on oneself, to give or to bring more attention to the one praying than the *One* to whom the prayer is offered. The wrong way to pray is to have more concern for the effect of the prayer on the people than it does on God, to concentrate on the form of the prayer, or the length of time spent in prayer.

The right way to pray is to exclude, as far as possible, all distracting elements, to shut out things and forget people. Proper prayer is based on the realization that praying ushers one into the presence of a holy, sovereign God. Acceptable prayer eventuates in confidence and trust in God and peace and faith within man.

c. Holiness presents proper motivation for fasting. In the area of fasting, holy motives are also essential (Matt. 6:16-18). Self-discipline, as represented by fasting, is an activity sanctioned by Christ, but such self-discipline should not be an occasion for spiritual display nor an event for mournful appearance. When a person is fasting he does not need to announce it in billboard fashion.

Fasting was a sign of penitence, particularly among the pious Jews who were accustomed to fast each Monday and Thursday (Luke 18:12). "Centuries before, Isaiah, deploring insincere fasting, had condemned those who bowed down their heads like a bulrush, and grovelled in sackcloth and ashes (Isa. 58:5)."[41] Jesus condemned those who sought to establish a reputation for piety by smearing ashes on their faces and parading in public, in order to hear the murmur of the crowd, "There goes a godly man." "And that, says Jesus, is their reward, the reward they bargain for, and all the reward they are ever going to get."[42]

3. *Dedicated Affections*

Because man's affections tend to dominate his activities, they should be holy affections. "Lay not up for yourselves treasures upon earth . . . but lay up for yourselves treasures in heaven . . . for where your treasure is, there will your heart be also" (Matt. 6:19-21). Toynbee has pointed out that, in regard to the world, religion can take one of three directions. Some religions, as Islam, identify religion and the social order. Others, such as monasticism, are anti-worldly or excessively otherworldly. Some, like Christianity, are in the world, but not of the world.[43]

Jesus warned against the attitude that derived its main satisfaction in life from things that belong to this world only. Not only love of money, but love of honor, the love of position, the love of status, the love of one's work in an illegitimate sense—whatever it

[41] A. M. Hunter, *A Pattern for Life* (Philadelphia: The Westminster Press, 1953), p. 75.

[42] *Ibid.*

[43] Arnold Toynbee, *Christianity Among the Religions of the World* (New York: Charles Scribner's Sons, 1957), pp. 8-10.

may be, anything that stops with this life and this world is not worthy of unreserved affection.[44]

To lay up treasures in heaven is to view life from the perspective of holiness. Vital holiness means death to the love of money, the end of coveting honors, the cessation of idolatry of position, freedom from slavish devotion to personal gain. Holiness lays up treasures in heaven because it focuses a person in a position of stewardship and appreciation for eternal values.

4. *Open Allegiance*

The Christian's supreme loyalty is to God. "Ye cannot serve God and mammon" (Matt. 6:24). Spiritual schizophrenia is ultimately impossible. Holiness is healthy because it operates on the level of open and consistent allegiance, resulting from complete submission to God's will. The literature of present-day psychiatry, contemporary educational theory, and current philosophical discussion all point to the fact that man commits suicide when he operates from a base of divided loyalty, and that man attains the highest degree of personal self-realization and satisfaction when he deliberately transcends his own experience to support or work in behalf of a cause. Holiness is the springboard of open allegiance to Christ.

5. *Generous Evaluation* (Matt. 7:1-5)

Wesley suggested that the chief hindrances to holiness arose from a lack of generous evaluation.[45] Holiness brings an appreciation of all personality that refuses to exercise spiritual judgment or discrimination "without full, clear, certain knowledge, without absolute necessity, and without tender love."[46] Only a person with an exalted sense of his own importance detects insignificant faults or weaknesses (the mote) in others while remaining ignorant of glaring flaws in his own life (the plank, joist, rafter). Holiness is not naive in its approach to problems, nor is it gullible in dealing with unpleasant or unjust action, but holiness does reserve judgment or render judgment in a spirit of generous evaluation.

6. *Absolute Commitment*

"Enter ye in at the strait gate" (Matt. 7:13). "Not every one that saith unto me, Lord, Lord, shall enter into the kingdom of

[44]D. Martyn Lloyd-Jones, *Studies in the Sermon on the Mount* (Grand Rapids, Mich.: Wm. B. Eerdmans Pub. Co., 1960), II, 81.

[45]*Notes*, p. 41.

[46]*Ibid.*

heaven, but he that doeth the will of my Father which is in heaven" (Matt. 7:21). The strait gate is the holiness described in the Sermon on the Mount, says Wesley.[47] The gate to this holy way is narrow. Not only is the gate narrow, but the way is narrow all along—holiness to gain entrance and holiness to remain.

Such things as eloquent professions or noteworthy success are not sufficient to assure entrance into the Kingdom. Holiness builds character, and all character is inevitably tested. When the test arrives, holiness is the one quality of Christian experience that guarantees stability and endurance. One can make the ultimate, absolute commitment only in the expression of a dedicated, purified life which is called holiness.

III. Holiness: The Standard of Acceptable Service

The Gospel of Matthew presented the ideal of holy character in the kingdom of God. The Christian life, however, is not a cloistered withdrawal from life. True holiness arrays itself in the garments of righteousness and strides out to meet the issues of life head on. The Gospel of Mark and the Gospel of Luke present a picture of the outreach of holy service. Writers such as J. Wesley Bready, W. W. Sweet, and Timothy L. Smith have shown that true holiness has always had a concern for social and individual service.

Christian service involves at least four principles, all related to holiness. The first of these principles is that love is the source of Christian service. The second principle is that holy service is the norm for Christians here and now, rather than a goal of future life; the third principle illustrates the necessity of self-discipline in Christian service; while the fourth principle states that only holiness is adequate to meet the grinding challenge of sin and depravity in this life.

A. Holy Love and Christian Service

The standard for Christian service is complete dedication to God. "And thou shalt love the Lord thy God with all thy heart, and with all thy soul, and with all thy mind, and with all thy strength . . . Thou shalt love thy neighbour as thyself" (Mark 12:30-31). "Love," said Richard Baxter, "is the final act of the soul."

Literally, the idea is to love God *out of thy whole* heart. Love to

[47] *Ibid.*, p. 43.

God is to drain not one area of the heart only, or several, but the entire length and breadth of the domain. The word *heart* us not used here in its modern popular import of the special seat of the affections. It has the more primitive meaning of the interior of our nature, the very center or core of our complex being, as distinguished from the physical periphery.[48] Holiness is wholeness and such wholeness makes possible Christian service.

The total man is to love God—his affections, aspirations, intellectual powers. In a wartime broadcast the Archbishop of Canterbury said to the people of Great Britain: "This world can be saved from political chaos and collapse by one thing only, and that is worship."[49] At first glance such a statement may suggest an ecclesiastical cliché. But the archbishop meant more than church attendance, for he continued: "To worship is to quicken the conscience by the holiness of God, to feed the mind with the truth of God, to purge the imagination by the beauty of God, to open the heart to the love of God, to devote the will to the purpose of God."[50] The Spirit-baptized life produces the greatest service to God and man.

B. Contemporary Holiness

Holiness is a contemporary experience—it is for the "here and now." "That we being delivered out of the hand of our enemies might serve him . . . in holiness and righteousness . . . all the days of our life" (Luke 1:74-75). There are four ideas about the possibility of holiness. One is that holiness is an ideal toward which we are to strive, but which we never attain. A second idea is that the concept of holiness applies to the millennial Kingdom to be established after the second coming of Jesus Christ. A third interpretation is that the beatific vision of God is impossible in any earthly existence and must wait for the completely spiritualized life in God's eternal kingdom. A fourth position is that holiness is a requirement and an experience that can be realized in contemporary experience.

The words of Zacharias might be regarded as a postlude to the Magnificat of Mary. Mary's song magnified God for the gift of Christ, while Zacharias praised God for what the gift of Christ could

[48]James Morrison, *A Practical Commentary on the Gospel According to Mark* (London: Hodder and Stoughton, 1900), p. 341.

[49]Quoted by Ralph W. Sockman, *The Higher Happiness* (New York: Abingdon-Cokesbury Press, 1950), p. 148.

[50]*Ibid.*

do for man—enable him to serve God in holiness and righteousness, in this present life.

C. Holiness, Service, and Self-discipline

The service of God requires strong self-discipline, and holiness encourages such service. "Whosoever will come after me, let him deny himself, and take up his cross, and follow me" (Mark 8:34). Buddhism emphasizes the elimination of all desire, with the goal being *self-negation.* Communism stresses the equality of all people, with public ownership of all property, or *self-identification.* Liberalism, in politics, education, and religion, has advocated free expression which results in *self-exaltation.* Christianity, when it highlights holiness, points to a self-discipline which brings *self-realization.*

As Jesus spoke there was an eagerness among many to come after Him. The people were recalling Old Testament Messianic predictions and were now filled with great expectancy. Jesus wiped out their false hopes with one incisive statement. The followers of Christ were to renounce themselves, to say an everlasting *No* to the strongest cravings of their natures in the direction of earthly ease, comfort, dignity, and glory.

Self-discipline not only included self-renunciation, but moved on to the deliberate assumption of the cross. The follower of Christ must take up his own personal cross, and stagger with it, if need be, to the place of execution, ready for the last extremity.

D. The Clash of Opposites

Sin is man's greatest flaw. Holiness is God's greatest remedy. "I know thee who thou art, the Holy One of God" (Mark 1:24). Religion may take the form of intellectualism, ceremonialism, rationalism, legalism, or mysticism—or vital experience which incorporates some features of each of these types, but which transcends all of them in a meaningful relationship to God. The common feature of ceremonialism, rationalism, legalism, or mysticism is their failure to cope with sin in the raw.

The remarkable thing about the ministry of Christ was His ability to meet the polar opposite of holiness, demon-possessed people, and conquer them. Jesus met, *in the synagogue,* a man with an unclean spirit. And whether it was the man with the unclean spirit in the synagogue, the leper in Galilee, the blind man of Bethsaida, the woman taken in adultery, or the religious hypocrites of the day,

Jesus was able to master the situation and to exert His power.

Not only biblically, but historically, holiness has been the supreme antidote to sin. John Wesley left Georgia a discouraged failure because he felt helpless in the face of primitive expressions of sin. Among the Christian ministers and teachers on the American frontier, the circuit riders were most successful in dealing with sin as they presented the gospel of holiness.

Holiness meets the requirements for citizenship in the Kingdom and answers the qualification for ideal character in the Kingdom. Holiness is the springboard to service in the Kingdom. The crowning point of holiness is in the area of Christian fellowship.

IV. Holiness: The Source of Christian Fellowship

The highest point of ecumenical expression in the New Testament is found in the prayer of Christ in John's Gospel, chapter 17. The basis of ecclesiastical unity is found in the concept of individual unity, and personal unity is the result of the experience of holiness. Any spiritual unity, individual or corporate, must be based on the highest possible principle, not the lowest common denominator of all groups.

On the eve of His period of suffering and death the Teacher becomes the Intercessor, and the Prophet becomes the High Priest. The prayer is the epitome of priestly intercession:

> *Neither pray I for these alone, but for them also which shall believe on me through their word; that they all may be one; as thou, Father, art in me, and I in thee, that they also may be one in us: that the world may believe that thou hast sent me. And the glory which thou gavest me I have given them; that they may be one, even as we are one* (John 17:20-22).

In the High-Priestly prayer three things are considered: the persons for whom the prayer was offered, the purpose of the prayer, and the results hoped to be achieved by the prayer.

A. The Prayer Was for Disciples

Christ was praying for the sanctification of His disciples—and for the Church to follow. Thus the prayer was for the regenerate. Notice the evidences of their regeneration in this chapter. *(a)* They had already been given to Him by the Father (vv. 6, 9, 11). *(b)* They had already obtained eternal life (v. 2). *(c)* Christ had revealed the divine name to them because they were spiritual (v. 6). *(d)* They belonged to God in a peculiar sense (vv. 6, 9). *(e)* They had been obedient to God (v. 6). *(f)* They had knowledge of divine things which comes from experience (vv. 7, 25). *(g)* Christ had entrusted His truth to them as He was about to leave the world (vv. 8, 14). *(h)* They had received Jesus by saving faith (v. 8). *(i)* Jesus was glorified in them (v. 10). *(j)* They were not of the world (vv. 14, 16). *(k)* The world hated them because they were of another world (v. 14). *(l)* They had already received of His glory (v. 22).

B. The Purpose of the Prayer

Jesus prayed: "Sanctify them through thy truth: thy word is truth" (John 17:17). These central words of the prayer are a revelation of what Jesus desired and willed for men. As Westcott puts it: "The prayer is that the consecration which is represented by admission into the Christian society might be realized in fact."[51] The act by which the disciples were to enter into a full fellowship was sanctification. The word *sanctification (hagiosune),* as it is used in the Bible, means four things: (1) separation, (2) dedication, (3) consecration, (4) purification. The Latin equivalent to the Greek noun *hagios* is *sanctus,* meaning "holy," or "pure." Combined with the Latin verb *facere,* "to make," and the suffix *tion,* which indicates "the act of," the word is sanctification, the act of making holy, or pure.[52]

To *sanctify* thus means to set apart for sacred use, or to purify, depending upon the object or person being sanctified. If an unholy being, as man, is to be set apart to a sacred use, he must be rendered internally as pure as the use to which he is appropriated. When an object is set aside for sacred use there can be no purification, except a physical one, and the sanctity ascribed to the object is emblematical. "Where a holy being, such as Christ, is set aside for a holy work, no inward purification is possible, for He is already perfectly pure. It is a consecration of the holy to the holy."[53] It is possible for a human being to be divinely consecrated for service and to be dedicated to the sanctuary of heaven, but to attain this use, his entire purification must be perfect.

[51]B. F. Westcott, *The Gospel According to St. John* (Grand Rapids, Mich.: Wm. B. Eerdmans Pub. Co., 1950), p. 245.

[52]C. W. Ruth, *Entire Sanctification* (Chicago: The Christian Witness Co., 1903), pp. 19-20.

[53]D. D. Whedon, *Commentary on the Gospels of Luke and John* (New York: Nelson and Philipps, 1866), p. 385.

Notwithstanding the apparent loyalty and sincerity of the disciples, Jesus prayed for their sanctification, "having in view not only their perseverance, growth, and maturity in grace as private Christians, but more especially their spiritual equipment for the office of the apostleship."[54]

C. The Results of the Prayer

The results of sanctification would be personal unity—that they, each one, should be wholly (one) a unit. "The oneness here is not merely harmony of will or of love, but oneness by the indwelling of the Spirit of Christ, and ultimately, oneness of nature."[55] The unity would also be spiritual unity—a unity of faith and life in God. The unity prayed for is not unanimity of doctrine, as desirable as that might be. The unity is the type prayed for by the Apostle Paul, who echoes the words of Christ, "Till we all come in the unity of the faith, and of the knowledge of the Son of God, unto a perfect man, unto the measure of the stature of the fulness of Christ" (Eph. 4:13). William Temple refers to such spiritual unity in the words: "The way to the union of Christendom does not lie through committee-rooms, though there is a task of formulation to be done there. It lies through personal union with the Lord so deep and real as to be comparable with His union with the Father."[56]

Summary

Holiness is the key to the Kingdom. It is through the experience of holiness that aliens to God's kingdom are brought to a place of full citizenship. Holiness is the ideal of Christian citizenship and is attainable in the present mode of the Kingdom. All acceptable conduct in the Kingdom is either the direct or indirect expression of the life of holiness. True Christian service finds its source of inspiration and maturation in the experience of holiness. Finally, the fellowship of the saints finds its unity and harmony in the life of holiness. The royal road to both individual wholeness and to ecclesiastical unity is the sanctification of believers—the Spirit-filled life.

[54]A. B. Bruce, *The Training of the Twelve* (New York: Richard R. Smith, 1930), p. 458.

[55]Alford, *op. cit.*, I, 878.

[56]*Readings in St. John's Gospel* (London: Macmillan and Co., Ltd., 1959), p. 327.

CHAPTER VII /

Sanctification as Crisis

In the previous chapter the point of emphasis was the work of the Holy Spirit at Pentecost and after Pentecost. The baptism in or with the Holy Spirit brings a spiritual experience called entire sanctification. In discussing the experience of entire sanctification a few new terms are introduced, such as cleansing and the second crisis. The introduction of these new terms also indicates that the emphasis on the work of the Holy Spirit, often called the baptism with the Holy Spirit, recedes after Pentecost and the state of sanctification and purity move to the foreground.

It should also be stated that up to this point the procedure has been to study the doctrine of holiness in chronological fashion, following a biblical outline. Now the discussion will follow a topical outline for practical purposes.

I. Kinds of Sanctification

Entire sanctification is a crisis experience even as regeneration is a crisis experience. To point to a second crisis is in harmony with both Scripture and with the experience of sanctified people. To regard entire sanctification as a crisis does not minimize the revolutionary nature of regeneration. Nor does a second crisis nullify the possibility of further growth in grace. Sanctification as a crisis conserves the work of regeneration, magnifies the power of God, and makes possible the greatest spiritual growth.

Sanctification, however, has many facets: there is *official* and *religious* sanctification, *social* sanctification, *initial* sanctification, *instantaneous* or *personal* sanctification, and *progressive* sanctification. In the Old Testament the people sanctified themselves; Moses sanctified them; and the priests, Levites, kings, and assemblies sanctified objects and people (Ex. 19:10; Lev. 11:44; John 17:19). This type of sanctification is called *official* or *religious* sanctification. Paul said that an unbelieving husband, or wife, was sanctified by a believing spouse (I Cor. 7:14). Similarly, the children of a home with at least one Christian parent were said to be holy. This is called *social* sanctification.

A. Initial or Partial Sanctification

Initial or *partial* sanctification is another term for regeneration (cf. chap. I). The regenerated person is said to be sanctified (partially) but not wholly, or entirely (I Cor. 1:2; I Cor. 6:11). In this first work a person experiences repentance, saving faith, justification, regeneration, adoption, and the witness of the Spirit. These are all aspects of one instantaneous work which is partial sanctification. All of the spiritual graces in the regenerated, however, have a carnal opposite which is fighting for expression. The presence of these carnal opposites to spiritual graces threatens the spiritual life, or the *eternal life*, of the regenerated.

When the sinner is regenerated he is in possession of eternal life. But eternal life has nothing to do with time or duration. The biblical concept of eternal life is relational and experiential: "And this is life eternal, that they might know thee the only true God, and Jesus Christ, whom thou hast sent" (John 17:3). To know God redemptively *is* eternal life. "Life eternal" refers to a quality of duration, but not to duration itself.

B. Entire Sanctification

Entire sanctification, as a second crisis, is a distinct work of grace. In stating its position on entire sanctification as a second crisis the *Manual* of the Church of the Nazarene reads as follows:

> We believe that entire sanctification is that act of God, subsequent to regeneration, by which believers are made free from original sin, or depravity, and brought into a state of entire devotement to God, and the holy obedience of love made perfect.[1]

[1]*Manual, Church of the Nazarene* (Kansas City: Nazarene Publishing House, 1968), p. 31.

This statement of belief is in harmony with both biblical teachings and practical Christian experience.

In developing a perspective regarding the time element in sanctification it seems necessary to treat the problem from two points of view: (1) biblical examples of entire sanctification as a second crisis; (2) an exegetical analysis of biblical passages regarding sanctification as a second crisis, along with a grammatical analysis of words and phrases which are used in biblical terminology. The latter will be discussed in the next chapter.

II. Biblical Examples of Entire Sanctification

To accept entire sanctification as a second crisis is scriptural. Since revelation is the accepted authority by evangelicals, and since the burden of proof rests most heavily on those who deny the "secondness" of sanctification, the procedure in the following discussion will be to allow the Bible to speak for itself. Several examples will be cited of New Testament personalities who knew God in personal experience, yet had a second crisis which lifted them to the level of Spirit-filled living.

The distinction between *initial* sanctification and *entire* sanctification must be kept clearly in mind in order to avoid confusion in interpreting the Scripture. Paul, in particular, uses the words interchangeably. Thus in Rom 1:7 he writes: "To all that be in Rome, beloved of God, called to be saints." The word "saints" does not indicate either a process of cleansing or a state of holiness. "Saint" is simply a term applied to Christians generally, as those who are called and owned of God.

Again in I Cor. 1:2, Paul writes: "Unto the church of God which is at Corinth, to them that are sanctified in Christ Jesus, called to be saints." Paul certainly did not have in mind any advanced state of purity, since the subsequent description of the Corinthian church is far removed from a highly spiritual, even ethical, church. Paul's use of the term in connection with regeneration is clarified in I Cor. 6:11 when he writes: "But ye are washed, but ye are sanctified, but ye are justified in the name of the Lord Jesus, and by the Spirit of our God." The idea here is that initial sanctification is synonymous with regeneration, and that the process of sanctification begins in regeneration, when one becomes a new being and is set aside as distinctly and uniquely belonging to God.

Concrete examples of a second crisis, following regeneration, are found in the lives of the disciples, the disciples at Samaria, the church at Ephesus, the experience of Paul, and by inference in the experience of Cornelius.

A. The Disciples Before and After Pentecost

The classic example of a second work of grace in the New Testament is the experience of the disciples. There are only four possible ways to regard the condition of the disciples before Pentecost: (1) They were simply highly moral Jews who were inspired by a human leader; (2) They were sanctified before Pentecost; (3) They were regenerated men who were sanctified by the baptism with the Holy Spirit on the Day of Pentecost; (4) They were backslidden believers who were reclaimed at Pentecost. The biblical evidence for the fact of the regeneration of these disciples before Pentecost and sanctification at Pentecost seems overwhelming.

1. *Evidences of Salvation Before Pentecost*
    - *a.* They were not of the world (John 17:14).
    - *b.* They were kept by Christ and were not lost (John 17:12).
    - *c.* Their names were written in heaven (Luke 10:20).
    - *d.* They belonged to God and Christ (John 17:9-10).
    - *e.* They were empowered to cast out devils (Luke 9:1; 10:1, 20).
    - *f.* They were ordained and commissioned (Matt. 28:19; Mark 3:14-15).
    - *g.* They spent 10 days praising God and waiting in prayer (Luke 24:53).
2. *Evidences of Need*
    - *a.* They were sometimes unstable and disloyal (Mark 14:50).
    - *b.* They were at times carnally selfish and carnally ambitious (Mark 10:28; 10:37-41; Matt. 19:27).
    - *c.* They were sometimes carnally sectarian (Matt. 15:22-23).
    - *d.* They were occasionally vindictive in spirit (Luke 9:54-55).
3. *Evidences of a Change After Pentecost*
    - *a.* Their hearts were purified by the baptism with the Holy Spirit (Acts 2:4; 15:8-9).
    - *b.* They were changed from man-fearing, unstable people to bold, courageous witnesses for Christ (Acts 2:14).
    - *c.* Oneness of heart (Acts 2:44).
    - *d.* Spiritual illumination (Acts 2:14-40).

It is evident that the disciples were Christians before Pentecost and that something happened at Pentecost which dramatically changed their inner spiritual response as well as their outer spiritual expression. The biblical record contains no further witness to such a radical change in these men and women who had been confused, unstable, and mediocre prior to Pentecost. After Pentecost the thread runs without variation and without break in the direction of Spirit-filled and Spirit-directed people who "turned the world upside down." Even the resurrection of Christ did not produce the change that was brought by Pentecost. It was the crisis of Pentecost, a crisis in the lives of those already enjoying a personal relationship to Christ, that launched the Early Church on its conquering career. As such, Pentecost was more than a climactic event in the transition from one dispensation to another. It was an intensely personal second crisis in the transition from one level of spiritual living to a higher level of spiritual living.

B. The Disciples at Samaria

However one may explain the coming of the Holy Spirit on the disciples at Samaria, there is no denying the "secondness" of their experience. Jesus himself had felt it necessary to go to Samaria to preach to them and He had preached at Sychar for two days. His conversation with the woman of Samaria at Jacob's Well revealed the strong Messianic expectations of the Samaritans (John 4:25). The preaching of Jesus was fruitful in Samaria, for "many of the Samaritans of that city believed on him" (John 4:39).

1. *The Samaritan Revival*

When Philip went to Samaria to preach after Pentecost, he was going to a group which had a prior knowledge of Christ. The following observations may be made about this first evangelistic endeavor outside of Jerusalem, as described in Acts 8:5-13: (1) Many were cleansed of unclean spirits (v. 7); (2) They gave heed to the things spoken by Philip (v. 6); (3) The leading sinner of the community was converted and baptized (v. 13); (4) Many men and women accepted Philip's teachings concerning the kingdom of God and were baptized (v. 12); (5) "There was great joy in that city" (v. 8).

2. *The Second Crisis*

The news of the revival reached Jerusalem and caused some concern. For the founders of the Church were Jews, and to the Jews, "the Samaritans were worse than aliens. They were heretics, schismatics, more to be hated than infidels."[2] Peter and John were sent as spiritual ambassadors to evalutate the new development in the Early Church. Four things are highly significant in the ministry of Peter and John in Samaria: (1) The first thing Peter and John did upon reaching Samaria was to pray for them "that they might receive the Holy Ghost" (Acts 8:15). (2) As yet the converted Samaritans had not received the Holy Spirit (Acts 8:16). No doubt the reference here is to receiving the Holy Spirit in an outpouring similar to that of Pentecost, for all the spiritual work done in the human life is done by the Holy Spirit. (3) When Peter and John laid their hands on them, they received the Holy Spirit (Acts 8:17); (4) much later, a dissension regarding the necessity of circumcision for converts to Christianity threatened to split the thriving church. Paul and Barnabas, with others, were elected to go to Jerusalem to present the case for the Gentiles against the requirements of circumcision. But it was Peter who settled the issue by declaring: "And God, which knoweth the hearts, bare them witness, giving them the Holy Ghost, even as he did unto us; and put no difference between us and them, purifying their hearts by faith" (Acts 15:8-9). If there were no other reference in the New Testament to a second crisis, the example of the Samaritans alone would be enough to support the idea.

C. The Disciples at Ephesus

Paul had visited Ephesus briefly on his first missionary journey and had left Aquila and Priscilla to do home mission work in the great metropolis (Acts 18:18-21). Later Apollos came to Ephesus to preach. Apollos was a powerful preacher and "was instructed in the way of the Lord; and being fervent in the spirit, he spake and taught diligently the things of the Lord" (Acts 18:25). Since Apollos knew only of the baptism of John, he was given an intense course in the new Christology, with Aquila and Priscilla as his personal tutors (Acts 18:24-28). It was the work of Aquila and Priscilla, plus the preaching of Apollos, that produced the Christian converts at Ephesus.

Because their spiritual knowledge regarding the Holy Spirit was limited, and because they had received only the baptism of

[2]Richard B. Rackham, *The Acts of the Apostles* (London: Methuen and Co., 1951), p. 112.

John, some have denied that they were in a state of regeneration. But again, when the Bible speaks for itself, several significant things may be said about the disciples at Ephesus.

1. *These Men Are Regarded as Disciples.* (Acts 19:1)

F. F. Bruce states that it may be presumed that they were "disciples of Christ, in accordance with the meaning elsewhere of *mathetes* thus used absolutely; had they been disciples of John, we should have expected this to be explicitly stated."[3] And since "the disciples were first called Christians at Antioch" (Acts 11:26), the New Testament generally uses the words interchangeably, unless otherwise indicated.

2. *They Had Believed on Christ.*

When Apollos left Ephesus to go to Achaia (Acts 18:27), "he mightily convinced the Jews, and that publicly, shewing by the scriptures that Jesus was Christ" (Acts 18:28). So it might be assumed that the instruction of Aquila and Priscilla was effective and that any believers Apollos persuaded would be in the direction of believing in Christ.

3. *Paul Accepted Their State of Faith.*

When Paul came to Ephesus, he apparently accepted the fact that these people were in a state of grace, for he regarded them as believers (Acts 19:2). It may be true that Paul was not satisfied with their spiritual state. As one writer suggests: "Possibly after the example of the Baptist they were living the life of rigid ascetics, severe and gloomy, without Christian joy; or again they may have failed to understand Paul's spiritual teaching."[4] Also, Paul did not ask them about their knowledge of Christ; he seemed to take their belief in Christ as a starting point. He wanted to add another dimension to their experience.

So Paul asked a pointed question: "Have ye received the Holy Ghost since ye believed?" (Acts 19:2) This question is translated differently in versions other than the King James. Regarding the difference in translation the comment of W. T. Purkiser is incisive:

> Whether the original be translated as it is thus in the Authorized Version, or translated as it is in the Revised and Revised Standard Versions, "Did you receive the Holy Spirit when you believed?" makes not the slightest difference so far as this point

[3]*The Acts of the Apostles* (Grand Rapids, Mich.: Wm. B. Eerdmans Pub. Co., 1960), p. 353.

[4]Rackham, *op. cit.*, p. 346.

is concerned. In either case, it is admitted that they had believed, and it is evident that they had not received the Holy Ghost in the sense in which Paul speaks.[5]

4. *Paul Baptized the Ephesians.*

Paul baptized the Christians at Ephesus in the name of the Lord (Acts 19:5). Paul apparently did not press the issue of baptism, for in writing to the church at Corinth he states that, insofar as he could recall, he had baptized only Crispus and Gaius and the household of Stephanus (I Cor. 1:14-16). He also asserts that "Christ sent me not to baptize, but to preach the gospel" (I Cor. 1:17). Yet Paul baptized the Ephesian disciples without any hesitation or reservation. If these men were still sinners when Paul came to Ephesus, then Paul was guilty of baptizing unregenerate men. "That such has often been done since, we will not debate; but that Paul began the practice, we cannot admit."[6]

Thus when Paul laid his hands upon them he was placing his hands on men who were disciples, who believed on Christ, who were accepted by Paul as being in a state of grace, and who had been baptized by Paul. And when the Holy Spirit came on them, He came instantaneously, as a second crisis on men who were entitled, by the Scriptures, to be called Christians. Later, in his personal letter to the Ephesians, Paul again stressed the importance of a Spirit-filled life.

D. The Apostle Paul

Paul's conversion is unusual and unique. No other biblical character experienced such a sudden and dramatic change in his life as did Paul. It is true that the time element in Paul's case is extremely short. It must be stated, however, that the major concern at this point is to present biblical examples of those who had a second crisis subsequently to regeneration. Paul is another such example, if the biblical record is accepted as it is given.

1. *Paul's Conversion*

Paul was converted on the way to Damascus (Acts 9:3-8). Almost all Bible scholars agree as to the validity of his conversion at that time. The dramatic reversal in Paul's life was an experience which truly was a "shaking of the foundations." Most people experience a time of great joy and sense of release upon their regen-

[5] *Conflicting Concepts of Holiness*, p. 40.

[6] *Ibid.*, p. 41.

eration. Not so with Paul. When he was taken to Damascus, "he was three days without sight, and neither did eat nor drink" (Acts 9:9). Paul's conversion led to a three-day fast. There is no intimation of what happened in Paul's thinking during these three days of intense spiritual exercise and no indication of what or how he felt.

2. *Paul's Reception of the Holy Spirit*

At the end of three days Ananias visited Paul and greeted him with these words: "Brother Saul, the Lord, even Jesus, that appeared unto thee in the way as thou camest, hath sent me, that thou mightest receive thy sight, and be filled with the Holy Ghost" (Acts 9:17). It may be granted that Paul did receive the Holy Spirit at this time. On his first missionary journey, Paul faced a severe challenge in the city of Paphos (Acts 13:6) in the person of a false prophet named Bar-jesus. Paul was equal to the occasion. "Then Saul, (who also is called Paul,) filled with the Holy Ghost, set his eyes on him" (Acts 13:9).

Because some scholars point to the extremely brief time lapse of only three days between Paul's conversion and his baptism with the Holy Spirit, it might be advisable to summarize the principles learned from the biblical examples presented thus far regarding the time element between regeneration and entire sanctification.

a. God, presumably, could regenerate and sanctify a person in one work of grace. However, man is a free moral agent, and nothing significant can happen to human personality without an awareness of need, personal interest and desire, and personal commitment. Man, not God, is the one who necessitates a time element between the crisis experiences. This idea shall be dealt with more fully in a later discussion.

b. The length of time is not set by the Bible, but by man himself. Men vary in their spiritual sensitivity and in their grasp of spiritual truth.

c. The disciples took approximately three years to come to a full grasp of the truth regarding the nature of Christ-centered, Spirit-directed living.

d. Peter's preaching after Pentecost suggests that the time could be brief (Acts 2:37-39).

e. The leaders of the new Church thought the time could be short, for Peter and John led the Samaritans to the experience shortly after their conversion under Philip (Acts 8:5-17).

f. Ananias thought Paul could be filled with the Holy Spirit within a few days after his conversion (Acts 9:17-19).

g. Paul himself urged the Thessalonians to be sanctified within a short time after their entrance into spiritual life (I Thess. 4:3; 5:23-24).

h. Paul at Ephesus also urged immediate action (Acts 19:1-7).

i. There is danger in either direction—urging action before people are aware of a need or waiting until they have lost their first love.

E. The Case of Cornelius

Before leaving New Testament examples of those who received the Holy Spirit as a second, instantaneous crisis experience, it might be stated that Cornelius also could be used (Acts 10). Since there is no record of Cornelius' conversion and since the previous discussion refers to those who had two works of grace, Cornelius is presented as an example by inference, rather than an example by direct assertion. It is true that Wesley regarded Cornelius as an unbeliever, for he writes: "And yet it is certain, in the Christian sense, Cornelius was then an unbeliever."[7] Adam Clarke refers to Cornelius as a Gentile, a "*proselyte of the gate* though not a *proselyte of justice,* because he had not entered into the *bond of the covenant by circumcision.*"[8]

However, it is one thing to state that Cornelius was not a Christian, in the technical sense, and a completely different thing to state that he had no vital, experiential relationship to God which would be comparable to regeneration. Some Old Testament personalities were able to touch the "faith line" and attain a position in grace comparable to regeneration and sanctification. God is not limited to prescribed forms nor to particularized channels. God meets a person whenever a sincere soul seeks Him, according to the best knowledge he has. As Rackham observes in regard to the Holy Spirit coming upon Cornelius before his baptism: "It proves that God is free, and that his grace is not confined to any channels."[9]

1. *Christian Qualities of Cornelius*

Several things are stated about Cornelius in Acts 10:2-3 which indicate the presence of a vital piety that made him a devout man enjoying a vital personal relationship with God. He was a God-

[7] *Notes,* p. 432.
[8] *Op. cit.,* V, 760.
[9] *Op. cit.,* p. 159.

fearing man. He had led his entire household into a reverential worship of God. He prayed continually and consistently. He was liberal in financial matters. He was honored with a heavenly vision. His spiritual response was acceptable in the sight of God. Would this man not meet the crystallized summary of spirituality as expressed by Micah: "And what doth the Lord require of thee, but to do justly, and to love mercy, and to walk humbly with thy God?" (Mic. 6:8) And would not Paul's statement regarding the faith relationship as the basis of an acceptable relationship to God be applied to Cornelius as well as to Abraham: "But to him that worketh not, but believeth on him that justifieth the ungodly, his faith is counted for righteousness" (Rom. 4:5). And Peter sanctioned the spiritual status of Cornelius, for when the two met, Peter exclaimed, "Of a truth, I perceive that God is no respecter of persons: but in every nation he that feareth him, and worketh righteousness, is accepted with him" (Acts 10:34-35).

2. *Cornelius and the Second Crisis*

The second crisis in the experience came to Cornelius instantaneously, interrupting a sermon by Peter, for "while Peter yet spake these words, the Holy Ghost fell on all them which heard the word" (Acts 10:44). Thus Cornelius was lifted to the New Testament norm of Spirit-filled Christian living by an unforgettable experience.

If the Scriptures are permitted to speak for themselves, they do present examples of those who were followers of Christ, called disciples, who experienced the coming of the Holy Spirit subsequent to their conversion. The biblical historian also points to the conversion of 3,000 in Acts 2:41 (who received the Holy Spirit in Acts 4:31). It is possible to state that there are sufficient examples of a second crisis in the New Testament to make it as valid as a first crisis, or regeneration. Evangelicals, in particular, should be extremely reluctant to reject the biblical teaching of a "second blessing," for if their logic were reversed on themselves, they might find it difficult to sustain the concept of regeneration in the New Testament!

But experience as such, even biblical experience, is not quite sufficient to sustain a doctrine in the ultimate sense. For biblical hermeneutics requires a general, comprehensive, underlying theme before any truth can become all-embracing. The doctrine of holiness has the great advantage that the general tenor of biblical revelation contains the idea of holiness. It is thus possible to add exegetical analysis to experiential example in discussing sanctification as a second work of grace.

CHAPTER VIII /

An Exegetical Analysis of Entire Sanctification

The life of holiness is the New Testament norm for the Christian. The examples listed in the previous chapter indicate that the Christian norm is reached in two stages, or in two crises, regeneration and entire sanctification. Now the discussion turns to a study of scriptures which teach the dual nature of the process of reaching the level of Spirit-filled living. By symbol, by direct command, by promise, by prayers, by provision, by exhortations, and by grammatical inference the New Testament points to holiness as the Christian norm and to the act of entire sanctification as God's method of making men holy.

I. Symbol of Vine and Branch

In John 15, Jesus presents the nature of spiritual life by the symbol of the vine and the branches. In this image from the realm of nature spiritual life is more than a "divine-human encounter," more than an "I-Thou" relationship, more than "human commitment." In the symbol of the vine and the branch spiritual life is presented as a union with Christ, a life which is sustained by the life-giving stream of life embodied in God himself.

Jesus speaks of three types of branches in the first two verses of John 15. The first is the branch which bears no fruit. This branch is rejected. The second branch is the one "that beareth fruit." Certainly this branch represents the regenerated Christian, for Jesus said: "As the branch cannot bear fruit of itself, except it abide in the vine; no more can ye, except ye abide in me" (John 15:4).

Something happens, however, to this fruit-bearing Christian. For "every branch that beareth fruit, he purgeth it, that it might bring forth more fruit" (John 15:2). Commenting on this verse Adam Clarke writes: "The verb *kathairo*, from *kata (intens.)*, and *airo (I take away)*, signifies ordinarily to cleanse, purge, purify, but is certainly to be taken in the sense of pruning, or cutting off, in this text."[1]

Since biblical figures or symbols point to spiritual realities, then this pruning or purging is a reality in the lives of those already engrafted into Christ. The purpose of the pruning is to produce a more vigorous, more productive spiritual branch. This branch, the sanctified person, is he "that bringeth forth more fruit." From a biblical point of view, then, a second crisis seems normal and desirable.

II. The Living Sacrifice

Paul was a Jew who made the transition from old-covenant forms to new-covenant life quickly and completely. But he used terms from both traditional Judaism and from his Graeco-Roman environment to convey the truth of the Christian life. When Paul spoke of "a living sacrifice," the spiritual truth involved would be immediately plain to both Jew, Greek, and Roman. Thus he said:

> *I beseech you therefore, brethren, by the mercies of God, that ye present your bodies a living sacrifice, holy, acceptable unto God, which is your reasonable service. And be not conformed to this world: but be ye transformed by the renewing of your mind, that ye may prove what is that good, and acceptable, and perfect, will of God* (Rom. 12:1-2).

H. Orton Wiley, in discussing this passage from Romans, makes several observations which show that it points to a work of grace subsequent to regeneration. These observations of Wiley are presented as follows:

> Nothing can be clearer than (a) that this exhortation is addressed to those who were at the time Christians; (b) that an appeal to the mercies of God would mean nothing to those who have not already experienced His pardoning grace; (c) that the sacrifice was to be presented holy, as initially sanctified by the cleansing from guilt and acquired depravity; (d) that it was to

[1] *Op. cit.*, V, 627.

> be acceptable, that is, those who presented it must have been justified; all of which the apostle deems a reasonable source . . . (e) that there remained in the hearts of the believers, a bent toward worldliness, or a bias toward sin; (f) that this tendency to conform to the world was to be removed by a further transformation, or a renewal of their minds; and (g) that they were thereby to prove, or experience, the good, and acceptable, and perfect will of God.[2]

In using the term, or symbol, of "living sacrifice" Paul certainly indicated a crisis experience, or an instantaneous work. The sacrifices in the Old Covenant were presented, slain, and burned or eaten as a definite event, which was completed at a given time. It is true that in Paul's figure the sacrifice is to remain alive—as a testimonial to the redemptive power of God. But the "living sacrifice" must first be presented, offered, and accepted. Then it develops and more perfectly reflects the spirit of true holiness.

III. The Call to the Ephesians

In the Ephesian letter Paul does again what he had done previously in writing to the Thessalonian, Corinthian and Roman Christians. He first points to their present state of spiritual grace and enumerates their spiritual qualities. Second, he points out their weaknesses, failures, and deficiencies. Third, he urges them to become partakers of the divine holiness through the act of sanctification. This act of sanctification is the normal New Testament method of lifting Christians to the level of Spirit-filled living.

A. Evidence of Spiritual Standing at Ephesus

Paul, as was his custom, began by listing the qualities which distinguish the Ephesians as Christians.

1. *The Ephesians Are Called Saints* (Eph. 1:1).

"Saints" is the title usually used by Paul to designate Christians. It did not signify any particular group of believers, but was applied to all members of the Church in general. As the Church became older the name "became associated with those virtues which are becoming to saints, such as purity and devotion and godliness, so that the notion of personal holiness became attached to the term."[3]

[2] *Christian Theology*, II, 445-46.

[3] Charles R. Erdman, *The Epistle of Paul to the Ephesians* (Philadelphia: The Westminster Press, 1931), p. 23.

However, when used as Paul used it, the term was "the language of charitable presumption."

2. *The Ephesians Were Faithful to Christ.*

The letter was written to "the faithful in Christ Jesus" (Eph. 1:1). The *faithful* here are not those who merely believe in Christ The faithful "denotes those who are steadfast in their Christian life and profession."[4] Faith was much more than intellectual belief or mental assent to Paul. To Paul, faith "was an act in which the intellect, the heart, the conscience, and the will acknowledged Christ as the Redeemer and Ruler of men."[5] The Ephesians were honored by Paul by being called loyal and faithful to Christ.

3. *The Ephesians Were in Christ.*

Paul refers to these Ephesian Christians as being "in Christ." Some deny any idea of "a personal, mystical union with Christ"[6] in this phrase. But most scholars agree that "in Christ" refers to a vital union and a personal fellowship with Christ. "Possibly it is the most significant and characteristic of all the phrases used by the apostle."[7] The phrase "in Christ" appears 33 times in Paul's Epistles.[8] Variations of the phrase, with slight differences in meaning, occur approximately 240 times.[9]

The general meaning of the term, as suggested by John Nielson, is as follows: "Paul uses the phrase *in Christ* to describe all the experience, feeling, thought, and will of the believer as taking place in Christ."[10]

As followers who were "in Christ," these Ephesians had trusted in Christ (1:12); they had been sealed with the Holy Spirit of promise (1:13); they had expressed faith and love to all (1:15); they had been made alive spiritually (2:1, 5); they had experienced a "heavenly" relationship with God (2:6). According to Westcott, "the three characteristics, *saints, faithful, in Christ Jesus,* give a complete and

[4]*Ibid.*, p. 24.

[5]R. W. Dale, *The Epistle to the Ephesians* (London: Hodder and Stoughton, 1888), p. 20.

[6]F. C. Synge, *St. Paul's Epistle to the Ephesians* (London: Society for Promoting Christian Knowledge, 1941), p. 2.

[7]Erdman, *op. cit.*, p. 25.

[8]John B. Nielson, *In Christ* (Kansas City: Beacon Hill Press, 1960), p. 42.

[9]H. R. Mackintosh, *The Doctrine of the Person of Christ* (Edinburgh: T. and T. Clark, 1912), p. 56.

[10]*Op. cit.*, p. 43.

harmonious view of those to whom St. Paul writes."[11] Westcott adds this comment: "He addresses men who are consecrated to God in a Divine Society (saints), who are inspired by a personal devotion towards Him (faithful), who are in Him in whom the Church finds its unity and life (ch. IV.16). Thus the order saints, faithful, is seen to be perfectly natural. The thoughts are complementary: God's will, man's answer."[12]

While the Ephesian Christians were clearly in a state of spiritual union with Christ, they had specific needs which were of grave concern to Paul. Paul was concerned for the spiritual improvement of these people. The condition of the Ephesians, in contrast to the Corinthians, was a condition of sound and vigorous spiritual life. Thus it is evident that the experience of holiness is not only for those, like the Corinthians, who are beset with carnal struggles. The experience of holiness is a clarion call to the best people in the church to move up to the full potential of life "in Christ."

B. Paul's Concern for Spiritual Improvement

Paul's concern for the spiritual advance of the Ephesians was expressed in prayer and in exhortation. Paul prayed for their spiritual illumination and for their spiritual strengthening. He also exhorted them to a practical expression of their heavenly citizenship by moral and spiritual living.

1. *Paul's Prayer for the Ephesians*

Paul prayed for the spiritual enlightenment of the Ephesian Christians: "The eyes of your understanding being enlightened; that ye may know" (1:18). Paul was not praying for an increase in their theoretical knowledge. "The knowledge for which Paul asks is therefore definitely spiritual and practical. His request is for an awakened and an enlarged moral perception, for a clearer spiritual vision."[13] Paul was a master of doctrine, but when he prayed here it was for the purpose of "having the doctrine transmitted into actual experience. He would have them enjoy the full scope of their inheritance in Christ."[14] This full inheritance was the experience of holiness.

[11]Brooke Foss Westcott, *Saint Paul's Epistle to the Ephesians* (Grand Rapids, Mich.: Wm. B. Eerdmans Pub. Co., n.d.), p. 4.

[12]*Ibid.*

[13]Erdman, *op. cit.*, p. 38.

[14]Lehman Strauss, *Devotional Studies in Galatians and Ephesians* (New York: Loizeaux Brothers, 1957), p. 130.

The coming of the Holy Spirit is the occasion of spiritual enlightenment, for one task of the Holy Spirit is to reveal the meaning of truth (John 14:26; 16:12-15; I Cor. 2:10).

2. *Paul's Prayer for an Increase in Their Spiritual Strength*

In Paul's first prayer (1:15-23) he had prayed for increased spiritual illumination. Personal enlightenment leads to spiritual strength and stability. Thus Paul also prayed (3:14-19) that the Ephesians might "be strengthened with might by his Spirit in the inner man . . . being rooted and grounded." Westcott sums up the intent of this prayer of Paul as follows: "The object of the prayer is expressed in another and a final form, even the continual indwelling of Christ according to His promise (John XIV. 23) which is the most perfect strengthening. *Kataiothenai* is parallel with *krataiothenai,* and in both cases the aorist marks the decisive act by which the blessing is conveyed."[15]

Ellicott states that Paul's prayer here, as in 1:17, is "for the gift of the Spirit."[16] Adam Clarke also states that spiritual strength is derived from "the sovereign energy of the Holy Ghost. This fountain of spiritual *energy* can alone supply the spiritual strength which is necessary for this spiritual work and conflict."[17] A more recent writer stated that "the source of this strength is the Holy Spirit, who is to communicate the desired power."[18] Spiritual strength, like spiritual enlightenment, comes from an experience of the fullness of the Spirit. Spiritual illumination and spiritual power enable the Christian to walk worthy of his Christian vocation.

3. *Paul's Concern for Holy Christian Vocation*

To Paul, the Christian vocation involved practical expression, "I . . . beseech you that ye walk worthy of the vocation wherewith ye are called" (4:1). Speaking of Paul's sudden shift of emphasis after the first three inspiring chapters of Ephesians, one writer stated: "The transition from Paul's lofty and impassioned account of the present glory of the church and of its infinite hopes to these exhortations to *'lowliness,' 'meekness,' 'longsuffering'* and mutual forbearance is sudden and unexpected."[19] To Paul, faith and righteousness were the Siamese twins of Christian experience. They were

[15]*Saint Paul's Epistle to the Ephesians,* p. 51.
[16]*Op. cit.,* III, 35.
[17]*Op. cit.,* VI, 447.
[18]Erdman, *Op. cit.,* p. 67.
[19]Dale, *op. cit.,* pp. 260-61.

inseparable, for faith produced practical good works, and practical ethical qualities came from faith.

Thus Paul made a strong plea that the heavenly citizenship of the Christian would be expressed in personal integrity, unpretentious devotion, social forbearance, and peaceful unity. To achieve the ideal spiritual life, or vocation, Paul states that God has a plan of spiritual power and helps ranging from the personal presence of the triune God (4:4-6) to various gifts and talents in the Church (4:11-13).

C. Holiness and Heavenly Citizenship

The letter to the Ephesian church is often called the Epistle of "the heavenlies." It speaks of "heavenly places in Christ" (1:3; 2:6); it refers to the Christians as "fellowcitizens with the saints, and of the household of God" (2:19); it exhorts the Christians to "walk in love" (5:2) and to "walk as children of light" (5:8); it presents the ideal for the Church as "a glorious church, not having spot, or wrinkle, or any such thing; but that it should be holy and without blemish" (5:27); it challenges to Christian warfare and for perseverance (6:10-18). Such heavenly citizenship can be lived in the day-by-day confrontation with the world only in the life of holiness. The holiness which is the privilege and the obligation of the Christian has both negative and positive aspects.

1. *The Negative Aspect—Putting Off the "Old Man"*

In the beginning of his letter Paul had reminded the Ephesians that the eternal purpose of God for all Christians is that they "should be holy and without blame before him in love" (1:4). In his intensely practical approach to the relationship of holiness to heavenly citizenship Paul writes:

> *That we put off concerning the former conversation the old man, which is corrupt according to the deceitful lusts; and be renewed in the spirit of your mind; and that ye put on the new man, which after God is created in righteousness and true holiness* (4:22-24).

a. The "old man" as the former self. The meaning of the "old man" is a much debated issue. The phrase "old man" appears only three times in the New Testament: in Rom. 6:6; in Eph. 4:22; and in Col. 3:9. Some writers interpret the "old man" as a simple reference to the unregenerate state, to the state of the sinner prior to conversion. For example, Erdman describes the "old man" as the "former self, unregenerate, and fashioned according to the life of the heathen world."[20] Another writer states that "the 'old man' is the unregenerate, natural man, and his manner of life is corrupt, deceitful, and lustful."[21] William Barclay also indicates that the "old man" is simply the unregenerate man. In his discussion of baptism as a symbol of the new birth Barclay says: "Baptism was symbolically like dying and rising again. The man died to one kind of life and rose to another kind of life. He died to the old life of sin and rose to the new life of grace."[22] Westcott refers to the "old man" as "the old life which was summed up in 'selfishness.'"[23]

b. The old man as depraved human nature. Other commentators make the term "old man" much more radical than simply the unregenerate, selfish man. To many writers the term "old man" is related to the basic depravity of human nature. Martin Luther called the "old man" a defect in human nature which caused man to act wickedly. Man's wickedness, according to Luther, is not due to stubbornness, but is the result of "the defect that is in man by inheritance and because of the poison that is in him from the beginning of his days and infects the depths of his nature."[24] John Calvin, commenting on Eph. 4:22, writes: "As we are first born of Adam, the depravity of nature which we derive from him is called the *Old* man."[25] John Wesley adds a delicate touch when he comments on the "old man" in Rom. 6:6. Wesley regards Paul's use of the term "old man" as "a strong and beautiful expression for that entire depravity and corruption which by nature spreads itself over the whole man, leaving no part uninfected."[26]

Lexicographers throw little light on the proper interpretation of the meaning of "old man." Thayer interprets "our old man . . . as we were before our mode of thought, feeling, action, had been changed."[27] Cremer states that the term *old man* "designates a particular mode or manifestation of human nature . . . human nature . . . as the individual is naturally."[28] Kittel remarks that the "old

[20]*Op. cit.*, p. 88.

[21]Strauss, *op. cit.*, p. 182.

[22]*The Letter to the Romans* (Philadelphia: The Westminster Press, 1955), p. 84.

[23]*Saint Paul's Epistle to the Ephesians*, p. 66.

[24]Wilhelm Pauck, ed., *Luther: Lectures on Romans*, The Library of Christian Classics (Philadelphia: The Westminster Press, 1964), XV, 182.

[25]*Commentaries on the Epistles of Paul to the Galatians and Ephesians*, trans. William Pringle (Edinburgh: T. Constable, 1854), pp. 294-95.

[26]*Notes*, p. 540.

[27]*Op. cit.*, p. 474.

[28]*Op. cit.*, p. 105.

man" denotes "the sinful being of the unconverted man."[29] Arndt and Gingrich use the term to indicate the earlier, unregenerate man.[30]

c. The ultimate concern—holiness. However one may interpret the term *old man*, the ultimate goal of the Church is holiness. For after the *old man* is put off, then the *new man* "is created in righteousness and true holiness" (Eph. 4:24). This holiness which is imparted to man rests upon the atonement of Christ. Christ died to *sanctify the church* (Eph. 5:25-26) as well as to bring spiritual life to the sinner (John 3:16). Both regeneration and sanctification are dependent on the atoning death of Christ. In regard to the verb "to sanctify," as it appears in Eph. 5:26, Bishop Ellicott remarked: "*hagiase* here neither implies simple consecration . . . on the one hand, nor expiation, absolution, on the other, but the communication and infusion of holiness and moral purity."[31] The word for "cleanse" in the passage is used as an active aorist participle, which means "having cleansed." Commenting on the verse in Eph. 5:26, Winchester remarks:

> Just as Christ gave himself for the world that He might redeem it and that it through His death might be saved, so did He give himself for the Church that He might "sanctify it, having cleansed it." Both verbs are aorist in tense. The purpose for which He sanctifies and cleanses His church is that He may "present" it to himself "holy and without blemish." Only thus can it really be glorious in His sight and happy in His presence.[32]

Thus the life of holiness involves the complete renovation of the personality, the putting off of the "old man," which may be interpreted as the unregenerate life which was rooted in a corrupt nature. Since Paul was exhorting Christians in a good state of grace to move to a higher level of living, the "putting off" of the former nature was to be achieved through the cleansing activity of the Holy Spirit, based on the sacrificial death of Christ. The negative aspect of holiness thus invovles a "putting off," a cleansing. Both in Eph. 4:22, and in Eph. 5:26 the language used "indicates the sudden resolve of the will, inspired and empowered by the Holy

[29]Kittel, *op. cit.*, p. 365.

[30]*Op. cit.*, p. 610.

[31]Charles J. Ellicott, *A Critical and Grammatical Commentary on St. Paul's Epistle to the Ephesians* (Andover: Warren F. Draper, 1884), p. 133.

[32]Olive M. Winchester and Ross E. Price, *Crisis Experiences in the Greek New Testament* (Kansas City: Beacon Hill Press, 1953), p. 71.

Spirit, to be no longer under the dominion of these terrible passions. Once and forever let us divest ourselves of them; as the beggar his rags, or as Lazarus the garments of death."[33]

2. *The Positive Aspect—Putting on the New Man*

The experience of holiness also has positive aspects. Holiness produces the "new man"—the New Testament Christian. The character of the life of man is determined by its source. Character determines conduct. "Life in the new sphere is traced to its source, 'the new man,' and the conduct is righteous and holy because the character is so. The fountain determines the flow."[34] Several positive aspects of holiness are presented by Paul. These aspects pervade the entire personality of the Christian and are expressed in practical, ethical, and moral living.

a. Holiness in character. When writing to the Ephesians, Paul was specific about the norm for the New Testament Christian. The standard for the Christian was holiness. Thus Paul wrote: "He hath chosen us in him . . . that we should be holy" (1:4). Again he wrote: "Put on the new man . . . created in righteousness and true holiness" (4:24). And again he exhorted: "That he might present . . . to himself a glorious church, not having spot, or wrinkle, or any such thing; but that it should be holy and without blemish" (5:27). The words "righteousness" and "holiness" sum up the believer's life before man and God. "'Righteousness' expresses the right behavior of the Christian before men; 'holiness,' his behavior before God. The former is an outward attitude expressed in words and deeds; the latter is the attitude of heart and mind toward God."[35]

b. Holiness in conduct. Paul dealt in specifics when it came to the practical expression of holiness. These specifics left no room for doubt regarding the overt expression of Christian character in Christian conduct. Thus the Christian was to be truthful (4:25); free from "any smoldering fires of unjudged temper or the inward burning of unrighteous indignation";[36] honest in all his relationships (4:28); devoid alike of unclean talk and unwise joking (4:29); sensitive to the leadership of the Holy Spirit (4:30); without sour-

[33]F. B. Meyer, *Ephesians: A Devotional Commentary* (Fort Washington, Pa.: Christian Literature Crusade, 1953), p. 107.

[34]Ruth Paxson, *The Wealth, Walk, and Warfare of the Christian* (Westwood, N.J.: Fleming H. Revell Co., 1939), p. 107.

[35]Strauss, *op. cit.*, p. 183.

[36]Paxson, *op. cit.*, p. 116.

ness, ill feelings, or carnal clamorings (4:31); and marked by the tenderness that is inherent in holiness (4:32).

c. Holiness in personal relationship. Holiness is another name for love in practical operation. Holiness is manifested in love or it is not New Testament holiness. Holiness expresses itself in sexual integrity (5:3), in a love for and acceptance of the truth (5:6-8), in creative labor (5:16), in Spirit-produced joy and contentment (5:18-19), in a spirit of thankfulness (5:20), and in a cooperative spirit (5:21).

The holiness that Paul presented to the Ephesians was the privilege and the responsibility of those already Christian in every sense of the term. This holiness was attained as a second crisis by the Holy Spirit. As a second crisis, called entire sanctification, the experience of holiness contained both negative and positive aspects. The negative aspect was cleansing of the taint of original sin, which Paul labels the "old man." The positive aspect of holiness was the fullness of the Spirit, resulting in the presence, and continued development, of all the Christian graces.

IV. The Pauline Imperative

In writing to the Thessalonian Christians, Paul said: "For this is the will of God, even your sanctification, that ye should abstain from fornication" (I Thess. 4:3). In explaining this passage, two things are essential. First, it must be shown that these Thessalonians were already members of the body of Christ. Second, it is necessary to show that Paul exhorts them to a higher level of living, resulting from sanctification.

A. Christian Qualities of the Thessalonians

There were several qualities about the people in the church at Thessalonica which made it apparent that they were Christians. These qualities are presented in the early chapters of Paul's first letter to them. (1) Paul continually thanked God for them, consistently referring to them in prayer (I Thess. 1:2). Paul's prayer "is constant, and he speaks of giving thanks for them all, so there were apparently no disaffected members."[37] Paul's prayer of thanksgiving was threefold.

[37]Leon Morris, *The Epistles of Paul to the Thessalonians* (Grand Rapids, Mich.: Wm. B. Eerdmans Pub. Co., 1956), pp. 33-34.

1. *Paul Notes Their Works of Love and Faith.*

"They had faith, not *speculative* and *indolent,* but *true, sound,* and *operative:* their *faith worked.*"[38] Second, Paul expressed thanks for their "labour of love" (I Thess. 1:3). It is easy to misunderstand the phrase "labour of love," for it is often used to denote small services rendered without hope of recognition or reward. "But Paul's term is a strong one, and he means that, out of love, they have labored to the point of weariness. The word expresses the cost of their love, not its result."[39] The third part of Paul's prayer of thanksgiving referred to the "patience of hope" of these early Christians. By "patience of hope" is meant, "not a quiet, passive resignation, but an active constancy in the face of difficulties."[40] Or, as William Barclay says: "It is the spirit which can bear things, not simply with resignation, but with blazing hope."[41] Paul's prayer indicates that those Thessalonian Christians were in a good state of grace. In addition to praying for them, Paul calls them "brethren beloved."

2. *They Were Well-loved Fellow Christians.*

Paul calls the members of the church "brethren beloved" (I Thess. 1:4). As far as Paul was concerned, "the practical evidence of the Spirit in their lives showed that God had willed to enroll them among His chosen people."[42] As well-beloved brethren they were of the "elect of God." Adam Clarke interprets *election* in its broad sense. Since the Jews "had rejected the offers of the Gospel, God has now elected the Gentiles in their stead. This is the *election* which the Thessalonians *knew.*"[43] These people were valid members of the kingdom of God.

3. *They Had Been Converted* (I Thess. 1:5).

The gospel had come to the Thessalonians "in word . . . but also in power, and in the Holy Ghost, and in much assurance." Another evidence of the regenerated state of these individuals was the way they had responded to the gospel. "The crowning evidence was in

[38]Clarke, *op. cit.,* VI, 540.

[39]Leon Morris, *The First and Second Epistles to the Thessalonians* (Grand Rapids, Mich.: Wm. B. Eerdmans Pub. Co., 1959), p. 51.

[40]*Ibid.,* p. 53.

[41]William Barclay, *A New Testament Word Book* (London: SCM Press, 1955), p. 60.

[42]W. Robertson Nicoll, ed., *The Expositor's Greek New Testament* (Grand Rapids, Mich.: Wm. B. Eerdmans Pub. Co., n.d.), IV, 24.

[43]*Op. cit.,* VI, 540.

the way the Word was received."[44] First, it was received in power, and "power," as it is used here, refers to "the power of grace unto salvation."[45] Through the work of the Holy Spirit they had become followers of Paul, and more importantly, of Christ. Second, they had "received the word in much affliction" (I Thess. 1:6). In the New Testament the word "affliction" does not mean "mild discomfort, but great and sore difficulty."[46] Third, these Christians expressed joy rather than self-pity in the face of unwarranted persecution (I Thess. 1:6).

4. *They Were Examples to Others.*

Because of their joyful witness in the midst of affliction the Thessalonians became an example of triumphant Christian living to the believers in Macedonia and Achaia (I Thess. 1:7-9). A summary of the impact of the Thessalonian church on other Christians is given in the following statement:

> The gospel was received by them with such eager zeal, its words were so constantly in their mouths, and so wrought in their hearts, that it swelled . . . into a mighty trumpet-call that was heard of all men sounding forth from Thessalonica.[47]

B. Spiritual Deficiency of the Thessalonians

Paul was definite regarding the nature of the spiritual deficiency of the Thessalonian church. Paul warned them against fornication (I Thess. 4:3). He also warned them against fraud (I Thess. 4:6). He exhorted them to refrain from noisy meddling (I Thess. 5:11). The church was deficient in perfect love—in holiness. Paul was equally specific regarding the method of meeting this spiritual lack. The method was sanctification. The method of meeting spiritual deficiency was presented both as a fraternal request ("I beseech you") and as a reiterated commandment: "For this is the will of God, even your sanctification, that ye should abstain from fornication" (I Thess. 4:3). Sanctification *(hagiasmos)* in this exhortation of Paul may be said to carry a double meaning. Some writers stress the idea of separation, as suggested by Lenski:

[44]John F. Walvoord, *The Thessalonian Epistles* (Findlay, Ohio: Dunham Publishing Co., 1955), p. 15.

[45]R. C. H. Lenski, *The Interpretation of St. Paul's Epistles to the Colossians, to the Thessalonians, to Timothy, to Titus and to Philemon* (Minneapolis: Augsburg Publishing House, 1964), p. 226.

[46]Morris, *The First and Second Epistles to the Thessalonians,* p. 27.

[47]Ellicott, *op. cit.,* p. 27.

> This thing that God wills is the condition of the Thessalonians in which they are set wholly apart for God and are separated in life and conduct from the world which is not thus set apart and does not even know God.[48]

But more than a setting aside is involved in sanctification, for the mere act of setting aside would not supply the spiritual deficiency about which Paul was concerned. So a second meaning must be added to the word sanctification. John Wesley interprets it in this case (I Thess. 4:3) as "entire holiness of heart and life."[49] Adam Clarke refers to this passage in these words: "God has called you to holiness; he requires that you should be holy."[50] God's call is to holiness *outwardly* and *inwardly*, for the "spirit and soul and body" are to be preserved blameless (I Thess. 5:23).

Both separation outwardly and holiness inwardly are not only permissible as renditions of the word sanctification but are actually required in the total context of this first letter to the Thessalonians. For near the end of the letter Paul again expresses his deep concern for their sanctification: "And the very God of peace sanctify you wholly; and I pray God your whole spirit and soul and body be preserved blameless unto the coming of our Lord Jesus Christ" (I Thess. 5:23). Then Paul drove home the idea of present, attainable holiness with the declaration: "Faithful is he that calleth you, who also will do it" (I Thess. 5:24).

From a study of the Pauline exhortation to the church at Thessalonica it is evident that there is a higher level of spiritual living than that of regeneration. This higher level of spiritual life is the New Testament norm of the Christian life. It is attained, or received, by the act of the Holy Spirit called sanctification. This act of sanctification is clearly shown to follow regeneration and is therefore validly called a second crisis. Other passages from the pen of New Testament writers are also precise in their teaching of a second crisis. One such passage is found in the letter to the Hebrew Christians.

V. THE HEBREW CHALLENGE

The writer of the Book of Hebrews also suggests a second crisis in these words: "Therefore leaving the principles of the doctrine of

[48] *St. Paul's Epistles*, p. 308.
[49] *Notes*, p. 759.
[50] *Op. cit.*, VI, 548.

Christ, let us go on unto perfection" (Heb. 6:1). The writer was concerned about the lack of spiritual progress in the Hebrew Christians. There is little doubt that these people were Christians. "That they had been 'illuminated,' had 'endured a great fight of affliction,' and had been made a 'gazing-stock' (10:32-33) is sufficient evidence of their conversion."[51] Further, these people had already laid the foundation for a Christian life by "repentance from dead works, and of faith toward God, of the doctrine of baptisms, and of laying on of hands, and of resurrection of the dead, and of eternal judgment" (6:1-2). But they had not gone on to perfection.

A. Learning First Principles

A detailed exegesis of this text (Heb. 6:1) is helpful in strengthening the biblical basis of holiness. Each of the significant words, or phrases in the text is analyzed in the following discussion.

1. *A Transition Needed*

The Hebrew Christians needed a transition to a higher state of grace. The Greek word *dio* may be translated as "therefore," or "for this reason"; or again "by denoting that the influence is self-evident."[52] Thus the word "links this verse with the exhortation of of the previous chapter which sets forth the shamefulness of the lack of spiritual progress among the Hebrew Christians."[53]

The participle *aphentes* means "to leave behind,"[54] but since it is used in the aorist in this passage, it may be translated "having left." One writer says that it is used "frequently, as here, applied to quitting a thing for the sake of going to some different place, or of engaging in some different employment."[55]

2. *The Principles of the Doctrine of Christ*

Ellicott suggests that "'the principles of the doctrine of Christ' is actually 'the doctrine of first principles' or the word of the beginning."[56] These basic principles "are summed up under three main heads, represented by three important Greek terms: (1) *metanoias,*

[51]H. Orton Wiley, *The Epistle to the Hebrews* (Kansas City: Beacon Hill Press, 1959), p. 199.

[52]Arndt and Gingrich, *op. cit.,* p. 197.

[53]Wiley, *The Epistle to the Hebrews,* p. 202.

[54]Arndt and Gingrich, *op. cit.,* p. 510.

[55]Moses Stuart, *A Commentary on the Epistle to the Hebrews* (Andover: Warren F. Draper, 1876), p. 344.

[56]Charles John Ellicott, ed., *A New Testament Commentary for English Readers* (London: Cassell and Co., 1897), IV, 301.

repentance; (2) *pisteos*, faith; and (3) *didaches*, doctrine or teachings."[57] Repentance is a personal expression of sorrow and the act of turning away from sin, while faith is the active, personal response in accepting the grace of God in forgiveness and justification. The doctrines referred to are the initial ones of the beginning of the Christian life, such as baptism, the laying on of hands, the belief in such future events as the resurrection of the dead and a final judgment. Certainly no one could be a Christian without meeting these initial, basic conditions.

3. *On to Perfection*

The Christians were exhorted to "go on." "Let us go on," means, "Let us press on to perfection." "There is a sense of urgency in these words which is missed by the ordinary rendering."[58] Adam Clarke states that the verb in the original is very emphatic, meaning, "Let us be carried on to this perfection"; and again, "Let us never rest till we are *adult Christians*—till we are saved from all, and are filled with the Spirit and power of Christ."[59] Whedon also emphasizes the urgency of going on to Christian perfection in these words: "When [Heb. 6:1] . . . is adduced as an exhortation to advancing to a perfected Christian character, it is no misquotation."[60]

The word for perfection used here is *teleioteta*. It appears only in Heb. 6:1 and in Col. 3:14. Moulton and Milligan give the secular background of the word as meaning "full-grown, mature; four full-grown cocks; in good working order or condition; one perfect Theban mill; a complete lampstand; final verdict."[61] In all these references *perfect* means a mature state.

a. Perfection as soundness. In the case of men the secular meaning stated above is that of one who has attained a legal maturity. In the case of chickens, as suggested by Wuest, it means "soundness, freedom from sickness and physical defect; in reference to a grain mill, it means to be in dependable working order so that the grain may be produced when needed or desired; in the case of a lampstand, it means that all the necessary parts needed to give light

[57]Wiley, *The Epistle to the Hebrews*, pp. 199-200.

[58]Ellicott, *A New Testament Commentary for English Readers*, III, 301.

[59]*Op. cit.*, VI, 723.

[60]*Commentary on the New Testament, Titus—Revelation*, p. 76.

[61]James H. Moulton and George Milligan, *The Vocabulary of the Greek Testament* (London: Hodder and Stoughton, 1930), p. 629.

are present."[62] In summary, the term means, in a secular sense, mature, in sound health, dependable workability, and completeness.

In the light of its biblical context, the term perfection must be interpreted to mean more than maturity in the sense of a well-balanced Christian personality, where the various Christian graces and virtues are expressed in proper proportion. For Paul refers to the Corinthians as "babes," that is, as spiritually immature people. This spiritual immaturity on the part of the Corinthians did not refer to their recent conversion nor the time limit of the experience as Christians. When Paul used the term "babes," or immaturity, he indicated that this was a state of spiritual childishness, or carnal qualities, of lack of spiritual graces (I Cor. 3:1). So spiritual maturity would at least point to the absence of carnal qualities and the presence of spiritual graces.

b. Perfection as purity. However, the perfection that the Hebrews were urged to seek was not a state of grace in which they were magically elevated to a state of moral and spiritual completeness where there was no room for growth and development. Nor was it a state from which they could not fall and lapse back into sin. Andrew Murray suggests the general idea of the perfection possible to the Christian:

> It is not difficult to know what perfection means here. Perfect is that which corresponds to what its maker intended . . . God has set before us in His word the life He actually means us to live, and He calls every true child of His to leave the beginnings, and to press on to perfection.[63]

In the larger context of the term perfection, its meaning becomes even more sharply defined. In a later passage (Heb. 7:19) the writer states that the law made nothing perfect. Here the word for *perfect* means *entire.* In explaining this term Richard Trench writes: "The *holokleros* perfect is one who has preserved, or who, having once lost, has now regained, his *completeness.*"[64] In describing the use of the two terms for perfect *(holokleros* and *teleios),* Trench draws the following conclusion: "In the *holokleros* [entire] no grace which ought to be in a Christian man is deficient; in the *teleios* [perfect] no

[62]Kenneth S. Wuest, *Treasures from the Greek New Testament* (Grand Rapids, Mich.: Wm. B. Eerdmans Pub. Co., 1941), p. 113.

[63]*The Holiest of All* (New York: Fleming H. Revell Co., 1894), p. 205.

[64]*Op. cit.,* p. 771.

grace is merely in its weak imperfect beginnings, but all have reached a certain ripeness and maturity."[65] In the light of its context, it may be said that the writer was using terms which meant that a person should go on to a state of spiritual fitness, or fullness, or completeness—to a state in which one has been given divine power to attain a level of practical, operational, dependable living. Such a state is the state of holiness.

In the still larger context of the entire Hebrew letter the meaning of the term *perfection* becomes even more sharply defined. Following the exhortation, "Let us go on to perfection," there is a detailed analysis of the superiority of the priesthood of Christ to all preceding priests and to all past sacrifices. From the point of view of the spiritual impact in man, the essential superiority of the priesthood of Christ points directly to holiness as a contemporary possibility. Following is a list of references to Christ's priesthood which indicates that this priesthood was designed to produce holiness in man.

c. Purging the conscience. "How much more shall the blood of Christ . . . purge your conscience from dead works to serve the living God?" (Heb. 9:14) This is a continual future promise with a permanent present application. For the purging work of Christ was already completed (Heb. 1:3) insofar as the provision was concerned. And the purging described meant "to bring about purification from sin."[66] The purging of the conscience thus meant "to free from the guilt of sin, to purify."[67] As Wiley points out, the word for "cleanse" or "purge" is *kathariei,* and is "an ancient Hellenic verb which was generally used in a ceremonial sense."[68] In addition to the text, the word is used in only two other places in the New Testament. One is found in Matt. 3:12, where it is said that "he will throughly purge his floor"; the other in Jas. 4:8, which reads, "Cleanse your hands, ye sinners." The usage of the word "makes it clear that the Blood not only cleanses from actual sin, but purges the very sin nature itself."[69]

d. Contemporary sanctification. "By the which will we are sanctified through the offering of the body of Jesus Christ once for all" (Heb. 10:10). In the previous verse (10:9) the writer has shown that

[65] *Ibid.*
[66] Arndt and Gingrich, *op. cit.,* p. 388.
[67] Thayer, *op. cit.,* p. 312.
[68] *The Epistle to the Hebrews,* p. 300.
[69] *Ibid.*

Christ had manifested the will of God perfectly when He offered himself as a Sacrifice. In this passage (10:10) the writer shows that the permanent result of the obedient sacrifice is sanctification. The word "we are sanctified" *(hegiasmenoi)* is the periphrastic perfect passive indicative of the verb *sanctify (hagiazo).* Since the particular verb form may denote "existing state or . . . completed action,"[70] it is interpreted "we have been sanctified." Contemporary sanctification is thus included in the sacrificial work of the perfect High Priest—Jesus Christ.

Contemporary sanctification is also indicated in Heb. 10:14: "For by one offering he hath perfected for ever them that are sanctified." Dr. Wiley, after a technical analysis of the Greek terms used in this passage, draws the following conclusion:

> These words affirm not only that the heirs are included in the will, but that they have been brought actually into possession of that which was bequested them. They "are sanctified," as a present, inner, spiritual experience wrought by Christ through the great sacrifice of himself. Furthermore, the writer links the term "sanctified" with the *teleiosis* or "perfection" which the Levitical system could never achieve, but which now has been accomplished by Christ. The word used here is *teteleioken,* the perfect active indicative of *teleioo.* "He has perfected and continues to keep perfect."[71]

Contemporary sanctification is again declared in one of the classic references to this aspect of the work of Christ. "Wherefore Jesus also, that he might sanctify the people with his own blood, suffered without the gate" (Heb. 13:12). This passage is the climax of the Epistle to the Hebrews. The writer has actually presented an interpretation of redemptive history, with particular emphasis on the results of the work of Christ. The writer of Hebrews would agree with the statement that "God's holiness is the fundamental and moulding principle of the whole revelation of redemption in all its elements."[72]

Since the Hebrew letter deals extensively with the sacrificial system of the Old Testament, the writer would also agree that holiness is "the principle of the covenant made between Him and them."[73] Since "God's holiness becomes historically manifest in

[70]Ernest DeWitt Burton, *Syntax of the Moods and Tenses in New Testament Greek* (3rd ed.; Grand Rapids, Mich.: Kregel Publications, 1955), p. 40.

[71]*The Epistle to the Hebrews,* p. 324.

[72]Cremer, *op. cit.,* p. 46.

[73]*Ibid.,* p. 43.

sanctification,"[74] it is essential to ascertain the meaning of the term. Cremer presents a precise definition: "To sanctify means, to make anything a participator, according to its measure, in God's holiness, in God's purity as revealed in His electing love."[75] Sanctification, according to Cremer, involves two things: (1) ". . . the setting up, advancing, and preserving of the life of fellowship with the God of grace and righteousness . . . sanctification, as the removal of existing impurity, accompanies and characterizes the calling; (2) the preservation and nurture of the divine life-fellowship on the part of the man who has become the subject of divine influences."[76]

Through Christ all past acts of sacrifices, priestly ritual, ceremonial presentation, dedication and consecration, the feasts and the fasts, "all these find their culmination in the one great act of sanctification, by which Christ purifies the hearts of the people and takes up His abode within them through the Holy Spirit."[77]

In addition to biblical *examples* of a second crisis, and added to biblical *commands* and *exhortations* pointing to a second crisis, biblical *terms* also point to a second crisis. To be sure, an analysis of grammar does not carry equal weight with biblical examples and biblical exposition, yet such an analysis is significant, for it rounds out the circle of biblical teachings regarding a second crisis. In the following analysis, key words and verb forms are analyzed to show their relation to a second crisis.

VI. Sanctification Implied in Semantical Analysis

At this point it might be well to observe that the two experiences, regeneration and entire sanctification, do not automatically and magically elevate one to a kind of ephemeral sainthood. The purpose here is to show that the norm of New Testament living involves a crisis subsequent to regeneration. Having reached this New Testament norm, the Christian is prepared for unlimited spiritual development and for consecrated Christian service. For the purpose of the discussion that follows, the grammatical analysis will be confined to a few significant terms related to sanctification, and to a study of the structure of verbal forms, which in the original language are doctrinally significant.

[74] *Ibid.*, p. 47.
[75] *Ibid.*, p. 54.
[76] *Ibid.*, p. 56.
[77] Wiley, *The Epistle to the Hebrews*, p. 418.

A. Biblical Terminology Points to a Second Crisis

Many terms in the New Testament suggest a second crisis. Thus any list selected is representative rather than exhaustive. The terms selected for discussion here are baptism, crucifixion, gift, sacrifice; and the verb forms for such words as purify, cleanse, destroy, purge, and sanctify.

1. *Baptism*

As has been suggested, the act of entire sanctification is often referred to as a baptism: "For John truly baptized with water; but ye shall be baptized with the Holy Ghost not many days hence" (Acts 1:5). As Purkiser points out, "Gradual baptism is an absurdity—whether it be a baptism with water or a baptism with the Holy Spirit."[78] In fact, gradual baptism with water could be a tragedy! Baptism is a term which always implies an act which is undertaken and completed at a given point. Certainly one would not continue to be gradually baptized, with the act being finally completed at death. Both water baptism and the baptism with the Holy Spirit are instantaneous and completed.

2. *Crucifixion*

Much criticism has arisen from the use of eradication in connection with entire sanctification. This criticism has arisen for two reasons—because it is not a biblical term and because it implies the elimination of a physical something from an individual. The objections are hardly valid; for some words, such as *trinity*, are not biblical terms, yet are accepted as permissible terms in expressing biblical ideas. Then, too, it is extremely naive to think that any reputable thinker would conceive of sin as a physical something which is removed from the soul. For if the soul is a spiritual entity, it would not incorporate physical substance.

If there is an objection to the use of the word eradication, then an even stronger term is at hand—crucifixion. Sanctification is sometimes referred to in a negative sense as a crucifixion or death, as indicated by the following references: "Knowing this, that our old man is crucified with him, that the body of sin might be destroyed, that henceforth we should not serve sin" (Rom. 6:6). "Mortify [treat as dead] therefore your members which are upon the earth" (Col. 3:5). "I am crucified with Christ: nevertheless I live; yet not I, but Christ liveth in me: and the life which I now live in the

[78]*Conflicting Concepts of Holiness*, p. 34.

flesh, I live by the faith of the Son of God, who loved me, and gave himself for me" (Gal. 2:20). Since crucifixion was a method of eliminating criminals from society, it was not a gradual or extended process. It is true that a criminal would agonize in the throes of death several hours, or even days, but crucifixion was an event which was completed and ended—death had come, and the criminal was no longer a threat to society. Also, in this connection Paul speaks of the "body of sin" being destroyed. To destroy does not mean to suppress, to weaken, or to render inactive—it means the destruction, the removal, the demolition of something which stands in the way. So here again the figure is that of an instantaneous, completed act.

3. *Gift*

Sanctification is frequently referred to as a "gift," to be "received." Jesus said: "If ye then, being evil, know how to give good gifts unto your children: how much more shall your heavenly Father give the Holy Spirit to them that ask him?" (Luke 11:13) After Pentecost, Peter echoed the words of his Master when he said: "Repent, and be baptized every one of you in the name of Jesus Christ for the remission of sins, and ye shall receive the gift of the Holy Ghost" (Acts 2:38).

The very nature of a gift is that it is bestowed instantly rather than progressively. One may develop a gift, exercise stewardship regarding a gift, or even abuse a gift. But if one receives a gift, he is aware of a possession which he did not have the day before.

4. *Sacrifice*

A sacrifice was presented once and for all. In the Old Testament it was an act, an event, a ritual which was anticipated with intense preparation and remembered with inner peace. When Paul exhorted the Roman Christians to present themselves as living sacrifices, he was asking them to complete the act immediately, once and for all. Regarding the finality of the presenting of oneself as a sacrifice in Rom. 12:1, one scholar commented: "Self-surrender to God is to be conceived as a momentary act concluded at once and forever, which reveals its effects continuously in a walk well-pleasing to God."[79] Daniel Steele interprets it as "a single act, never needing to be repeated."[80] Adam Clarke indicated the finality of the act in his

[79]Friedrich A. Philippi, *Commentary on St. Paul's Epistle to the Romans* (Edinburgh: T. and T. Clark, 1878), II, 250.

[80]Daniel Steele, *Milestone Papers* (New York: Phillips and Hunt, 1878), p. 69.

remarks on Rom. 12:1: "They are exhorted to give themselves up in the spirit of sacrifice; to be wholly the Lord's property as the *whole burnt-offering* was, no part being devoted to any other use."[81]

B. Verb Forms and the Second Crisis

Sanctification as an instantaneous second crisis also finds significant support from the study of verb forms in the New Testament writing. One of the earlier studies in this area was presented by the Methodist scholar, Daniel Steele. In his *Milestone Papers*, Steele included a section entitled "The Tense Readings of the Greek New Testament." Another impressive study dealing with the same line of thought is the research done by Olive M. Winchester, edited by Ross E. Price, entitled *Crisis Experience in the Greek New Testament*. Another Wesleyan writer, Charles E. Brown, also presents sound, biblical evidence for a second crisis, based on Greek verb forms, in his book *The Meaning of Sanctification.*

The significance of verb forms in relation to sanctification as a second crisis is that the tenses in Greek grammar had a meaning quite different from the tenses of contemporary language. Referring to the difference in the Greek use of tense as contrasted to modern languages, one scholar commented:

> It is somewhat unfortunate that we are compelled to use the name *tense* in connection with the forms of the Greek verb. It directs our attention too much to the time of the action, whereas it was the state of the action, rather than the time, that was most prominently before the mind of a Greek.[82]

In the English language, verb tenses indicate primarily the *time* of the action—as past, present, or future. While Greek tenses also signify time sequence, they point mainly to the *kind* of action or the *state* of the action. The two basic *kinds* or *states* of action are described as linear action or punctiliar action. When action is regarded as a continuing action, or process, it is linear action. When action is regarded as a past event viewed in its entirety simply as an event, or a single fact, it is called punctiliar action. Thus the Greek uses the present or the imperfect tense to denote continued action or a state of incompleteness. This is linear action. On the other hand, the Greek uses the *aorist* to denote momentary, completed, or punctiliar ac-

[81] *Op. cit.*, VI, 136.

[82] H. P. V. Nunn, *A Short Syntax of New Testament Greek* (Cambridge: The University Press, 1956), p. 66.

tion. "The imperfect refers to continuous action in past time, while the aorist is the simple past tense."[83] G. B. Winer describes the aorist as referring to "the simple occurrence of an event at some time past, considered as a momentary act."[84] Generally, then, the aorist refers to actions "thought of merely as events or single facts without reference to the time they occupied."[85] The exception in regard to time is the aorist indicative, which does indicate past time. But, however it is used, the aorist "always means point action"[86] —or momentary action.

The relevance of all this technical discussion of verb tense is seen in the following lengthy quotation from Steele's *Milestone Papers*. Relating the use of the aorist tense in the Greek New Testament to a second crisis, he writes:

> 1. All exhortations to prayer and to spiritual endeavor in resistance of temptation are usually expressed in the present tense, which strongly indicates persistence. . . .
>
> 2. The next fact which impresses us in our investigation is the absence of the aorist and the presence of the present tense whenever the conditions of final salvation are stated. Our inference is that the conditions of ultimate salvation are continuous, extending through probation, and not completed in any one act. The great requirement is faith in Jesus Christ. A careful study of the Greek will convince the student that it is a great mistake to teach that a single act of faith furnishes a person with a paid-up, non-forfeitable policy assuring the holder that he will inherit eternal life, or that a single energy of faith secures a through ticket for heaven, as is taught by the Plymouth Brethren and by some popular lay evangelists. The Greek tenses show that faith is a state, a habit of mind, into which the believer enters at justification. . . .
>
> 3. But when we come to consider the work of purification in the believer's soul, by the power of the Holy Spirit, both in the new birth and in entire sanctification, we find that the aorist is almost uniformly used. This tense, according to the best New Testament grammarians, never indicates a continuous, habitual, or repeated act, but one which is momentary, and done once for all.
>
> We have looked in vain to find one of these verbs (denoting

[83]J. Gresham Machen, *New Testament Greek for Beginners* (New York: The Macmillan Co., 1923), p. 81.

[84]*A Treatise on the Grammar of New Testament Greek* (Edinburgh: T. and T. Clark, 1870), p. 331.

[85]James Hadley, *A Greek Grammar for Schools and Colleges* (New York: D. Appleton and Co., 1877), p. 264.

[86]A. T. Robertson, *A Grammar of the Greek New Testament in the Light of Historical Research* (4th ed.; Nashville: The Broadman Press, 1923), p. 835.

> sanctification and perfection) in the imperfect tense when individuals are spoken of. The verb *hagiazo*, to sanctify, is always aorist or perfect. . . . The same may be said of the verbs *katharizo* and *hagnizo*, to purify. Our inference is that the energy of the Holy Spirit in the work in entire sanctification, however long the preparation, is put forth at a stroke by a momentary act. This is corroborated by the universal testimony of those who have experienced this grace.[87]

Further discussion of the aorist tense as it relates to a second crisis will be considered in a later chapter.

Summary

Biblical evidence points to entire sanctification as a second crisis. Particularly in the New Testament, there are numerous examples of believers being baptized with the Holy Spirit subsequent to regeneration. This spiritual baptism is synonymous with sanctification. An intensive study of New Testament passages, especially from the writings of Paul, also indicates that there is an "also" experience for the Christian. Finally, New Testament terms and grammatical construction make the idea of a second crisis a valid biblical doctrine. Thus on the basis of biblical example, biblical exegesis, and biblical terminology, it is possible to accept the validity of entire sanctification as a second crisis, subsequent to regeneration.

[87]Pp. 57-90.

CHAPTER IX /

The Time Element in Sanctification

All Christian groups believe in sanctification. The reason is simple. First, most churches accept the Bible as the source of authority and inspiration for Christian living. And there can be no doubt that the doctrine of sanctification is biblical. Second, perfection must be the goal, or end, of religious experience. Otherwise religion becomes largely a matter of emotional preference or of human achievement. But when divine redemption enters the picture, then holiness becomes the normal and natural purpose of religious being. So the idea of holiness, or of perfection, is not, in itself, a primary cause of disagreement among Christian churches.

The "great divide" among Christian groups in the matter of personal holiness is the time element. To state it another way, the source of disagreement concerns the *when* of entire sanctification. To phrase it still another way, the problem is: Can a person experience a crisis of personal redemptive grace which makes possible a state of holiness here and now? The holiness churches of the Wesleyan heritage have always presented the possibility of personal holiness as the result of a second crisis. Other groups have denied this possibility. Thus the time element becomes crucial.

In regard to the time element in sanctification, there are, or have been, at least eight positions held within the Church. Before presenting these eight positions, it might be suggested that in most cases they are mutually exclusive. That is, to accept any one of the eight means the rejection of the others. So no one group can be commended for being more tolerant nor be condemned for being more dogmatic than the others. The eight positions to be discussed are: (1) the postmortem or Roman Catholic position; (2) the simultaneous or Moravian theory; (3) the positional, or holy-in-Christ doctrine; (4) the idea of sanctification by growth or progressive sanctification; (5) the "dying grace" teaching; (6) the suppression or counteraction theory; (7) the Oberlin theory; (8) the Wesleyan doctrine.

I. The Postmortem Theory

Roman Catholic theology places the time of sanctification for most people after death. According to Catholic teaching a person may die in one of three states.[1] First, a person may die "thinking of sin." Such a person may die without having received the grace of God in baptism or, having received it, he may have rejected it and dies in mortal sin. Such a person is shut out from heaven forever. His destiny is hell. Second, a person may die "filled with the love of God and free from all stain of sin, and therefore pass straight to behold God in heaven. Such was our Lady's soul; such also are the souls of babes baptized who die before they can sin."[2] Third, a person may die with God's love in him, and with a determination to serve and to love God. But his love and his service are hindered by bad habits and small sins. A person dying in this state goes to purgatory.

A. Purgatory

Purgatory serves two purposes, according to Catholic thinking. The first purpose in *punitive*. Every sin, they say, carries both *guilt* and *punishment*. God forgives the guilt of original sin in baptism and forgives the guilt of committed sins by absolution, based on personal confession. But the penalty of sin remains and must be paid for by penance in this life or by suffering in purgatory. A second purpose of purgatory is *purification*. Thus "purgatory (Lat., *pugare*, to make clean, to purify), in accordance with Catholic teaching, is a place or condition of temporal suffering for those who, departing this life in God's

[1]George D. Smith, ed., *Teaching of the Catholic Church* (New York: The Macmillan Co., 1951), p. 1146.

[2]*Ibid.*

grace, are not entirely free from venial faults, or have not fully paid the satisfaction due to their transgression."[3] Another statement defines purgatory as follows: "Purgatory is the name given to the state of purgation where such souls are, by suffering, brought to that perfection of their being which is essential if they are to be united to God, to know Him even as they are known."[4]

The *Catholic Catechism* is precise at the point of stating the purifying work of purgatory, for it reads: "The souls in purgatory must still suffer in order to be purified from the effects of their sins."[5] From the theoretical point of view, it is possible to avoid purgatory by the special assistance of God. Such, according to Catholic teaching, was the case of Mary and possibly John the Baptist. Practically, however, no one escapes altogether from venial sin. Thus the method of arriving at a state of holiness, or perfection, is the result of the sufferings of purgatory. In reference to the trying of man's works by fire in I Cor. 3:13, one commentator wrote as follows:

> The last words clearly imply some penal suffering, and as Paul connects it so closely with God's judgment, it can hardly be confined to suffering in this world, but seems to include the idea of purification suffering after this life, i.e., in purgatory.[6]

Protestants in general and the holiness movement in particular reject the concept of person purification in purgatory.

B. Objections to the Idea of Purgatory

There are several objections to the idea of purgatory and to the concept of purification through purgatorial sufferings. Among these are: (1) It is not biblical; (2) It is contrary to spiritual principles; (3) It encourages a lax attitude toward sin.

1. *It Is Not Biblical.*

Protestants generally reject the doctrine of purgatory since the evidence on which it is based is found not in the Bible but "in the Apocrypha, in II Macc. 12:39-45."[7] Catholic scholars also refer to I Cor. 3:13-15. However, this part of Paul's letter draws a picture of

[3] *Ibid.*, p. 1147.

[4] Philip Hughes, *The Catholic Faith in Practice* (Wilkes-Barre, Pa.: Dimension Books, Inc., 1965), p. 117.

[5] *A Catholic Catechism*, p. 163.

[6] Don B. Orchard, ed., *A Catholic Commentary on Holy Scripture* (New York: Thomas Nelson and Sons, 1953), p. 1087.

[7] George D. Smith, *op. cit.*, p. 594.

the *work* of men, not of the *men* as such. Thus it is the work which is tried in the fires of life or in the white light of judgment.[8]

2. *It Is Contrary to Spiritual Principles.*

First, it is the grace of God, mediated by the suffering and death of Christ, which secures men's restoration. If Christ paid the full penalty of sin, then man can do nothing to further meet the demands of divine justice. Second, there is no evidence either in the Bible or in human experience that suffering as such is a redemptive or purifying agency. Third, the body is left behind at death and the soul enters a spiritual life. Thus the major purpose of purgatory has been removed, namely, the purification of the physical body and its appetites. For, according to Catholic teaching, suffering cleanses in the following way: "The bodily appetites, overgrown and unhealthy, have to be brought back to their natural limits; the soul's control over the body is to be restored; and the soul itself is to be freed from all wrong habits and desires."[9] Since man does not have a physical body after death, the problem of bodily appetites and wrong habits is eliminated. Also, Paul taught that all such works of the flesh were to be put off in this present life (Col. 3:8-10; Eph. 4:25-32).

3. *It Encourages a Lax Attitude Toward Sin.*

While *mortal* sins condemn a person to hell, yet *venial* sins are recognized as part of the Christian life. Thus a person may profess a love to God and yet commit the sins of the flesh, such as adultery, lying, etc. But since these sins are done impulsively or through the weakness of the flesh, they do not cause a rupture in one's relationship to God. Historically, the Roman Catholic church has removed personal sanctity from the realm of everyday living and has placed it in the cloister, the convent, the monastery. Personal sanctity may thus be the spiritual goal of the select few. But the vast majority of God's people are left in a state of spiritual laxness or weakness. Such a two-track system of personal piety is contrary to both biblical teachings and a rational understanding of the nature of redemption.

II. The Simultaneous Theory

The simultaneous theory of sanctification teaches that both regeneration and sanctification occur in the experience of conversion. From this point of view a person receives the basic spiritual

[8]Wesley, *Notes*, p. 594.

[9]George D. Smith, *op. cit.*, p. 1144.

benefits of regeneration and sanctification at the same time. There is no crisis beyond the first crisis of regeneration. After the first, and only, crisis, a person grows in grace and develops in Christian maturity. Holiness in the Christian life is thus the result of regeneration. This teaching was advocated by pietistic groups in Germany, mainly the followers of Menno Simons and the Moravians. Both of these groups emphasized a practical holiness, which was the result of regeneration.

A. The Mennonites

The Mennonites represent the pietistic element in the early years of the Protestant Reformation. In listing the reasons for the Mennonite church withdrawing from the Roman Catholic church, a church historian wrote: "The essential character of the Christian life is holy obedience to Christ and His word, not ceremonialism, church feasts, pilgrimages, adoration of relics, making the sign of the cross, using the rosary, and the like."[10] The holy life has always been a part of the religious life of this group. To the Mennonites, the holy life is the result of regeneration. In speaking of regeneration as a spiritual resurrection Menno Simons declared: "This resurrection includes the new creature, the spiritual birth and sanctification, without which no one sees the Lord."[11] The holiness which regeneration produces is of a revolutionary nature, for it means being "godly, holy, clean, obedient unto God, serving all mankind, powerful in truth, showing faith in righteousness, dead unto sin, living by the Spirit, yes, in all things Christian, heavenly, and unblamable in Christian love."[12] However, such holiness is not to be identified with perfectionism of any kind, for the same author writes: "Think not . . . that we boast of being perfect and without sin."[13]

A contemporary scholar of this group repeats the historic position of the Mennonite church in these words:

> There is no second crisis to be experienced with the Holy Spirit. What crisis experience could transcend baptism with the Spirit which brought into being the new life in Christ Jesus? There

[10]John Christian Wenger, *Glimpses of Mennonite History and Doctrine* (Scottdale, Pa.: The Herald Press, 1949), p. 5.

[11]John Christian Wenger, ed., *The Complete Writings of Menno Simons* (Scottdale, Pa.: The Herald Press, 1956), p. 54.

[12]*Ibid.*, p. 447.

[13]*Ibid.*, p. 506.

> is no biblical language that speaks of experiences with the Holy Spirit which surpass these just mentioned. With all respect to the sincerity and zeal of those who profess a second crisis of entire sanctification wrought by baptism with the Holy Spirit, it must be said that this baptism is the crisis experience which marks the beginning of the Christian life. All later experiences have their origin through the energizing of the indwelling Spirit.[14]

Before attempting to answer the implications of this position, let us examine the Moravian concept, which is similar to that of the Mennonites.

B. The Moravians

The Moravian church, or the *Unitas Fratrum,* "dates from the year 1457; Bohemia was the land of its birth; and the more spiritually-minded followers of John Hus were its first members."[15] Bohemia, Moravia, and Poland were the areas of its earliest outreach. Due to intense persecutions many of these people migrated to Saxony, Germany, in the early years of the eighteenth century. Here they found refuge in the estate of Count Nicolaus Ludwig von Zinzendorf. In 1723, Zinzendorf and three companions entered into an association which became known as the "Covenant of the Four Brothers." "The four pledged themselves to the cultivation of holiness in themselves and throughout the land."[16] Count Zinzendorf was one of the earliest Protestant leaders to develop a missionary program. In fact, "missions proved to be his greatest monument."[17] Personal holiness was a major emphasis among the Moravians.

1. *Wesley and the Moravians*

It was the missionary work of the Moravians that brought about an acquaintance with Wesley. There were 26 Moravian missionaries traveling to Georgia on the boat that carried Wesley on his missionary work in 1735. Wesley was impressed with their conduct on the journey and was particularly impressed with Mr. Spangenberg, one of the German pastors. When Wesley returned to England in 1738 another Moravian pastor, Peter Bohler, was instrumental in leading Wesley toward his Aldersgate experience. Wesley paid a short visit to the Moravians at Herrnhut and was greatly impressed with their devotion to Christ. In England the early

[14]Lehman, *op. cit.,* p. 178.
[15]*ERE,* VIII, 837.
[16]John R. Wernlick, *Count Zinzendorf* (New York: Abingdon Press, 1957), p. 65.
[17]*Ibid.,* p. 93.

followers of Wesley met and worshipped in the same "societies" as the Moravians. However, a break came between the Moravian Methodists and the Wesleyan Methodists in 1740.

2. *Differences Between Wesley and the Moravians*

There were several areas of disagreement between Wesley and the Moravians, but one of the sharpest was in the area of holiness and perfection. Wesley accused the Moravians of universalism, quietism and antinomianism. But the problem of holiness also entered the picture. In a letter to George James Stonehouse in November, 1750, Wesley listed his points of disagreement with the Moravians. Included in the list were the following points of Moravian doctrine with which Wesley disagreed:

> 5. That we are sanctified wholly the moment we are justified, and are neither more nor less holy to the day of our death.
> 6. That a believer has no holiness in himself at all; all his holiness being imputed, not inherent.[18]

Wesley's doctrine of Christian perfection was as much a stumbling block to the Moravians as holiness and "stillness" were to the Methodists. "I recognize no inherent perfection in this life,"[19] said Zinzendorf. And again Zinzendorf said: "This is the error of errors—Christ is our sole perfection. Whoever seeks perfection denies Christ."[20] According to a letter written by Wesley to Joseph Benson, the headmaster of Lady Huntingdon's school at Trevecca on December 26, 1769, Zinzendorf declared that he would accept no one in *his* Society who even *thought* of perfection. Wesley's laconic reply to this assertion of Zinzendorf was: "However, I trust you shall not only think of it but enjoy it."[21] All these points of practical and doctrinal matters brought about the separation between Wesley and the Moravians.

C. Objections to the Simultaneous Theory

The followers of Wesley echo his stand in rejecting the simultaneous nature of regeneration and sanctification. The reasons for these objections are biblical, psychological, and practical.

1. *Biblical Objections*

There are three serious weaknesses in the simultaneous theory.

[18]Telford, *op. cit.*, III, 53-54.

[19]Quoted by Clifford W. Lowlson, *Moravian and Methodist* (London: The Epworth Press, 1957), p. 114.

[20]*Ibid.*

[21]Telford, *op. cit.*, V, 166.

First, the Bible *does* present examples of some people who certainly would be accepted as Christian who had a second crisis. Second, if a person is sanctified at the time he is regenerated, then all the commands and exhortations to be holy are given to sinners, who are prospects for salvation. This idea is unsound, for a sinner must be made alive spiritually before he has any concept of holiness and righteousness. Third, the New Testament recognizes that many were Christians, such as the Corinthians, Ephesians, and Thessalonians, and yet exhorts them to go on to a life of cleansing and of holiness.

2. *Psychological Objections*

Psychologically, sanctification cannot normally take place at the same time as regeneration. This does not mean that *God* is *unable* to sanctify an individual at the same time as He regenerates the individual. But the hindrance is in *man*, not God. For nothing significant can happen in personality unless at least two elements are present—a sense of need and a volitional response. Thus when a person comes to the place of repentance and confession, his sense of need and volitional response center on forgiveness, submission, and the impartation of spiritual life. It is only *after* a person has been born again that a sense of need develops in the area of the holy life. Thus a second crisis is no reflection on God's power nor does it indicate God's reluctance to impart His holiness to man. But even as God cannot resurrect a person from the death and the power of sin until man has a sense of need and makes a volitional response, so God cannot sanctify a man until a similar sense of need is felt and a volitional response is made. God could impute holiness to man when He regenerates him but personal holiness is the result of recognized need and volitional response.

3. *Practical Objections*

Practically, the simultaneous theory has several weaknesses. First, the existence of *sin* in *believers* is almost universally accepted. Second, the Bible indicates that the New Testament norm of Christian living is freedom from the power of sin. So either the New Testament standard for Christian living is an impossible and irrational ideal or the Christian is under obligation to "perfect holiness in the fear of God." Third, many Christians witness to a second crisis, which is called *entire sanctification*. Either these people are deluded or they are hypocritical. To level such a criticism of these people from the time of Wesley until the present is a rather large assignment. Fourth, those who have accepted the simultaneous theory have tended to interpret holiness in terms of external legalism rather than in terms of internal life and power.

III. Positional Holiness

According to W. T. Purkiser, "The essential point of the doctrine of entire sanctification is this fact of heart purity as an actual purging of the soul."[22] However, Purkiser recognizes that there is a strong challenge to the position of the Wesleyan doctrine of Christian holiness, for he writes:

> One of the major challenges to which this faith is subjected is from a very numerous group of Bible teachers, evangelists, Bible institutes, and radio preachers who assert that no such cleansing is possible, and that the holiness of the New Testament is a positional holiness wherein the believer, who is in Christ, is said to be accounted holy while actually morally impure.[23]

Although the idea of positional holiness was included in the introduction, it is elaborated here for the sake of emphasis.

A. Luther's Idea of Positional Holiness

The concept of being "holy in Christ," that is, positionally holy, was a feature of Luther's theology, who taught that holiness was "a thing that is common to all churches and all Christians in the world."[24] Thus, in Luther's thinking, holiness is the universal mark of all Christians, and comes as the result of faith: "For Christian holiness, or the holiness of universal Christendom, is that which comes when the Holy Spirit gives people faith in Christ."[25] According to Luther there is no state of grace which is holier than that of the ordinary Christian. A contemporary interpreter of Luther phrases it as follows:

> Because faith receives and accepts the gift of God and thus men become saints through faith, "holy" becomes the equivalent of "believing." The saints, or holy ones, are the believers and "to make holy" means to be made a "believer." In Luther's explanation the emphasis is shifted from sanctity and sanctifying to faith and being brought to faith except that there is no real difference between the two.[26]

[22]*Conflicting Concepts of Holiness*, p. 15.
[23]*Ibid.*
[24]Luther, *Works*, V, 266-67.
[25]*Ibid.*, p. 267.
[26]Girgensohn, *op. cit.*, p. 180.

B. Contemporary Teaching of Positional Holiness

Another supporter of the idea of positional sanctification writes that "positional perfection is revealed to be the possession of every Christian. . . . It is therefore absolute perfection which Christ wrought for us. There is no reference here to the quality of the Christian life. The issue of sinlessness is not in view. All saints (sanctified ones) are partakers of the perfection accomplished by the death of Christ."[27] Thus positional perfection is synonymous with positional sanctification, which is "wrought by Christ for every believer, and which is the possession of the believer from the moment of saving faith."[28]

From the point of view of positional sanctification, sanctification is the "ascription of sanctity to persons by virtue of their relationship to God. It is in this lowest sense that all Christians are said to be holy, or to be saints. The Christian church is regarded as separated community, the nature of which is to be holy."[29] In his analysis of positional sanctification, W. T. Purkiser states that the foundation of the teaching is laid on at least five interrelated theses:

> First, the Christian is possessed of two natures throughout his whole earthly Christian life—the seed of God, and the mind of the flesh or the carnal nature. These two natures are said to coexist in such a fashion that the believer's actual conduct may be now under one, now under the other, without in any way improving or disturbing his standing with God.
>
> Second, since the believer is in Christ and Christ is holy, the believer is holy in Christ, but not necessarily holy in character or conduct. That is, not only is the righteousness of Christ—His perfect obedience to God's law—imputed in justification to cover the believer's confessed sins; but the holiness of Christ—His conformity of nature to the character of God—is likewise supposed to be imputed to the believer. God is alleged to look at the believer through Christ, and to see him as holy even as Christ is holy although in point of fact the believer may at that very moment be full of carnality and sin.
>
> Third, the believer's sin nature can never be destroyed in this life, thus leaving him under the partial, and sometimes the full, dominion of the mind of the flesh. However, the sins which result from this sinful nature are not, in the case of the believer, supposed to be subject to condemnation at the judgment bar of God.

[27] Walvoord, *Doctrine of the Holy Spirit*, p. 208.
[28] Turner, *op. cit.*, p. 87.
[29] *Ibid.*

> These are, allegedly, dealt with at the judgment seat of Christ in the dispensation of rewards.
>
> Fourth, the justification or forgiveness granted the believer when he first accepts Christ is a permanent justification and encompasses all the future sins he may commit, as well as all his past sins. Faith only is the ground for justification; and repentance, if mentioned at all, is the transient sorrow of the sinning Christian when he realizes he has lost fellowship or broken communion with God.
>
> Fifth, it follows from the foregoing that the believer's standing his moral state may be. This, now known as the doctrine of eternal security, is basically the claim that any individual who is once saved can never be finally lost, regardless of his faith or lack of faith, his sinfulness or righteousness of life.[30]

There is no objection to the concept discussed above regarding the imputation of Christ's righteousness to the believer as long as it is equated with *justification*, which denotes a change of status rather than a change within the person. It is thus valid to regard all saints as called to sanctity, for those who are "sanctified in Christ Jesus" (I Cor. 1:2) are called to saintliness. From the Wesleyan point of view, however, the concept of sanctification includes more than merely objective relationship to God. To the Wesleyans both regeneration and sanctification include subjective, experiential changes which are derived from the presence of the Holy Spirit. It is possible to list several authentic objections to the idea of positional sanctification.

C. Objections to Positional Holiness

1. *It May Make Regeneration Positional.*

If sanctification is regarded as merely positional, then it is possible to regard regeneration as also positional, or relational. This would mean accepting the sacramental idea of regeneration. Biblical language addresses men in identical language in both cases. Further, if regeneration and sanctification are merely formal, then Christianity is only a slight improvement over Judaism. But the New Testament points to both regeneration and sanctification as much more than formal, or relational. In both cases there is a vital and effective change through union with Christ.

2. *The New Testament Regards Holiness as Contemporary.*

The New Testament speaks of personal holiness as something promised, something to be desired, something to be effected in the

[30]*Conflicting Concepts of Holiness*, pp. 17-18.

believer, as something which is obligatory on all believers. Thus it cannot be merely positional.

3. *It Minimizes the Power of God.*

To regard sanctification as positional minimizes the redemptive power of Christ and magnifies the destructive power of sin. The total activity of redemption is designed to free man from sin. The greatest testimony to the power of God is a holy life.

4. *It Denies Historic Experience.*

Positional sanctification denies the experience of hundreds and thousands who have witnessed to *entire* sanctification by a humble and pious walk with God.

Entire sanctification is, to the Wesleyan, a second crisis which results in a state of holiness. The believer is now freed from the everlasting battle against the *presence* of sinful attitudes and qualities within. He is fully "in Christ." The Christian may feel the pressure resulting from the natural appetites of the body and he may be tempted by a hundred things a day. But his keynotes are joy and victory.

IV. Progressive Sanctification

Perhaps the most popular concept of sanctification is that of progressive sanctification. This also was referred to in the introduction.

A. Statements Concerning Progressive Sanctification

Charles Hodge, noted Calvinistic theologian, expressed the idea of progressive sanctification in these words:

> Sanctification in the Westminster Catechism is said to be "the work of God's free grace, whereby we are renewed in the whole man after the image of God, and are enabled more and more to die unto sin and live unto righteousness."[31]

Another writer suggests the same thought in these words:

> Mere regeneration does not sanctify his inclination and disposition; nor is it able of itself to germinate the holy disposition. But it requires the Holy Spirit's additional and very peculiar act, whereby the disposition of the regenerated and converted sinner is brought gradually into harmony with the divine will; and this is the gracious act of sanctification.[32]

[31]*Op. cit.*, III, 213.
[32]Kuyper, *op. cit.*, p. 449.

Another writes that "sanctification is the growth of the soul toward maturity."[33] And still another observes that "sanctification is thus the perfecting or the progressive cleansing of the soul."[34] The Dutch theologian, G. C. Berkouwer, writes that progressive sanctification has four elements:

1. Increasing knowledge of our sinful nature.
2. Increasing earnestness in seeking remission of sin and the righteousness of Christ.
3. Prayer to God for the grace of the Holy Spirit and a constant endeavor to be renewed more and more after the image of God.
4. The eschatological prospect: the goal of perfection.[35]

"How remote this is," he says, "from any moralistic sanctification." But, as has been suggested, the Wesleyan view of entire sanctification is ethical and spiritual rather than moralistic.

B. Objections to the Idea of Progressive Sanctification

In connection with the doctrine of progressive sanctification it is possible to present a number of conclusions that show its basic weakness.

1. *Little or No Historic Evidence*

From a historical point of view, those individuals or groups which advocate "growth toward perfection" never seem to make much progress toward the goal, and do not generally exhibit a vital, consistent concern for spiritual development.

2. *Essentially Humanistic*

It is in essence a matter of sanctification by works and human achievement. It is not holy actions which make a person holy, but a holy heart which makes actions holy.

3. *Not Supported by Biblical Terminology*

Biblical terminology does not support the idea of a lifelong growth, with a gradual and prolonged subjugation of sin. Such terms and phrases as *crucify* (Rom. 6:6; Gal. 2:20); *cleanse* (II Cor. 7:1; Eph. 5:26; Jas. 4:8; I John 1:7-9); *purify* and *purifying* (Acts 15:9; Titus 2:14; Heb. 9:13); *purge* (Ps. 51:7; Matt. 3:12; Heb. 9:14; Isa. 6:7; John 15:2); *sanctify* and *sanctification* (Rom. 15:16; I Thess. 5:23; Heb. 13:12; I Pet. 1:2), all point to a contemporary state resulting from an act, not to a lifelong struggle with sin. Both contextual

[33]A. A. & J. A. Hodge, *op. cit.*, p. 62.

[34]Cox, *op. cit.*, II, 11.

[35]G. C. Berkouwer, *Faith and Sanctification* (Grand Rapids, Mich.: Wm. B. Eerdmans Pub. Co., 1952), p. 109.

examination and grammatical analysis point to a specific act and a spiritual state called holiness.

4. *Nature of Depravity Makes Growth Impossible.*

Spiritual depravity is not an *act* or a *deed,* but is a quality of human nature which lies at the fountainhead of all personal response and character. "This original, inborn sin, cannot be imperceptible, grown out, without a supernatural, conscious operation of the Holy Spirit."[36] Depravity is not eliminated gradually any more than sins are forgiven gradually.

5. *Nature of Sanctification Makes Growth into It Impossible.*

According to scripture, sanctification or purification is primarily the work of the Holy Spirit. Even as a person is unable to earn or to merit justification and regeneration, so is he unable to secure or attain his own sanctification. Sanctification is not a process of moral refinement by human, moral means. It is supernatural in its provision, supernatural in its method, and supernatural in its nature. As such it is the result of the activity and presence of the Holy Spirit. And as the result of the work of the Holy Spirit it is instantaneous. A person cannot *grow clean.* He must be *washed clean.* J. A. Wood quotes Wesley regarding the instantaneous aspect of entire sanctification as follows:

> Indeed, this is so evident a truth, that well-nigh all the children of God scattered abroad . . . generally agree in this: that although we may "by the spirit, mortify the deeds of the body;" *resist and conquer both natural and inward sin;* although we may *weaken our enemies* day by day;—*yet we cannot drive them out.* By all the grace which is given at justification, *we cannot extirpate them.* Though we watch and pray ever so much, we cannot wholly cleanse either our hearts or our hands. Most sure we cannot till it shall please our Lord to speak to our hearts again, to speak the SECOND TIME, BE CLEAN: and then *only the leprosy is cleansed* . . . and *inbred sin subsists no more.*[37]

A person may grow *in* grace, but it is not possible to grow *into* it. As man's inherent sinfulness was derived from Adam, so must man's inherent righteousness, or purity, be derived from Christ, the Second Adam. This inner holliness is a supernatural work called entire sanctification.

6. *Analogy with the New Birth Disproves Growth Idea.*

One of the clearest points of disagreement with the growth

[36]Wood, *Purity and Maturity,* p. 133.
[37]*Ibid.,* pp. 139-40.

theory is presented by W. T. Purkiser, by drawing an analogy between the new birth and entire sanctification. He writes as follows:

> Consider . . . the analogy found in the Bible between justification or the new birth and sanctification or holiness. There are great points of similarity between these two works of divine grace . . .
>
> Now, virtually all Bible-believing Christians recognize that the new birth, justification, is not gradual but instantaneous. It is an act of God which takes place at a given point in a believer's life. But if both justification and sanctification are products of the same divine love, the same will of God, the same Holy Word, the same blessed Spirit, the same redeeming Blood, and the same human condition, faith—is there any valid reason for supposing that one is instantaneous while the other is gradual? If justification is instantaneous, there is certainly no reason why sanctification, wrought by the same agency, should not be equally the act of a moment.
>
> As a matter of fact, every argument which proves the instantaneity of regeneration is just as forceful when applied to sanctification. If the evidence for the immediacy of sanctification be rejected, there is no logical ground on which to base proof for the immediacy of justification.[38]

V. The "Dying Grace" Theory

Closely associated with the idea of growth into, or toward, the state of holiness is the idea of dying grace. According to this view both the presence and the power of sin remain with a person throughout life. At the time of death, "in the hour and article of death," the soul is set free from sin and enters God's presence holy and pure. This idea, part of a great branch of traditional Protestant theology, was taught by Luther and Calvin, and later by many of their adherents.

A. Luther's Idea of Dying Grace

Speaking of the struggle between the flesh and the Spirit as discussed by Paul in Gal. 5:17, Luther writes: "Whence comes this evil lust in men who are baptized and saints? Without doubt from the fleshly birth, in which this inherited sin of evil desire is born with them; and it continues even unto death, and offers battle and resistance to our spirit as long as we live."[39] In his "Treatise on Baptism" Luther speaks even more precisely to the point of

[38] *Conflicting Concepts of Holiness*, pp. 32-34.
[39] *Op. cit.*, III, 25.

purification at death when he declares: "The dying or drowning of sin, is not fulfilled completely in this life, nay, not until man passes through bodily death also, and utterly decays to dust."[40] For Luther the redemptive work symbolized in water baptism was not ended until death. "Only then will that be finished which the lifting up out of baptism signifies. Then shall we arise from death, from sins and from all evil, pure in body and soul, and then shall we live forever."[41] To Luther man struggled with inner sin until he was released from the struggle by death.

B. Calvin's Idea of Dying Grace

Calvin expressed a thought similar to that of Luther in his discussion of the perfection possible to the believer. Though recognizing the possibility of progress toward the goal of perfection in the present life, he said: "We shall never reach the goal until we have laid aside the body of sin, and been completely united to the Lord."[42] Contemporary scholarship echoes the historic ideas of Luther and Calvin regarding the time of personal purification. Thus Berkouwer refers to the Wesleyan emphasis on present, experiential holiness as a "premature seizure of the glory that will be."[43] Here again the stress is on holiness as an eschatological prospect, for it is only "after this life we arrive at the goal of perfection."[44] Brunner also presents the idea of positional holiness combined with growth toward the ideal of holiness, for he writes: "Certainly in the sight of God sanctification is an indivisible unity, and in its character as justification through Jesus Christ a unique and total event. But as a matter of experience it is accomplished in the individual man in a series of acts, as it were by means of forward thrusts by God into man's sinful nature."[45] To Brunner, sanctification is "a lifelong process which never comes to its completion in the earthly historical world."[46] Wesleyans will be quick to agree that man cannot arrive at a state of glorified perfection before he is a subject for glorification. But yet there is an experience, says the Wesleyan, where the believer reaches a state of experiential holiness here and now.

[40] *Ibid.*, I, 57.
[41] *Ibid.*, p. 58.
[42] *op. cit.*, II, 118.
[43] *Op. cit.*, p. 67.
[44] *Ibid.*, p. 97.
[45] *Dogmatics*, III, 293.
[46] *Ibid.*, p. 296.

C. Objections to the "Dying Grace" Theory

In rejecting the historic concept of "dying grace" several potent reasons come into play.

1. *The Idea Is Not Biblical.*

Nowhere does the Bible state that death is the gateway to purification. The reverse is true. The Bible regards death as the last enemy to be overcome (I Cor. 15:26). But if death brings about purification and restores one to the image of God, then death is man's greatest friend. Also the Bible presents death as a point of character fixation, not of character transformation (Rev. 22:11; Luke 16:24).

2. *It Regards Sin as Something Physical.*

The teaching of "dying grace" appears to incorporate the ancient Gnostic idea that sin is resident in the physical body. But the New Testament places sin squarely in the "heart," or at the center of selfhood, at the core of personality, as working in the soul. And since man's essential selfhood, his personality, the essence of his being, does not die, then physical death can bring no dramatic and revolutionary change in one's spiritual state.

3. *It Is Psychologically Unsound.*

The concept of purification at, or after, death is extremely weak psychologically. For a person may die instantly, or after a prolonged period of time. He may be unconscious for a long period. In this case death would work some kind of magical transformation by which a state of purity was granted to it. But, as has been stated, all significant personality changes involved two fundamental aspects—a sense of need and volitional choice. Neither of these would necessarily be present at death.

4. *Its Explanations Are Vague.*

Those who advance the idea of "dying grace" are vague in regard to how God elevates the person to a state of purity. Perhaps it should, and must, remain a mystery. But the New Testament is clear, unqualified, and precise in linking experiential holiness in man with the atonement of Christ and the presence of the Holy Spirit.

VI. The Counteraction Theory

The "counteraction" approach to holiness, also called suppressionism, is often associated with the Keswick movement.

A. The Keswickians

The Keswick movement was an outgrowth of the evangelical revivals that swept England in the last half of the nineteenth century. The first Keswick Convention was held June 29 to July 2, 1875, at Keswick, England, as the result of an invitation from Rev. Harford-Battersby, vicar of St. Johns, Keswick.[47] Since 1875 "the convention has met annually at Keswick, the last week in July, and year by year it has grown in numbers and influence."[48] The aim of the Keswick movement is "the promotion of practical holiness."[49] Its motto is "All One in Christ Jesus."

The practical biblical approach of the Keswickians is summarized by Arthur T. Pierson in seven statements:

1. Immediate abandonment of every known sin, doubtful indulgence, or conscious hindrance to holy living.
2. Surrender of the will and the whole being to Jesus Christ as not only Saviour, but Master and Lord in loving and complete obedience.
3. Appropriation by faith of God's promise and power for holy living.
4. Voluntary renunciation and mortification of the self-life that centers in self-indulgence and self-dependence, that God may be all in all.
5. Gracious renewal or transformation of the inmost temper and disposition.
6. Separation unto God for sanctification, consecration and service.
7. Enduement with power and infilling with the Holy Spirit, the believer claiming his share in the Pentecostal gift.[50]

B. Keswick Method for Realizing Personal Holiness

The method for realizing personal holiness, according to Keswick teaching, is through personal consecration, personal appropriation, and personal trust. Thus "the child of God . . . grows by the daily morifying of the deeds of the body, and the daily vivifying of the Spirit through Christ Jesus: the daily putting off the old man of sin, the daily putting on of the 'new man, which after God is

[47] Arthur T. Pierson, *Forward Movements of the Last Half Century* (New York: Funk and Wagnalls, 1900), p. 25.

[48] "Keswick Convention," *Schaff-Herzog Encyclopedia*, VI, 321.

[49] *Ibid.*

[50] *Op. cit.*, pp. 32-33.

created in righteousness and true holiness.'"[51] Speaking of overcoming the burden of sin, one Keswick scholar states that the Christian is victorious by "letting Christ have the whole weight of our load, which He counteracts by His superior power."[52]

Man is never free from original sin, for "it is constantly there," says the Keswick teaching. The Christian, however, may experience "perpetual deliverence from it" by a moment-by-moment cleansing by the atonement of Christ. This appropriation, consecration, and enduement is recognized among the Keswicks as the baptism with the Holy Spirit, and is generally regarded as being subsequent to regeneration. "It is not, however, in the strict sense a work of grace, for there is no cleansing from inbred sin."[53] So, while the Keswick teaching stresses the practical life of holiness, "it is in no sense entire sanctification as Wesleyanism defines this term."[54]

C. Differences Between Keswickians and Wesleyans

The essential difference between Keswickians and Wesleyans centers around the idea of the place that original sin has in the life of holiness.

1. *Suppression Versus Cleansing*

The Keswickians state that sin is suspended, made inoperative, and is rendered powerless by the counteraction of the power of the Holy Spirit. But while the power of sin is neutralized, the presence of original sin is inevitable. One of the popular Keswick lecturers of recent years has expressed the "suppression" theory in these words: "Nowhere in the Word are we taught that sanctification means the eradication of the old sinful nature so that we are rendered impossible of sinning and even delivered from the presence of sin."[55] So within every saint there are always two natures. One nature "always yields to the instigations of the devil, the enticements of the world, and the claims of the flesh; the other chooses to live under the Lordship of Christ, according to the divine calling

[51]Arthur T. Pierson, *The Heart of the Gospel* (London: Passmore and Alabaster, 1892), p. 91.

[52]Herbert F. Stevenson, *Keswick's Authentic Voice* (Grand Rapids, Mich.: Zondervan Publishing House, 1959), p. 165.

[53]Wiley, *Christian Theology*, II, 463.

[54]*Ibid.*

[55]Ruth Paxson, *Called unto Holiness* (London: Marshall, Morgan and Scott, 1936), p. 14.

for the Church, and under the control of the Spirit."[56] Man is always engaged in a struggle to suppress the power of sin.

2. *Counteraction Versus Freedom*

The life of victorious holiness is possible, in Keswick teachings, because of the counteraction of the Spirit to the sin which resides within the believer. A precise summary of the position is presented in the following statement:

> As the Spirit of Life He counteracts all the work of the flesh within. While the Christian is no longer in the flesh, the flesh is still in him and remains there through life. The flesh will do everything it can possibly do to regain possession, control and use of the life. But that wonderful Spirit of life is within to counteract all the workings of the flesh, and, when we let the Holy Spirit have absolute control, He can keep the flesh from having dominion and power over us.[57]

In referring to Rom. 6:6, where the Apostle Paul speaks of the body of sin being destroyed, the same writer interprets "destroy" to mean "rendered inoperative." In modern terms, "to be put out of employment, out of a job as ruler over your life."[58] So it is by continual vigilance and constant mortification that the believer is enabled to live the life of holiness.

D. Objections to the Counteraction Theory

The answer of the Wesleyans to the "counteraction" theory is based on biblical and experiential foundations.

1. *Biblical Terminology*

The biblical terms used in relation to holiness are much stronger and more inclusive than the Keswicks indicate. For instance, the word *destroy (katargeo)* is sometimes used to denote *inoperative* or *put out of order*. But authoritative lexicographers translate the word as used in Rom. 6:6 to mean *remove*[59] or *to be done away*,[60] and place it under the general meaning of *do away with, annul, abolish*.[61] Similarly, the word *cleanse (katharidzo)* and its cognates mean "to free from the defilement of sin and from faults; to purify from wickedness."[62] In the physical sense, to cleanse means "to remove something by or

[56]Paxson, *The Wealth, Walk, and Warfare of the Christian*, p. 109.

[57]Paxson, *Called unto Holiness*, p. 59.

[58]*Ibid.*, p. 52.

[59]Arndt and Gingrich, *op. cit.*, p. 418.

[60]Thayer, *op. cit.*, p. 336.

[61]*Ibid.*

[62]*Ibid.*, p. 312.

for the purpose of purification."[63] In the moral and religious sense it means to "cleanse, purify."[64] Again, the word sanctification *(hagiasmo)* in I Thess. 4:7 is presented as indicating "the removal of existing impurity."[65] Thus sanctification is a state, not a process: "Sanctification is not moral action on the part of man, but a divinely effected state."[66] Biblical terminology, from the standpoint of context as well as syntax, shows that holiness is a state of spiritual purity brought about by the Holy Spirit.

2. *Lack of Consistency*

Practically and experientially, the counteraction approach does not produce permanent, long-range results. A majority of those who seek to be holy by self-mortification appear to have periodic bursts of spiritual interest, only to relapse in a short time into the routine of ineffective and frustrating religious living.

The counteraction theory does have the advantage of calling attention to the need for consistent devotional habits. But it seems that much of the devotional life is spent in unhealthy introspection and spiritual analysis. Holiness should release the vital spirit of joyful and victorious Christian living. Holiness should provide a springboard to sustained Christian service, unhindered by the ever present threat of the upheaval of carnal actions.

3. *Limits the Power of God*

Finally, the counteraction theory limits the redemptive power of the Triune God. There is no biblical or logical reason why, if God can give power to paralyze sin, He cannot *remove* sin from the life completely. This does not mean a restoration to Adamic perfection, or to any kind of absolute perfection. The Bible indicates that the atonement of Christ provided an effective antidote to sin which brings about a perfect cure. The scars of sin may remain—but the wound is healed.

VII. The Oberlin Theory

Charles G. Finney, Asa Mahan, and James H. Fairchild represent men who were emphatic in preaching the possibility and the necessity of personal holiness. But they developed a peculiar and unique theology in attempting to explain the experience. They dif-

[63] Arndt and Gingrich, *op. cit.*, p. 388.
[64] *Ibid.*
[65] Cremer, *op. cit.*, p. 56.
[66] Kittel, *Theological Dictionary*, I, 112.

fered at two points with traditional holiness thought (1) regarding the nature of original sin and (2) the nature of sanctification. Because of their connection with Oberlin College, Cleveland, Ohio, their position has been called the Oberlin position.

A. Oberlin Theory of Depravity

Charles Finney placed depravity in the *action of the will.* To Finney "moral depravity is depravity of choice."[67] Thus depravity was a "depravity of free will, not of the faculty itself, but of its free action. It consists of a violation of moral law."[68] By placing depravity in the action of the will, Finney rejected the idea of a sinful nature in man. Since man did not possess a sinful nature, then "all sin consists, and must consist in selfishness, or in the choice of self-gratification as a final end."[69] Elaborating on the idea that moral depravity can be predicated only to selfish intention Finney writes:

> Moral depravity, as I use the term, does not consist in, nor imply a sinful nature, in the sense that the substance of the human soul is sinful in itself. It is not a constitutional sinfulness. It is not an involuntary sinfulness. Moral depravity, as I use the term, consists in selfishness; in a state of voluntary committal of the will to self-gratification. It is a spirit of self-seeking, a voluntary and entire consecration to the gratification of self. It is selfish ultimate intention: it is the choice of a wrong end of life; it is moral depravity, because it is a violation of moral law. . . . Moral depravity is sinfulness, not of nature but of voluntary state. . . . It is not a sinful nature but a sinful heart.[70]

To Finney, then, sin was a matter of aiming at the wrong goal, the making of self-gratification the supreme end of life.

B. Nature of Sanctification in the Oberlin Theory

Since depravity, according to Finney, was an act of the will, it followed that sanctification should also be an act of the will. He defines sanctification as follows: "Sanctification consists in the will's devoting or consecrating itself and the whole being, all we are and have, so far as powers, susceptibilities, possessions are under the control of the will, to the service of God. . . . Sanctification, then,

[67]Charles G. Finney, *Lectures on Systematic Theology* (London: William Legg and Co., 1851), p. 371.

[68]*Ibid.*

[69]*Ibid.*, p. 373.

[70]*Ibid.*

is nothing more nor less than entire obedience . . . to the moral law."[71]

When the Oberlin theology interpreted sanctification as a matter of the obedience of the will, it also regarded consecration as a second crisis. But here this theology follows the historic pattern of ultimately eliminating a second crisis entirely. One of Finney's successors at Oberlin states that there is no second crisis. There are only steps in the process of becoming more and more obedient. Thus James H. Fairchild writes:

> There seems to be no ground in the Scriptures for the idea of a definite experience, like a second new birth, which marks the line between a sanctified and an unsanctified state. There are successive experiences marking various steps of progress in the Christian life; but there is no propriety in calling a particular experience sanctification. It is only a step in the progress.[72]

The Oberlin position thus ends in a position closely akin to that of the Keswicks, insofar as the practical expression of holiness is concerned.

C. Objections to the Oberlin Position

There are a number of objections that may be made to the Oberlin idea of sanctification:

1. *It Has a Deficient View of Sin.*

Oberlin theology locates all sin of every kind in the will and accepts only one definition of sin, namely: "Sin is the transgression of the law." As Fairchild stated, "Sin and holiness pertain only to voluntary action."[73] However, the Bible pictures sin as a corruption of nature which indicates far more than a moral or legal relation to the Law. Biblically, sin is both *act* and *state.* The sinfulness of sin involves an ethical and spiritual relationship, or the absence of such a relation, to a holy God.

2. *It Has a Deficient View of Personality.*

Oberlin theology is at fault in its psychological analysis of man. Finney apparently accepted an atomistic concept of man with personality made up of different "faculties."[74] But psychology has long since discarded "faculty psychology." And from the theologi-

[71] *Ibid.,* p. 595.
[72] *Elements of Theology* (Oberlin, Ohio: Edward J. Goodrich, 1892), p. 285.
[73] *Ibid.,* p. 128.
[74] *Op. cit.,* p. 371.

cal point of view as well as the psychological, man must be considered as a whole, *in toto.* Thus it would be impossible for depravity to affect only the will. Depravity has touched every aspect of man's personality.

3. *It Confuses Consecration with Entire Sanctification.*

Consecration is a human act, and as such is part of the overall act of sanctification. In its deeper meaning, however, sanctification is God's act of cleansing the believer. Jesus prayed, "Father, sanctify them" (John 17:17); and Paul prayed, "And the very God of peace sanctify you wholly"(I Thess. 5:23). There is "no dependence here upon vows and renunciations and consecrations. It is the work of God in response to our consecrations and faith."[75] Man consecrates but God sanctifies. Thus sanctification cannot be *only* an act of human dedication; it must be also a matter of divine purification.

Oberlin theology taught that sanctification was a matter of growth. While Finney stressed an act of consecration which was climactic, the full impact of his teachings were expressed by Fairchild in these words: "The growth and establishment of the believer —the development in him of the grace of the gospel, is called sanctification."[76] The Wesleyan position on growth *into* sanctification has been discussed earlier in this chapter.

Finney and Fairchild, in denying that original sin was inherent in man's nature, logically and consistently denied the idea of purification in sanctification. This is a constant problem to holiness theology. For when original sin is defined as selfishness, pride, self-will, self-sovereignty, etc., then inevitably sanctification tends to become only consecration, rather than consecration plus purification.

4. *Practical Results Are Not Effective.*

Practically, as Asa Mahan's remark about Finney's concern for the spiritual failure of his followers indicates, the results of the Oberlin teachings were not effective.[77] For when the theology of individual sanctification becomes fuzzy and vague, then the experience of those who listen also becomes unclear.

[75]A. M. Hills, *Fundamental Christian Theology* (Pasadena, Calif.: C. J. Kinne, 1931), II, 254.

[76]*Op. cit.*, p. 280.

[77]Hills, *op. cit.*, p. 477.

VIII. The Wesleyan Doctrine

There are four distinctive elements in the Wesleyan view of entire sanctification: (1) That entire sanctification is a second crisis which produces a change in the believer in his present experience; (2) That heart purity, or cleansing, is the essential aspect of sanctification; (3) That the *only* perfection possible in this life is a perfection of love; (4) That continual growth *in* grace not only can, but must, be the trademark of the sanctified believer. The first two of these elements are discussed below. The other two were discussed in the previous chapter.

A. Entire Sanctification a Second Crisis

Asbury Lowrey has written: "We may open our definition of this great gift by asserting that the work of grace, of which the heart is the subject, has its inception, progress, and consummation in this life."[78] In a previous chapter a number of examples of sanctification as a second crisis were presented. At this point, then, it seems sufficient to give a few biblical references which point to a second crisis. Note that all of these passages were directed to people already in the Church—"babes in Christ," "saints," etc.

1. "I beseech you therefore, brethren, by the mercies of God, that ye present your bodies a living sacrifice, holy, acceptable unto God, which is your reasonable service. And be not conformed to this world: but be ye transformed by the renewing of your mind, that ye may prove what is that good, and acceptable, and perfect, will of God" (Rom. 12:1-2).

2. "And God, which knoweth the hearts, bare them witness, giving them the Holy Ghost, even as he did unto us; and put no difference between us and them, purifying [cleansing] their hearts by faith" (Acts 15:8-9).

3. "Having therefore these promises, dearly beloved, let us cleanse ourselves from all filthiness of the flesh and spirit, perfecting holiness in the fear of God" (II Cor. 7:1).

4. "Therefore leaving the principles of the doctrine of Christ, let us go on unto perfection" (Heb. 6:1).

5. "Husbands, love your wives, even as Christ also loved the church, and gave himself for it, that he might sanctify and cleanse it with the washing of water by the word" (Eph. 5:25-26).

[78] *Possibilities of Grace* (Chicago: Christian Witness Co., 1884), p. 209.

6. "For this is the will of God, even your sanctification, that ye should abstain from fornication [evil]" (I Thess. 4:3).

7. "Now when the apostles which were at Jerusalem heard that Samaria had received the word of God, they sent unto them Peter and John: who, when they were come down, prayed for them, that they might receive the Holy Ghost . . . Then laid they their hands on them, and they received the Holy Ghost" (Acts 8:14-17).

8. "He said unto them, Have ye received the Holy Ghost since [when] ye believed? And they said unto him, We have not so much as heard whether there be any Holy Ghost. And when Paul had laid his hands upon them, the Holy Ghost came on them" (Acts 19:2, 6).

Some of the passages quoted above do not appear at first reading to refer to a second crisis, but when a grammatical anlysis is made of the terms used, particularly of the verbs, and when consideration is given to the context of the passages, then a second crisis is indicated without equivocation. In his *Plain Account of Christian Perfection,* John Wesley presented a summary regarding the biblical position on sanctification. It reads as follows:

> (1) That Christian perfection is that love of God and our neighbour, which implies deliverance from all sin. (2) That this is received merely by faith. (3) That it is given instantaneously, in one moment. (4) That we are to expect it, not at death, but every moment; that now is the accepted time, now is the day of salvation.[79]

B. Entire Sanctification Includes Purification.

The verb to *sanctify* is derived from the Latin *sanctus* (holy) and *facere* (to make). Thus when it is used in the imperative mood it signifies, literally, *to make holy.* The Greek verb *hagiadzo,* derived from *hagios* (holy), also means *to make holy.* Both etymology and the biblical use of *sanctification* point to the fact of purification. This cleansing is designed to remove the inherited sin from the believer's heart. H. Orton Wiley states the Wesleyan position on sanctification as *cleansing* in these words:

> The extent of cleansing according to the Scriptures, includes the complete removal of all sin. Sin is to be cleansed thoroughly, purged, extirpated, eradicated and crucified; not repressed, suppressed, counter-acted or made viod, as these terms are commonly used. It is to be destroyed; and any theory which makes a place for the existence of inbred sin . . . is unscriptural.[80]

[79]*Works,* XI, 393.
[80]*Christian Theology,* II, 488-89.

A study of the Greek terms used in connection with *sanctification* as *cleansing* is conclusive. Several terms are discussed below.

1. One of the most common terms is *katharidzo*, which means to make clean, or to cleanse in general, both inwardly and outwardly; to consecrate by cleansing or purifying; or to free from defilement (Acts 15:9; II Cor. 7:1; Titus 2:14; I John 1:7).

2. Closely related to *katharidzo* is the word *katargeo*, which means to annul, to abolish, to put an end to, to cause to cease (Rom. 6:6).

3. Another strong term pointing to purification is the word *ekkathairo*, meaning to cleanse thoroughly, or to purge (I Cor. 5:7).

4. For those who object to the word *eradicate* it is suggested that the term has biblical support in the word *ekrizoo*, which means to root out, to pluck up by the roots (Matt. 13:29).

5. One of the strongest terms is *stauroo*, which means, in reference to the *flesh*, "to destroy its power utterly" (Gal. 5:24).

6. Closely related to *stauroo* is the word *thanatoo*, signifying to subdue, mortify, or kill (Rom. 7:4; Rom. 8:13).

7. The term *luo* is occasionally used in reference to freedom from sin. When it is thus used it means primarily to loose or free from, but it also means to break up, to destroy, to demolish (I John 3:8).

A study of such terms used in relation to the purification of the believer shows conclusively that the Scriptures teach the possibility of the cleansing of the heart from inbred sin—the complete destruction of the carnal self.

SUMMARY

This chapter has presented the various teachings of the "when" of entire sanctification. As has been suggested, most church groups support one of the positions to the exclusion of the others. Thus no one group can be accused of being more dogmatic than another. The distinguishing mark of Wesleyan theology has always been the belief that God's grace is sufficient to break completely the power of sin over the individual in present experiences. Wesleyans believe that their position is biblically true and practically sound.

CHAPTER X /

The Work of the Holy Spirit

The dynamic presence of the Holy Spirit is necessary for living the life of New Testament Christianity. Christian response, or Christian living, may be formal, intellectual, or experiential. Neither formal religion nor intellectual religion makes an essential place for the Holy Spirit. But when Christianity becomes experiential and significant in the religious life, then the work of the Holy Spirit is of utmost importance. As E. F. Scott puts it: "The belief in the Spirit has always sprung out of an experience. It has been strongest in times of religious awakening, when men have grown suddenly aware that the truths they had clung to half mechanically are the great realities."[1]

In the Old Testament the work of the Holy Spirit is usually considered in His relation to creation, in His bestowment of special gifts and particular abilities, and in His spiritual dealings with specific men. In the New Testament the work of the Holy Spirit may be discussed in His relation to Jesus the Messiah, in His coming on the

[1]*The Spirit in the New Testament* (London: Hodder and Stoughton, 1923), p. vi.

Day of Pentecost, and in His place in the life of the Christian and the Church. However, since the purpose of this study is to relate the work of the Holy Spirit to the life and the doctrine of holiness, the discussion that follows will be limited to four aspects of the work of the Spirit: (1) the Holy Spirit in regeneration or initial sanctification, (2) the Holy Spirit in entire sanctification, (3) the Holy Spirit in Christian growth, (4) the fruit of the Spirit.

I. THE HOLY SPIRIT IN REGENERATION

John Wesley interpreted religion primarily from the point of view of regeneration and sanctification.[2] Protesting against mere formalism, Wesley preached a religion of love. Religion, according to Wesley, is "the love of God and of all mankind; the loving God with all our heart and soul, and strength . . . and the loving every soul which God hath made, every man on earth, as our own soul."[3]

Broadly speaking, sanctification begins with the operation of prevenient grace and ends when the redeemed one stands in the presence of God. But as the term has been used in Wesleyan theology, sanctification has carried two distinct meanings—*initial sanctification,* or regeneration, and *entire sanctification,* or heart cleansing. It is important to realize that *all* born-again Christians have the Holy Spirit, for any spiritual work done in man is the result of the work of the Holy Spirit.

A. The Holy Spirit in Regeneration

Every regenerated Christian has the Holy Spirit dwelling within. To speak of an experience subsequent to regeneration which is called the baptism with the Holy Spirit does not minimize the revolutionary work of the Holy Spirit in regeneration. As John Wesley wrote, "The state of a justified person is inexpressibly great and glorious."[4] The testimony of the Scriptures affirms that all Christians have received the Holy Spirit. Four things may be said about the Holy Spirit in regenerated believers.

1. *The Holy Spirit Sustains Spiritual Life.*

It is impossible to remain in a regenerated state without the help of the Holy Spirit. Spiritual life comes through the Holy Spirit. In the conversation with Nicodemus, Jesus said: "Except a man be

[2]*Works,* V, 39-40.
[3]*Ibid.,* VIII, 3.
[4]*Ibid.,* V, 146.

born of water and of the Spirit, he cannot enter into the kingdom of God" (John 3:5). Paul writes that to belong to Christ is to have the Holy Spirit: "Now if any man have not the Spirit of Christ, he is none of his" (Rom. 8:9). In writing to the legalistically inclined Galatians, Paul writes: "Having begun in the Spirit, are ye now made perfect by the flesh?" (Gal. 3:3) In a strong admonition to the same church Paul writes: "Walk in the Spirit, and ye shall not fulfil the lust of the flesh" (Gal. 5:16).

2. *Relationship to God Is Dependent upon the Holy Spirit.*

A second truth related to the possession of the Holy Spirit by the regenerated is that the filial relationship of the believer to God is dependent upon the Holy Spirit. In his references to Christians as children of God, Paul makes the Holy Spirit the vital link in the relationship: "Ye have received the Spirit of adoption, whereby we cry, Abba, Father. The Spirit itself beareth witness with our spirit, that we are the children of God" (Rom. 8:15-16). In his Galatian letter Paul again relates sonship to the presence of the Holy Spirit. "And because ye are sons, God hath sent forth the Spirit of his Son into your hearts, crying, Abba, Father" (Gal. 4:6). To Paul the word "Abba" carried a much deeper meaning than mere biological relationship. The Aramaic title "Abba" was used in Christian terminology because it was the title which Jesus used to address His Father.[5] Thus the title carries the idea of profound spiritual relationship.

3. *The Holy Spirit Is Resident in All Believers.*

A third truth related to the activity of the Holy Spirit in regeneration is that the Holy Spirit dwells in every truly regenerated believer, even when the believer is carnal. In writing to the church at Corinth, Paul bluntly tells them that they are carnal (I Cor. 3:1). But almost in the same breath he encourages them to spiritual pursuits by reminding them of their relationship to God: "Know ye not that ye are the temple of God, and that the Spirit of God dwelleth in you?" (I Cor. 3:16) Later on, Paul again chides the Corinthians for their spiritual immaturity, yet he also reminds them that their "body is the temple of the Holy Ghost which is in you" (I Cor. 6: 19). Thus it is evident that the Holy Spirit is responsible for the work of regeneration, that the filial relationship of the Christian to God is sustained through the Holy Spirit, and that the Holy Spirit dwells within all true Christians, even those who are carnal.

[5]Vincent, *op. cit.*, IV, 138.

4. *Opposition to the Holy Spirit*

A final truth regarding the presence of the Holy Spirit in the regenerated is that there is a contrary power, force, or tendency opposing the work of the Holy Spirit. Even though the Holy Spirit sustains and resides in every true follower of Christianity, the presence and the power of the Holy Spirit are not able to achieve the spiritual potential which is the birthright of every Christian. "For the flesh lusteth against the Spirit, and the Spirit against the flesh: and these are contrary the one to the other: so that ye cannot do the things that ye would" (Gal. 5:17). In speaking of this conflict between the flesh and the Spirit, Wesley writes: "There are in every person, even after he is justified, two contrary principles, nature and grace . . . the *flesh* and the *Spirit*. Hence, although even babes in Christ are *sanctified*, yet it is only in part."[6] This *initial*, or *partial* sanctification was for Wesley a reality which was both biblical and experiential.

B. Regeneration an Initial Work

The doctrine of holiness, as taught by Wesley, includes the work of the Holy Spirit in regeneration. But it is a partial, an incomplete work. For "although we are renewed, cleansed, purified, sanctified, the moment we truly believe in Christ, yet we are not then renewed, cleansed, purified altogether; but the flesh, the evil nature, still *remains* (though subdued, *and wars* against the Spirit.)"[7] Daniel Steele points out that "while the Spirit in the new birth touches the whole nature, the thoughts, the feelings, and the will, so that the man is a new creature, his renewal is not complete in any part."[8]

The new birth, called *regeneration* or *initial sanctification*, is a transforming, renewing experience that is revolutionary and glorious. But it is in reality just what the word regeneration indicates—a new birth, a new beginning, a new creature, a new outlook, a new loyalty. But the spiritual babe must grow to maturity. Christian character must be nurtured. The obstacles to spiritual development must be removed. The soul must be freed from all carnal opposites of spirituality in growing as sons of God. Thus the necessity of entire sanctification, which is the result of the work of the Holy Spirit.

[6] *Works*, V, 155.
[7] *Ibid.*, p. 156.
[8] *The Gospel of the Comforter* (Boston: The Christian Witness Co., 1904), p. 104.

II. The Work of the Holy Spirit in Entire Sanctification

In the area of practical theology, the holiness movement has usually used a number of terms synonymous with entire sanctification, such as the "second blessing" and the "baptism with the Holy Spirit." In the discussion that follows, it seems desirable to use the biblical term "baptism with the Holy Spirit." In discussing this aspect of the work of the Spirit, two ideas are presented: (1) the time of a Christian's baptism; (2) the manifestation of the Spirit's baptism, or the results of the baptism with the Holy Spirit.

A. The Time of the Baptism with the Holy Spirit

In regard to the time when a person is baptized with the Holy Spirit, there are two major schools of thought. One school teaches that a person is baptized with the Spirit at the time of his regeneration. The other school holds that the baptism with the Holy Spirit is subsequent to regeneration.

1. *The Simultaneous Theory*

A strong statement from a contemporary scholar claims that "every Christian is baptized by the Holy Spirit at the moment of salvation. Salvation and baptism are therefore co-extensive, and it is impossible to be saved without this work of the Holy Spirit."[9] The same author again declares: "Never in Scripture is baptism by the Spirit recorded as occurring subsequent to salvation."[10] Another writer states: "There can be no doubt that we receive it when we turn to the Savior and accept Him."[11]

The problem in this position arises from equating the "birth of the Spirit" with the "baptism of the Spirit." Such a position seems difficult to sustain from a biblical point of view. For after the Resurrection, at the end of those unforgettable 40 days of fellowship with the risen Saviour, Jesus commanded His disciples to remain in Jerusalem until they received the promise of the Father. And this promise was: "Ye shall be baptized with the Holy Ghost not many days hence" (Acts 1:5). It does not seem credible that Jesus regarded these followers as potential subjects for the new birth, for they had followed Him for over three years.

[9]Walvoord, *The Doctrine of the Holy Spirit*, p. 139.

[10]*Ibid.*, p. 140.

[11]Rene Pache, *The Person and Work of the Holy Spirit*, trans. J. D. Emerson (Chicago: Moody Press, 1954), p. 73.

Another instance is the revival at Samaria, initiated under the preaching of Philip, who "preached Christ unto them." Philip's preaching was effective, for "the people with one accord gave heed unto those things which Philip spake" (Acts 8:6). Further, these good Samaritans were baptized because they believed the gospel Philip preached. The church fathers at Jerusalem were anxious to get a firsthand report of this revival in Samaria, so Peter and John were dispatched to evaluate the situation. Peter and John saw the work of God which had been done in these new converts, and "laid they their hands on them, and they received the Holy Ghost" (Acts 8:17). There is no question here that these Samaritans were converts to Christ before they were baptized by the Holy Spirit. Other references have already been cited.

2. *The Second Crisis Teaching*

The second view of the baptism of the Holy Spirit is that such a baptism occurs subsequent to regeneration. Some refer to this as a "filling with the Spirit," but there seems little reason to force such semantic distinction. For the baptism with the Spirit and the filling with the Spirit are *identical.* As has been suggested in an earlier chapter, the disciples certainly would qualify as *bona fide* followers of Christ prior to Pentecost. The Samaritans also had fully accepted Christ before they received the Holy Spirit. But another instance is at hand. When Paul met the 12 disciples at Ephesus, he asked the oft quoted question: "Have ye received the Holy Ghost since ye believed?" (Acts 19:2) Most modern versions render this question: "Did ye receive the Holy Spirit when ye believed?"

Commentators generally reject the rendition of the Authorized Version, "since ye believed." Meyer translates it "after ye became believers,"[12] but he appears to be in the minority, for practically all contemporary exegetes, including Elliott and Gray, translate the thought "when ye believed." However, it should be pointed out that the verb form used is the aorist participle, which generally means either a completed event or an action antecedent in time to the action of the principal verb.[13] Charles E. Brown has presented an impressive case for the position held by Meyer in an appendix to *The Meaning of Sanctification.* It is not possible to be dogmatic at the point for, as one writer suggested, "The precise meaning of the

[12]Heinrich August Wilhelm Meyer, *Critical and Exegetical Handbook to the Acts of the Apostles,* tr. Paton Gloag (New York: Funk and Wagnalls, 1883), p. 365.

[13]Burton, *op. cit.,* pp. 62-63.

statement of the apostle in 19:2 is elusive, for the Greek is inconclusive at this point."[14] However, as W. T. Purkiser points out, two things remain crystal-clear whichever translation is taken: "These men were believers, and their faith is acknowledged by the Apostle Paul; and they had not received the Holy Spirit in the sense in which Paul intended."[15] Thus when the question is answered in the light of its context, it does indicate that these 12 disciples had an experience subsequent to regeneration in which they were baptized with the Holy Spirit.

The comprehensive nature of the baptism of the Holy Spirit is summarized by J. B. Chapman as follows:

> Sanctification, holiness, Christian perfection, perfect love, the baptism with the Holy Ghost, Christian purity, and other such terms imply the same work and state of grace, and that work is wrought in the hearts of believers subsequent to regeneration, on the basis of the merits of the blood of Jesus, on condition of faith, and by the efficient agency of the Holy Ghost.[16]

B. The Manifestation of the Holy Spirit

In relation to the experience of holiness, there have been two kinds of manifestation of the baptism with the Holy Spirit, as indicated by the New Testament and by Christian experience. The first of these manifestations may be called the external physical demonstration, while the second may be called the internal spiritual manifestation.

1. *External Physical Evidence of the Holy Spirit*

On the Day of Pentecost there were three external evidences of the coming of the Holy Spirit, namely, the "sound as of a rushing mighty wind," "tongues . . . like as of fire," and the ability "to speak with other tongues" (Acts 2:2-4). What was the purpose of this physical display? Ralph Earle compares the spectacular physical demonstration at Pentecost with the dramatic events at Sinai, where "there were thunders and lightnings, and a thick cloud upon the mount, and the voice of the trumpet exceeding loud; so that all the people . . . trembled. . . . And mount Sinai was altogether on a smoke, because the Lord descended upon it in fire . . . and the whole mount quaked greatly" (Exod. 19:16-18). Both Sinai and Pentecost were epochal events which signified the initiation of a new revela-

[14]Frank Stagg, *The Book of Acts* (Nashville: Broadman Press, 1955), p. 196.
[15]*Sanctification and Its Synonyms*, p. 36.
[16]*The Terminology of Holiness*, p. 69.

tion of God's redemptive process. At Pentecost "a new era was being inaugurated—the dispensation of the Holy Spirit. The supreme importance of this event must be recognized."[17] Similarly, a strange and brilliant star flashed in the sky at the birth of Jesus the Christ, while an angelic choir introduced the birth announcement to man. And when the Redeemer died, the sun was darkened, and the earth trembled. The Apocalypse also indicates that the beginnings of the judgmental era will be accompanied by awesome physical manifestations.

As symbols of a new period in redemptive history, "these audible and visible signs were but passing phenomena; the presence and power of the Holy Spirit was the permanent and important reality."[18] Four words can be used to state the meaning of the external physical manifestations at Pentecost, "namely, *power,* the rushing of a mighty wind; *purity,* tongues parting asunder, like as of fire . . . ; *possession,* they were all filled with the Holy Spirit; and *proclamation,* they began to speak with other tongues, as the Spirit gave them utterance."[19] Generally, the sound of the wind has been accepted to symbolize the mysterious, creative, life-giving power of God.[20] The fire stands for the purifying power of God's holy presence, the burning zeal of love, and the light of divine inspiration,[21] while speaking in tongues "was symbolical of the coming universality of the gospel."[22] While the external symbols of Pentecost were important, the truly significant meaning of the coming of the Holy Spirit is the internal, individual aspect of the work of the Holy Spirit.

2. *The Internal, Individual Work of the Holy Spirit*

The primary work of the Holy Spirit is internal and personal. The basic results of the work of the Holy Spirit are spiritual, not physical. For the Holy Spirit is a Person and, as a Person, produces the greatest work in personality. The outstanding works of the Holy Spirit are: (1) spiritualized religion, (2) personal power and victory, (3) heart purity, (4) freedom from fear of public opinion,

[17]Charles W. Carter and Ralph Earle, "The Acts of the Apostles," *The Evangelical Commentary* (Grand Rapids, Mich.: Zondervan Publishing House, 1959), p. 29.

[18]Stagg, *The Book of Acts,* p. 53.

[19]Carter and Earle, *op. cit.,* pp. 29-30.

[20]Rackham, *op. cit.,* p. 18.

[21]*Ibid.,* p. 19.

[22]F. J. Foakes-Jackson, "The Acts of the Apostles," *The Moffatt New Testament Commentary* (New York: Harper and Brothers, 1931), p. 11.

(5) complete dedication to God's kingdom, (6) success in soul winning.

a. Spiritualized religion. Religion may be ceremonial, legalistic, intellectualistic, humanistic, or spiritual. The coming of the Holy Spirit stamped Christianity as a spiritual religion—a life in the Spirit. Prior to Pentecost the Holy Spirit had filled people occasionally and was intermittently present. But "Pentecost witnessed the introduction into the world of a new order of life—the life of the divine Spirit in humanity."[23] What had formerly come as distilled dew from heaven now came in a sweeping flood. What had formerly been seen as a haunting shadow now became a blazing flame in their lives. "The Spirit now so took possession of their souls, that they henceforth spoke His thoughts, throbbed with His sympathies, and acted out His will. He filled them. They had no thoughts but His, or such as agreed with His; no feelings but such as glowed with His inspiration; no will but His."[24] After Pentecost "the Holy Spirit became the dominant reality in the life of the early church."[25]

b. Personal power and victory. Jesus had promised: "Ye shall receive power, after that the Holy Ghost is come upon you" (Acts 1:8*a*). Carter lists the power of the personal indwelling presence of the Holy Spirit in the life of the Spirit-baptized Christian as follows:

> *First,* Pentecostal power is the assurance of the sanctified Christian's victory over temptation and sin.
>
> *Second,* the Pentecostal power is an effective enablement to the execution of the Christian witness.
>
> *Third,* the efficacy of Pentecostal power for the endurance of persecution is well exemplified by the first Christian martyr, Stephen.
>
> *Fourth,* the practice of demon expulsion by the Spirit-filled apostles dots the pages of the first-century Christian history.
>
> *Fifth,* Pentecostal power for Christian healing in the first-century Church is quite as much in evidence as is demon expulsion.

[23]Rackham, *op. cit.*, p. 15.

[24]David Thomas, *Acts of the Apostles* (Grand Rapids, Mich.: Baker Book House, 1956), p. 27.

[25]William Barclay, *The Acts of the Apostles* (Philadelphia: The Westminster Press, 1953), p. 12.

> *Sixth* and finally, death itself was made to give up its victim at the command of these Spirit-filled servants of God. The restoration of Dorcas to life at the hands of Peter is a familiar example.[26]

c. Heart purity. The great fact of the Pentecostal baptism is purity of heart. It is impossible to distort or to confuse the meaning of the work of the Holy Spirit if purity is the core of Pentecost. J. B. Chapman wrote that "baptism always means cleansing, and the baptism with the Holy Ghost means the cleansing of our hearts by the Holy Ghost."[27] In fact, heart purity was presented as the essential element of Pentecost by Peter in one of the first councils of the Apostolic Church. When a committee headed by Paul and Barnabas was summoned to Jerusalem to discuss certain legal requirements related to Christianity, the issue was settled on the basis of heart purity.

In the midst of fruitless debate about circumcision, Peter took the floor and drove home the idea that the supreme requirement of the Christian faith was heart purity. Peter declared that "God, which knoweth the hearts, bare them witness, giving them the Holy Ghost, even as he did unto us; and put no difference between us and them, purifying their hearts by faith" (Acts 15:8-9). Peter's declaration settled the issue—on the basis of heart purity as a result of the baptism with the Holy Spirit. Thus, heart purity became the rallying point between Jewish Christians and Gentile Christians. Purity of heart was the ecumenical principle of unity first adopted by the Christian Church.

d. Freedom from fear of public censure. One of the notable results of the work of the Holy Spirit is freedom from fear of public censure. After Pentecost, the disciples exhibited a freedom from "fear of the people" which released their powers and vitalized their lives. When "others, mocking said, These men are full of new wine" (Acts 2:13), Peter stood up, and "lifted up his voice" to preach to the people. When Peter and John were advised by the rulers to stop preaching, their answer was simple and final: "Whether it be right in the sight of God to hearken unto you more than unto God, judge ye" (Acts 4:19*b*). Later on Peter answered bluntly: "We ought to obey God rather than men" (Acts 5:29*b*). When Paul was commis-

[26]Carter and Earle, *op. cit.*, pp. 41-42.
[27]*Holiness Triumphant*, p. 100.

sioned as an apostle, his commission included a "delivering . . . from the people" (Acts 26:17).

Any normal person, even when filled with the Holy Spirit, will retain a healthy regard for public opinion, and will find satisfaction in being socially acceptable. Nor does the presence of the Holy Spirit remove the nervousness of "stage fright" which some persons experience when performing in public. But the presence of the Holy Spirit should produce a kind of holy boldness that refuses to be intimidated by social pressure, and which openly affirms its convictions even when it may be personally beneficial to remain silent. The charismatic movement of the second half of the twentieth century has shown that people do have a hunger to *feel* the divine presence, and that the presence of the Holy Spirit results in a type of response in which one is truly "delivered from the people." To a church overconscious of public opinion the presence of the Holy Spirit comes as a refreshing power and a dynamic presence.

e. Complete dedication to God's kingdom. Bonhoeffer has called "cheap grace the deadly enemy of our Church."[28] When he was hanged by Hitler's agents in 1945, he showed that the twentieth century can produce martyrs equal in courage to those in the first-century Church. When Dr. Paul Carlson died in the Congo with a bullet in the back in 1965, he revealed again that the Spirit of God brings about a complete dedication to God's kingdom. In a day marked by the drive to acquire and to possess material things, the Spirit-filled disciples of the Early Church, with their willingness to sell their possessions to promote the gospel, stand as a challenge to the contemporary Church. In a day characterized by a desire for security, the abandonment of the Early Church to God's will looms as a reminder that Christ is "Lord of all, or not Lord at all." In a day featured by a theology of relevance and a practice of conformity, the open and incisive distinction between the world and the Apostolic Church reminds modern disciples that the baptism of the Holy Spirit brings a complete dedication to God's kingdom.

f. Success in soul winning. After Pentecost, the Church seemed to be like a flood which carried all before it. Both public preaching and private testimony brought a ceaseless flow of converts into the newly born Church.

[28]Dietrich Bonhoeffer, *The Cost of Discipleship* (2nd ed.; New York: The Macmillan Co., 1959), p. 35.

III. The Holy Spirit in Christian Growth

The Holy Spirit is the inner Source of spiritual growth and development. There are many aspects of the Spirit-directed life which result in spiritual growth. Among the more important aspects of the Spirit-directed life are: (1) the witness of the Spirit, (2) the leadership of the Spirit, (3) the discipline of the Spirit, (4) prayer in the Spirit, (5) service in the Spirit, (6) worship in the Spirit.

A. The Witness of the Holy Spirit

The idea of inner assurance has always been prominent in holiness circles. This inner witness has been called the doctrine of assurance. For Wesley, the matter of assurance was basic, because what the Spirit accomplished, the Spirit would confirm. Wesley felt that this doctrine of the witness of the Spirit was part of Methodism's great contribution to the world, for he wrote: "It more nearly concerns the Methodists . . . clearly to understand, explain, and defend this doctrine; because it is one grand part of the testimony which God has given them to bear to all mankind."[29] The witness of the Spirit is both direct and indirect.

1. *Direct Witness*

Wesley describes the direct witness of the Spirit as follows: "By the testimony of the Spirit I mean an inward impression on the soul whereby the Spirit of God immediately and directly witnesses to my spirit, that I am a child of God."[30] Wesley's idea was based on Scripture, as found in Rom. 8:16: "The Spirit itself beareth witness with our spirit, that we are the children of God." Wesley would add other scriptural support, as did Daniel Steele, who stated the direct witness of the Spirit "does not rest upon one, two, or three cardinal proof texts, but upon a wide variety of scriptural proofs, such as the communion of the Holy Spirit, the revelation of Christ within the soul, the knowledge of God . . . the clear, certain, thorough and perfect knowledge of Christ."[31] In this sense the witness of the Spirit to sanctification comes in the same way that the witness comes to justification and regeneration.

2. *Indirect Witness*

There is also the indirect witness of the Spirit to sanctification.

[29] *Works*, V, 124.
[30] *Ibid.*
[31] *The Gospel of the Comforter*, pp. 136-37.

The direct witness may not always be strong and vibrant, due to loss of physical vitality, sudden and shocking personal tragedy, and to spiritual pressures. So there is the indirect witness of the Spirit. The indirect witness, according to Wesley, "is the result of reason, or reflection on what we feel in our souls. . . . Strictly speaking, it is a conclusion drawn partly from the word of God, and partly from our own experience."[32] For the Word of God states that all who have the fruit of the Spirit and have no condemnation are the children of God. Thus, the Christian has a dual witness which enables him to live in a state of constant assurance of his relationship to God. However, the spiritual, personal, direct witness of the Spirit always has priority over the rational and indirect witness based on Christian works. Otherwise the Christian might be tempted to pride, which is the very opposite of the presence and the work of the Holy Spirit.[33] The benefits of the witness of the Holy Spirit are suggested by Daniel Steele as follows:

> The advantages of the direct witness are, salvation from doubts on fundamentals, certainty with respect to adoption and forgiveness, the joy of the Lord and the strength which always springs therefrom. . . . It gives positiveness and convincing cogency to testimony. Conscious salvation attested by the voice of the Spirit crying, "Abba, Father," is a great safeguard against apostasy—the greatest next to the Spirit's work in entire sanctification.[34]

B. Leadership of the Holy Spirit

The Holy Spirit is a constant Guide. "If we live in the Spirit, let us also walk in the Spirit" (Gal. 5:25). The Christian life is a life filled with purpose, meaning, and development. The Spirit-filled life means walking with God in full cooperation with the divine Spirit. In the Spirit-filled life the only question that really matters is knowing God's will. There is no struggle in the Spirit-

[32]*Works*, V, 124-25.

[33]Lindstrom, in his classic book, *Wesley and Sanctification*, p. 176, writes: "In the two sermons on The Witness of the Spirit (1746 and 1767) the order is (1) God's love to us; (2) The witness to it of God's Spirit, which precedes our love to God and is immediate and direct. Through this we know we have been forgiven and are God's children. From this witness, love, like all other fruits of the Spirit, has its origin. (3) Our love to God, which is the root of all holiness. (4) Holiness in heart and life. (5) The witness of our own spirit from the fruits the Spirit has worked."

[34]*The Gospel of the Comforter*, p. 143.

filled life about *doing* God's will. This problem is settled. The problem is *finding* God's will.

There are numerous incidents of the Spirit's leadership in the Bible. When Philip met the Ethiopian's chariot, he was directed by the Spirit to "go near, and join thyself to this chariot" (Acts 8:29). The author of the Book of Acts shows how Peter, the man of action, was confused by a vision which appeared to him. The record in Acts relates how this problem was solved: "While Peter thought on the vision, the Spirit said unto him, Behold, three men seek thee. Arise therefore, and get thee down, and go with them, doubting nothing: for I have sent them" (Acts 10:19-20). When Paul planned to take the gospel into the East, his plans were changed because "the Spirit suffered them not" (Acts 16:7). There is no doubt that the scriptural testimony points to a direct leadership of the Spirit.

However, it is not always possible to receive clear-cut directions from the Holy Spirit. Sometimes the direction of the Spirit is as clear as a rainbow in the sky. At other times the leadership of the Spirit is like a shadowy form on a misty morning. Are there, then, any tests, or norms, by which one may test the leadership of the Spirit?[35] Rene Pache suggests the following:

> Normally, the Spirit guides us by means of God's word. When Scripture fails to supply sufficiently clear guidance, the Spirit will lead us . . . by *circumstances*. The Spirit can also guide us in negative fashion, by closing a door before us. The Spirit can lead us, for our own good, along the path of temptation and suffering.[36]

Everett L. Cattell also suggests several ways to test the leadership of the Spirit.

> First, Is the impression Scriptural? . . .
>
> Second, Is it right? . . .
>
> Third, Is it providential? . . .
>
> Fourth, Is it corroborated by trusted and Spirit-led friends? . . .
>
> Fifth, and finally, Does the impression become an ever more weighty conviction?[37]

[35]In addition to the sources quoted above, two very helpful books are: Martin Wells Knapp, *Impressions* (Kansas City: Nazarene Publishing House, n.d.), pp. 7-81; and Thomas C. Upham, *Principles of the Interior or Hidden Life*, abridged by Olive M. Winchester (Kansas City: Beacon Hill Press, n.d.), pp. 63-85.

[36]*Op. cit.*, pp. 158-59.

[37]E. L. Cattell, *The Spirit of Holiness* (Grand Rapids, Mich.: Wm. B. Eerdmans Pub. Co., 1963), pp. 57-58.

C. The Discipline of the Holy Spirit

By the sustaining and indwelling presence of the Holy Spirit the entire nature of the Christian is brought under the control of God.

> *For what the law could not do, in that it was weak through the flesh, God sending his own Son in the likeness of sinful flesh, and for sin, condemned sin in the flesh: that the righteousness of the law might be fulfilled in us, who walk not after the flesh, but after the Spirit* (Rom. 8:3-4).

The discipline of the Spirit refers to the proper exercise and the valid expression of the natural appetites and tendencies of human nature. The cleansing presence of the Holy Spirit eliminates all the self-recognized carnal opposites to God's grace. But the sanctifying presence of the Holy Spirit does not subtract anything from essential human nature. As William Greathouse writes: "We believe . . . that the Scriptures teach both *eradication* and *self-discipline*—the radical cleansing from sin and the discipline of our legitimate selfhood. The two truths are not contradictory but complementary."[38]

Because man is a biological and social creature as well as a spiritual creation, there will always exist some tension between the biological, social tendencies and the spiritual impulses. It is at these points that the Holy Spirit enables one to exercise discipline. As a mature Christian, Paul wrote: "But I keep under my body, and bring it into subjection: lest that by any means, when I have preached to others, I myself should be a castaway" (I Cor. 9:27).

Perhaps the greatest area of need for the discipline of the Spirit in the sanctified life is in the nonphysical areas where attitudes, aspirations, and imagination are operative. Certainly attitudes of envy, malice, jealousy, and conceit are eliminated when the Holy Spirit takes up His full residence in the soul. But the attitudes of self-pity, self-depreciation, or self-exaltation; the tendency to sarcasm or to criticism; the proneness to spiritual pride, to harsh, legalistic judgment, are all attitudes which require the discipline of the Holy Spirit.

The Early Church was born in a time of moral relativism, when the consciousness of sin had almost disappeared. But the Christians *overcame* the world, not by tailoring their gospel or their lives

[38]*The Fullness of the Spirit* (Kansas City: Nazarene Publishing House, 1958), pp. 16-17.

to the world, but by contagious, joyful, and disciplined lives which won converts by the sheer force of moral and spiritual vitality. Undisciplined sin will yield to disciplined holiness. Undisciplined holiness will fall prey to worldliness.

D. Prayer in the Spirit

The prayers of the nominal Christian are apt to be dominated by two themes—thanksgiving for personal salvation and petition for personal needs. Thus these prayers tend to lead back to the person himself. Such prayers indicate a lack of insight into the deeper nature of salvation as well as a lack of depth in spiritual development. Moreover, the prayers of the average professed Christians are too often cold and formal, performed as a lip service and uttered as a duty. Finally, the prayer of the unsanctified is apt to be spasmodic and intermittent. He may pray when his emotions are stable or when the pattern of his life is satisfying and rewarding. But when such a person is at a low ebb emotionally or is faced with a confused or shattered pattern of existence, he may neglect his prayer life. Prayer in the Spirit-filled life should be different. For—

> *The Spirit also helpeth our infirmities: for we know not what we should pray for as we ought: but the Spirit itself maketh intercession for us with groanings which cannot be uttered. And he that searcheth the hearts knoweth what is in the mind of the Spirit, because he maketh intercession for the saints according to the will of God* (Rom. 8:26-27).

Paul also revealed the fervency of the prayers of the sanctified when he wrote: "I beseech you . . . for the love of the Spirit, that ye strive together with me in your prayers to God for me" (Rom. 15:30). The word *beseech* is a strong word suggesting begging, pleading, persuasion, while the word *strive* has great force, implying agonizing, wrestling to the point of death. Prayer of such fervor and desperation comes only when the love of the Spirit lifts a person beyond himself and his own needs to a level of spiritual concern for God's redeeming love in the life of man. Paul also points out that the presence of the Spirit builds a consistent pattern of prayer: "Praying always with all prayer and supplication in the Spirit, and watching thereunto with all perseverance and supplication for all saints" (Eph. 6:18).

The presence of the Holy Spirit is the secret of effective intercessory prayer, the pathway to positive and persistent patterns of prayer which develop holy character and produce a holy Christian community.

E. Service in the Spirit

The holy life is a life of service. The life of service requires the fullness of the Holy Spirit for several reasons. First, the presence of the Holy Spirit can strengthen the motivation for Christian service. Since the Christian community is, above all other groups, susceptible to manipulation and exploitation, the purifying presence of the Holy Spirit is needed to guarantee proper motivation. Spirit-inspired motivation is the spirit of selflessness that acts out of interest for the good of others, without undue concern for credit. Spirit-inspired motivation is the impulse to do good simply because it is the thing to do and because such service adds to God's glory and to His kingdom.

Service in the Spirit may involve anything from washing a window in the local church to building a church in some mission field. Service in the Spirit may include a Spirit-filled sermon or a Spirit-filled testimony. Seven times in the seven letters to the seven churches in the Revelation the Lord said, "I know thy works." The possibility of Spirit-motivated service was declared by Christ: "'He who believes in me, as the scripture has said, "Out of his heart shall flow rivers of living water."' Now this he said about the Spirit, which those who believed in him were to receive" (John 7:38-39, RSV).

F. Worship in the Spirit

Worship is usually associated with a group of believers meeting in special buildings, participating in some kind of ritual. But the scriptural approach is that worship is adoration and praise mingled with awe and reverence. Such worship is "in spirit and in truth." The person not filled with the Spirit cannot worship fully and freely because he is inhibited by self-centered desires and hindered by selfish aspirations. No one can worship God and himself at the same time. True worship must lift a person out of himself. In this sense true worship is possible only when man follows the biblical injunction: "Worship the Lord in the beauty of holiness" (Ps. 29:2).

IV. THE FRUIT OF THE SPIRIT

The fulness of the Spirit produces the fruit of the Spirit. Jesus used two figures of speech that point directly to the relationship of the fullness of the Spirit and the practical results of the fruit of the Spirit. The first figure was that of the vine and gardener, found in John 15:1-2: "I am the true vine, and my Father is the husbandman. Every branch in me that beareth not fruit he taketh away: and every branch that beareth fruit, he purgeth it, that it may bring forth more fruit." The second illustration is taken from a scene at the Temple, early in the ministry of Jesus. At a dramatic moment of a festive occasion Jesus stepped out and with a loud voice cried to the multitude: "If any man thirst, let him come unto me, and drink. He that believeth on me, as the scripture hath said, out of his belly shall flow rivers of living water" (John 7:37-38). Commenting on this statement John wrote: "But this spake he of the Spirit, which they that believe in him should receive: for the Holy Ghost was not yet given; because that Jesus was not yet glorified" (John 7:39).

The Spirit-filled life may thus be like an orchard which is well-pruned, well-watered, and well-cultivated. And the orchard is to produce a variety of fruit. The life of holiness is not a life of sameness, tameness, and lameness. The life of holiness is a dynamic, growing, expanding life of exciting living. The fruit of the Spirit produces contagious Christian character. It is significant to note Paul's choice of the term *fruit,* as contrasted to works. "A fruit is something which is produced by a power which he does not possess. Man cannot *make a fruit.*"[39] Paul leaves no doubt as to the practical results of the presence of the Holy Spirit, for in his Galatian letter he writes: "But the fruit of the Spirit is love, joy, peace, longsuffering, gentleness, goodness, faith, meekness, temperance" (5:22-23).

A. Love, Joy, Peace

The first cluster of spiritual graces refers to the Christian's relationship to God. The doctrine of holiness exalts the holiness of a sovereign God who in love and mercy imparts His own nature to man. Thus the essence of holiness is the enjoyment of God.

1. *Love*

The life of holiness, the Spirit-filled life, is the life of love.

[39]William Barclay, *Flesh and Spirit* (Nashville: Abingdon Press, 1962), p. 21.

Since Paul made love the greatest quality, or aspect, of the Christian life, he naturally would present love as the choice product of Spirit-filled living. "Indeed, there is a sense in which Christian love is an all-inclusive category and uniquely the source of other fruit, even as a tree trunk bearing branches, or a prism as it reflects the various colors of light."[40] This love *(agape)* is an added dimension to life that is the result of God's redeeming activity. Love defines life in the Spirit. Love describes Christian motivation and prescribes Christian activities. This love is God's love, which was revealed in Christ and in which the Christian participates. "It may be God's love, love to fellow men, or love to God, but it is all of the same nature as God's love in Christ."[41]

Love as a fruit of the Spirit differs from other kinds, or types, of love. "It is not, like *philia,* attachment to a person independently of his quality and created by close intercourse. It is less *sentiment* than consideration. While *philia* contemplates the person, *agape* contemplates the *attributes* and *character* and gives an account of its inclinations."[42] This Spirit-produced love *(agape)* is also different from erotic love, *(eros)* which is primarily self-centered and sensual. Love is thus a concern, a consideration, a total response to God or man which seeks only the highest services or the highest good. Love is the *summum bonum,* the fulfillment of the law, the expression of the Christlike spirit. It is "the cord that unites the body of Christ."

2. *Joy*

It is noteworthy that the Roman Catholics consider joy an essential quality of sainthood. No one is elevated to the status of sainthood who has not lived a life of *joyous* service and piety. Thus the Roman Catholics have no gloomy saints! The Protestant church, and specially those believing in holiness, could benefit by the Roman conception of sainthood. Joy *(chara)* "means that spiritual gladness which acceptance with God and change of heart produces."[43] Another writer defines joy as "delight in God because of the salva-

[40]*Beacon Bible Commentary,* IX, 104.

[41]Ragnar Bring, *Commentary on Galatians* (Philadelphia: Muhlenberg Press, 1961), p. 262.

[42]Vincent, *op. cit.,* IV, 167.

[43]John Eadie, *Commentary on the Epistle of Paul to the Galatians* (rev. ed.; Grand Rapids, Mich.: Zondervan Publishing House, n.d.), p. 442.

tion in Christ, the reconciliation, and being received as children."[44]

The greatest joy in the Christian life comes to those who are sanctified wholly (John 17:13). Joy is constant in the sanctified life because guilt and condemnation are absent. Joy is a trademark of the life of holiness because the power of sin is broken and removed from the sphere of conscious activity and attitude. Jesus was so named because He would save the people "from their sins." The fullness of joy in Christ is the result of Spirit-filled living. It is also significant that even in the Old Testament the prophet related joy to strength: "for the joy of the Lord is your strength" (Neh. 8:10).

3. *Peace*

The life of holiness is the life of peace. The experience of holiness removes the three great areas of turmoil and strife—enmity against God, guilt within, and friction without. In the crisis of entire sanctification the believer makes a full consecration to God. This consecration, accepted and sustained by the Holy Spirit, results in peace with God. For God's will is paramount in the life of the sanctified. Peace comes when inner guilt and frustration over the power of sin are eliminated. Holiness brings peace because the tensions with others due to envy, malice, jealousy, etc., are gone. The peace of the Spirit-filled then is "peace with God primarily, and peace within them; and not simply so, but concord—peace with those around them."[45] Peace is not freedom from hardship and suffering, nor is it the automatic goodwill of man. Peace is the inner tranquility which comes from proper relationships and pure motives.

B. Long-suffering, Gentleness, Goodness

A second cluster of virtues is related to other people. "Peace can form the transition from *joy* to *long-suffering.*"[46]

1. *Long-suffering*

The need to be long-suffering suggests attack, provocation, and incentive to anger. "And the fruit of the Spirit makes for the preservation of love and peace despite these all."[47] Long-suffering may be patient endurance of uncalled for injuries inflicted by others or

[44]Herman N. Ridderbos, *The Epistle of Paul to the Churches of Galatia* (Grand Rapids, Mich.: Wm. B. Eerdmans Pub. Co., 1953), p. 207.

[45]Eadie, *op. cit.*, p. 423.

[46]Ridderbos, *op. cit.*, p. 207.

[47]*Ibid.*

the calm acceptance of the unexpected blows of man or nature. It is in the area of *long-suffering*, or *patience*, that the state of holiness should make a noteworthy difference in Christian living. For holiness should produce a kind of self-restraint which is possible only with the help of the Holy Spirit.

2. *Gentleness*

In regard to the exercise of gentleness, Wesley states it should be practiced "toward all men; ignorant and wicked men in particular."[48] Clarke suggests that gentleness is "a very rare grace, often wanting in many who have a considerable share of Christian excellence."[49] Gentleness may be associated with courtesy. And, as Harry E. Jessop writes. "While this experience will not impart a knowledge of the rules of etiquette, it will at least manifest the indwelling of Him who is the most gentle Person in God's great universe, the Holy Spirit himself."[50] A sanctified person is naturally gentle and courteous. Crude, ill-mannered, boorish conduct is incompatible with holiness. "A sanctified man, whatever his restrictions, is never a boor. There is no refining influence like the indwelling of the Holy Spirit."[51] Gentleness is a fruit of the Spirit. It springs from an inner power and a respect and concern for man. "Gentleness is thoughtful consideration, courteous and kindly action, the delicate ministering of love."[52] Holiness produces rugged character, but this strength of character is clothed with gentleness.

3. *Goodness*

Goodness is the practical expression of all Christian virtue. Holiness is thus to be expressed in practical deeds as the occasion is afforded. Goodness is love in action. Goodness is love applied to the normal affairs of life. Goodness is love rising to meet difficulties and emergencies. Goodness is the outreach of the soul to man and God.

C. Faith, Meekness, Temperance

The last cluster of fruit again turns to personal ethical qualities.

[48]Wesley, *Notes*, p. 697.
[49]Clarke, *op. cit.*, VI, 413.
[50]*Foundations of Doctrine* (Kansas City: Nazarene Publishing House, 1940), p. 65.
[51]*Ibid.*
[52]Strauss, *op. cit.*, p. 90.

1. *Faith*

One of the results of the coming of the Holy Spirit is stability and loyalty. The "old-timers" of the holiness movement loved to preach on sanctification as the *stabilizing* experience. The life of holiness should be indicated by loyalty, dependability, integrity, and trustworthiness. Christians are to be faithful to God (cf. I Cor. 4:2). But "faithfulness is not only to be found in holding true to God under test and duress, but also in being loyal to one's fellowmen."[53] Holiness comes from faith in God and results in faith in man.

2. *Meekness*

Meekness is difficult to define. Negatively, it is the reverse of arrogance, pride, egotism, and self-exaltation. But it does not mean an apologetic demeanor nor a crippling timidity. It does not involve a Saul-like shrinking from responsibility nor does it include a banal self-depreciation. It is "gentle, unassuming firmness."[54] Meekness is possible only where there is strength. True meekness is possible only where there is divine strength. Jesus was meek and lowly in heart (Matt. 11:29), but He never evaded issues nor did He shrink from a proper evaluation of His person and His work.

3. *Temperance*

Temperance suggests the idea of self-control. "Self-control is the fruit of the Spirit. *He* takes over and controls from within."[55] One writer interprets temperance as *chastity*. "Chastity is a better word than self-control or temperance because it includes more of the attitude rather than legalistic performance."[56]

The fruit of the Spirit represents the ethical and moral product of the presence of the Holy Spirit. Some of these virtues had been mentioned previously by pagan moralists. But the Pauline combination, totally omitting selfish or self-assertive qualities, "result in setting forth an ethical idea of a quite distinctive and peculiar type, which has ever since been the characteristic idea of Christian morals."[57] The doctrine of holiness avoids the pitfalls of legalism

[53]*Beacon Bible Commentary*, IX, 108.

[54]D. D. Whedon, *Commentary on the New Testament, I Corinthians—II Timothy* (New York: Eaton and Mains, 1875), p. 245.

[55]Strauss, *op. cit.*, p. 92.

[56]Joh. Ph. Koehler, *The Epistle of Paul to the Galatians*, trans. E. E. Sauer (Milwaukee, Wis.: Northwestern Pub. Co., 1957), p. 152.

[57]A. W. F. Blunt, *The Epistle of Paul to the Galatians* (Oxford: The Clarendon Press, 1960), p. 127.

by stressing the subjective, ethical aspect of religious experience. Love, as Wesley consistently pointed out, is essence of the state of holiness. The fruit of the Spirit as a variety of expressions related to love is aptly summarized in the following statement:

> Joy is love exulting; peace is love in repose; long-suffering is love on trial; gentleness is love in society; goodness is love in action; faith is love in endurance; meekness is love at school; and temperance is love in discipline and training—so then it is love in all the cluster and the circle of the Christian graces.[58]

The fruit of the Spirit is normal and natural in the life of holiness. Holiness is a gift of God to man. Any development of spiritual grace and power in human personality is the result of the work of the Holy Spirit.

SUMMARY

The spiritual dynamic in the Christian and in the Church comes from the dynamic presence of the Holy Spirit. The work of the Holy Spirit is indispensable to vital Christian living. The concept of inner holiness is completely dependent upon the work of the Holy Spirit. For the Holy Spirit is present and operative in both regeneration and entire sanctification. The Christian's growth in holiness depends upon the continuing presence of the Holy Spirit. The development of spiritual graces and the exercise of spiritual gifts rest squarely on the subjective work of the Holy Spirit.

[58] Bishop, *op. cit.*, p. 12.

CHAPTER XI /

Holiness as Spiritual Dynamic

Christianity was cradled in a Jewish heritage, and was born into a Roman society which had been drastically modified by Greek culture. Beginning with a few unknown men of common station, Christianity expanded so rapidly and with such explosive force that it had become the official religion of the Roman Empire by A.D. 325. The dynamic of spiritual conquest which enabled the Church to achieve such a dramatic victory over paganism was the life of holiness, which was the result of the baptism with the Holy Spirit.

I. The Pentecostal Outpouring

In this chapter, first the attempt is made to show that interpreters of church history as well as the author of the Acts of the Apostles have identified the baptism with the Holy Spirit, and its accompanying spiritual dynamic, as the outstanding characteristic of the Primitive Church. Drawing upon the description of the birth and the expansion of the Church in extra-biblical and in biblical sources, the discussion proceeds to show that through the Holy Spirit the Early Church was a victorious Church.

The Pentecostal outpouring resulted in a state of dynamic spiritual life which was characterized by spiritual purity, spiritual power, spiritual fellowship, and spiritual vision. Spiritual conquest depends upon spiritual dynamic. Spiritual dynamic depends upon spiritual purity, spiritual power, spiritual fellowship, and spiritual vision. From the divine point of view these four elements of spiritual dynamic are imparted by the Holy Spirit.

From the human point of view these four qualities—purity, power, fellowship, and vision—are the irreducible aspects of the experience of holiness. The experience of holiness is the direct result of the baptism with the Holy Spirit. The occasion for the initial outpouring of the Holy Spirit was the Day of Pentecost. Pentecost was, therefore, a day of prime significance both in the Old Testament and in the New.

A. The Old Testament Pentecost

Pentecost is directly related to one of the great Old Testament festivals, the Passover. Josephus describes the Passover in these words:

> In the month of Xanthicus, which is by us called Nisan, and in the beginning of our year, on the 14th day of the lunar month, when the sun is in Aries, (for in this month it was that we were delivered from bondage under the Egyptians,) the law ordained that we should every year slay that sacrifice which I before told you we slew when we came out of Egypt, and which was called the "Passover," and so we do celebrate this passover in companies, leaving nothing of what we sacrifice till the day following.[1]

On the fiftieth day after the Passover, another festival was celebrated which was the culmination of the "feast of weeks" (Exod. 34:22; Deut. 16:10). This festival was called "Asartha" by the Hebrews,[2] but "Pentecost" *(Pentekostos)* in the Greek, referring to the fiftieth day after the Passover. "It was the second of the three great yearly festivals, in which all the males were required to appear before God at the place of his sanctuary."[3] After the Exile the Day

[1]Flavius Josephus, *The Works of Josephus: Comprising the Antiquities of the Jews*, trans. William Whiston (Hartford, Conn.: The S. S. Scranton Co., 1905 [reprint]), p. 113.

[2]*Ibid.*, p. 114.

[3]John Kitto, ed. *The Cyclopedia of Biblical Literature* (New York: Hurst and Company, n.d.), II, 493.

of Pentecost became one of the great nationalistic as well as one of the great religious festivals in Judaism, "at which many of those who lived in remote sections of the Roman world returned to Jerusalem for worship (Acts 20:16)."[4]

B. Pentecost in the New Testament

In the historical life of the Church, Pentecost is the anniversary of the coming of the Holy Spirit in His fullness and power upon the followers of Christ. Before Jesus ascended He had commanded His disciples to remain in Jerusalem until they received the long awaited baptism with the Holy Spirit (Acts 1:4-5). The disciples obeyed the command of Jesus, spending the better part of 10 days praying in the Upper Room in Jerusalem. On the fiftieth day after the Crucifixion, the Holy Spirit baptized the waiting community of believers. Unusual phenomena accompanied the coming of the Spirit—the sound as of a hurtling gale of wind, the appearance of tongues similar to fire, and the speaking in other languages. "This tremendous manifestation of divine power marked the beginning of the church which has ever since regarded Pentecost as its birthday."[5]

The coming of the Holy Spirit at Pentecost "strikes the chief theological keynote of Acts."[6] However, the Holy Spirit is a vital personal presence, not a doctrine. As F. F. Bruce points out, "The doctrine of the Spirit is not presented simply for apologetic reasons in Acts; it is emphasized throughout the book for its own sake. The Christian community is Spirit-filled and Spirit-led . . . and the whole evangelistic enterprise, from Jerusalem to Rome, is directed by the Spirit."[7] Many scholars agree that the Day of Pentecost "is the beginning of the new spiritual life of the church."[8] All that Christ had done in the years of training and instructing the disciples "only laid the foundation, upon which the Spirit was to build."[9] All that the disciples and the Church were to accomplish in the future would

[4]Everett F. Harrison, Geoffrey Bromily, and Carl F. H. Henry, *Baker's Dictionary of Theology* (Grand Rapids, Mich.: Baker Book House, 1960), p. 401.

[5]*Ibid.*

[6]F. F. Bruce, *Commentary on the Book of the Acts* (Grand Rapids, Mich.: Wm. B. Eerdmans Pub. Co., 1955), p. 33.

[7]*Ibid.*, p. 24.

[8]Rackham, *op. cit.*, p. 15.

[9]D. Grant Christman, *Evangelistic Comments on the Acts of the Apostles* (Endicott, N.Y.: Eastern Bible Institute, 1923), pp. 19-20.

be the result of the coming of the Holy Spirit at Pentecost. The permanent heritage left to the Church by the baptism with the Holy Spirit was a spiritual dynamic that made the Church a conquering force. Included in this spiritual dynamic were spiritual purity, spiritual power, spiritual fellowship, and spiritual vision.

II. Holiness: The Dynamic of Spiritual Purity

Holiness appears to have been the outstanding quality of the Primitive Church, the cohesive force which held the rather small group together. The earliest Christians were well aware that the first business of life was to do the will of God and to present themselves as a holy community (Acts 2:38-39; 15:9). Both church historians and biblical scholars regard spiritual purity as one of the prominent features of the Early Church.

A. Life of Purity in Early Church

The earliest Christians were overwhelmed by their experience of the direct infilling and baptizing with the Holy Spirit. They became convinced that the first business of life was to do the will of God and to present themselves as a holy community. Thus Adolph Harnack noted: "Upon this their whole existence and their mission in the world were based."[10] Commenting further on the place of spiritual purity in the thought and lives of the early Christians, Harnack wrote:

> They took purity in the deepest and most comprehensive sense of the word, as the horror of everything that is unholy, and as the inner pleasure in everything that is upright and true, lovely and of good report. They also meant purity in regard to the body, for did not the Scriptures say, "your body is the temple of the Holy Spirit" (I Cor. 6:19)?[11]

In discussing the reasons for the amazing growth of the Primitive Church, John L. Mosheim lists the quality of "lives free from stain, and adorned with the constant practice of sublime virtue."[12] Referring to the antagonism of the Jews to Christianity, Mosheim again remarks about their spiritual purity: "The innocence

[10]*What Is Christianity?* trans. Thomas B. Saunders (New York: G. P. Putnam's Sons, 1903), p. 180.

[11]*Ibid.*, p. 181.

[12]*An Ecclesiastical History, Ancient and Modern,* trans. Archibald Maclaine (Cincinnati: Applegate and Co., 1858), I, Part I, 13.

and virtue that distinguished so eminently the lives of Christ's servants, and the spotless purity of the doctrine they taught, were not sufficient to defend them against the virulence and malignity of the Jews."[13]

Membership in the Early Church was granted to those who gave evidence of spiritual purity. Before one was permitted full membership, he was admitted as a catechumen. Catechumens were taught such doctrines as would "assist them in arriving at Christian perfection."[14] Such catechumens could not enjoy the privileges of the faithful until they had proved themselves, which was when, "through a considerable time of trial, they had evidenced the sincerity of their hearts by the sanctity and purity of their lives."[15] One historian quotes Origen on the matter of church membership as follows: "We initiate them into our mysteries when they have made a proficiency in holiness, and according to the utmost of their power have reformed their conversations."[16] The same author quotes Tertullian in regard to those who were baptized as part of their reception into the church: "We are not baptized that we may cease to sin, but because we have already ceased."[17] Personal holiness was the trademark of the early Christians, according to historians.

However, it is not from later historians that one is able to derive the best description of the life of the Early Church, but from New Testament writings. For, as Ernst Renan says, "the origin of every religion is known only by the narrative of the faithful."[18] From this point of view the "Acts of the Apostles appears as the chief source of information of the Apostolic age."[19] Thus the discussion turns to the biblical sources.

B. Spiritual Purity and the Baptism with the Holy Spirit

The Bible teaches that the outpouring of the Holy Spirit is

[13] *Ibid.*

[14] *Ibid.*, p. 25.

[15] Peter King, *An Inquiry into the Constitution, Discipline, Unity and Worship of the Primitive Church* (New York: G. Lane and P. P. Sanford, 1841), p. 101.

[16] *Ibid.*

[17] *Ibid.*

[18] Ernst Renan, *The History of the Origins of Christianity* (London: Mathieson and Co., 1890), II, xv.

[19] Ernst von Dobschütz, *Christian Life in the Primitive Church*, trans. George Bremmer (New York: G. P. Putnam and Sons, 1904), p. xxix.

directly related to heart cleansing, or purity. Among the impressive array of witnesses to the cleansing work of the Holy Spirit are David, Isaiah, Ezekiel, John the Baptist, Christ, Peter, and Paul.

1. *Purity and the Holy Spirit in the Old Testament*

In Psalms 51 the Holy Spirit is viewed as the agency of spiritual cleansing for the first time. Psalms 18 and Psalms 119 also refer to the creative, purifying work of the Holy Spirit. The prophets also emphasized the work of the Holy Spirit.

Isaiah's experience of sanctification came in the Temple (Isaiah 6). Later he witnessed to his experience in these words: "The Spirit of the Lord is upon me, because the Lord hath anointed me to preach good tidings unto the meek; he hath sent me to bind up the brokenhearted, to proclaim liberty to the captives, and the opening of the prison to them that are bound" (61:1). Hosea fully realized the prophetic concern for holiness. He was also called the prophet, "the man of the Spirit" (Hos. 9:7). Ezekiel made frequent references to the activities of the Spirit. The Spirit entered into him and lifted him up, taking him here and there for special work (Ezek. 2:2; 3:12; 8:3; 11:1). One of the sublime passages of the work of God in purifying His people comes from Ezekiel:

> *Then will I sprinkle clean water upon you, and ye shall be clean: from all your filthiness, and from all your idols, will I cleanse you.*
>
> *A new heart also will I give you, and a new spirit will I put within you: and I will take away the stony heart out of your flesh, and I will give you an heart of flesh.*
>
> *And I will put my spirit within you, and cause you to walk in my statutes, and ye shall keep my judgments, and do them* (Ezek. 36:25-27).

2. *The Holy Spirit and Purity in the New Testament*

In the New Testament baptism with the Holy Spirit is frequently associated with purity, or cleansing. One of the outstanding references on this is found in the words of John the Baptist, the forerunner of Christ. Anticipating the coming of the Holy Spirit, he said:

> *I indeed baptize you with water unto repentance: but he that cometh after me is mightier than I, whose shoes I am not worthy to bear: he shall baptize you with the Holy Ghost, and with fire: whose fan is in his hand, and he will throughly purge his floor, and gather his wheat into the garner; but he will burn up the chaff with unquenchable fire* (Matt. 3:11-12).

The important truth in these words of John the Baptist is that the main objective of the baptism with the Holy Spirit is the purging, the winnowing of the followers of Christ. "Christ's religion was to be a spiritual religion, and was to have its seat in the heart."[20] Thus the Holy Spirit, represented as a refining fire, was to produce the inward purity both possible and necessary in the followers of Christ.

That the primary result of the baptism with the Holy Spirit is a spiritual state of purity is also affirmed by Peter in Acts 15. In the middle of a crucial debate in the early Christian Church regarding the problem of Jewish ceremony in relation to Gentile Christians, Peter settled the question and silenced all opposition to the full acceptance of the Gentiles with these words: "And God, which knoweth the hearts, bare them witness, giving them the Holy Ghost, even as he did unto us; and put no difference between us and them, purifying their hearts by faith" (Acts 15:8-9).

C. Purity, the Irreducible Residue

Heart purity is the irreducible residue of the baptism with the Holy Spirit. Other things may or may not accompany the Pentecostal outpouring, but purity of heart is the one common denominator of all Pentecostal experience. For purity fulfills all the law and the gospel and is received by faith. Thus it is available to all.

1. *Purity—Pentecostal Common Denominator*

Heart purity is the common denominator of the Pentecostal outpouring. One writer states that Peter's phrase "purifying their hearts by faith" is one "of the most important statements in the New Testament. . . . The great lesson it teaches is that the blessing which the disciples obtained at Pentecost was purity of heart."[21] John the Baptist had promised the divine, purifying presence of the Holy Spirit (Matt. 3:11). The one feature of Pentecost which lingered in the mind of Peter was that Pentecost had produced purity. Commenting on Peter's speech before the Council at Jerusalem, Ralph Earle writes:

> It is sometimes said that while Acts has much to say about being filled with the Holy Spirit, it makes no mention of sanctification. But here Peter declares that when the hearers in Cornelius'

[20]Clarke, *op. cit.*, V, 53.

[21]G. A. McLaughlin, *Commentary on the Acts of the Apostles* (Chicago: The Christian Witness Co., 1915), p. 170.

> house received the Holy Spirit, they also experienced the cleansing [of] their hearts. These are two aspects of one and the same Christian experience.[22]

Since the first Jerusalem Council occurred at least 10 years after Pentecost, and since Peter equates the coming of the Holy Spirit at Pentecost with purity, it is sound to regard purity as the irreducible residue of Pentecost.

2. *Purity—Basis of Ecumenical Agreement*

The first ecumenical council of the Christian Church was held at Jerusalem (Acts 15:4). It was a tense situation, for there was "much disputing" (Acts 15:7). The fate of Christianity was at stake. The question was simple, yet far-reaching: Would the Church be a universal fellowship of Spirit-filled believers? The question arose because of the success of Paul and Barnabas in winning Gentiles to Christ. The source of the question was the Christian Pharisees. "These Christian Pharisees . . . were the leaders in insisting that Gentile converts should be instructed to submit to circumcision and the general obligation to keep the Mosaic law which that rite carried with it."[23]

Peter was the main speaker to address the first ecumenical council. His speech was as clear and concise as the question facing the council. He said that the Gentiles had received the word and God had received them. "By so doing God had declared that *the distinction* between . . . men did not depend upon external differences of birth and race, or upon accidental cleanness or uncleanness, but on purity of the heart."[24] In other words, Peter said that "the gospel, when believed, produced the same effect upon the Gentile as the Jew, and that effect was the *purifying* of the heart."[25] After Peter's speech, the assembly quieted down. "Peter, the head of the Twelve, having spoken, any argument to the contrary was out of the question."[26]

In addition to Peter, Paul and Barnabas addressed the ecumenical council, narrating the progress of the gospel among the Gentiles (Acts 15:12). James, apparently the chairman of the assembly,

[22]Carter and Earle, *op. cit.*, p. 211.

[23]F. F. Bruce, *The Acts of the Apostles* (Chicago: Inter-Varsity Christian Fellowship, 1952), p. 305.

[24]Rackham, *op. cit.*, p. 252.

[25]Thomas, *op. cit.*, pp. 232-33.

[26]Giuseppe Ricciotti, *The Acts of the Apostles* (Milwaukee: The Bruce Publishing Co., 1958), p. 235.

summed up the situation and presented an opinion that apparently settled the problem (Acts 15:13-29). James's final conclusion contains three points: "Liberty, for grace delivers the believer from legal Jewish bondage; Purity (verse 20), for they were to keep from pollution, fornication, etc.; Charity, for there was to be liberty of conscience."[27] Thus, purity of heart became the focal point of Christian unity in the first official meeting of Jewish and Gentile Christians. To those who still clung to the law as a means of purity, Peter stated that "God had done a far greater thing—by His Spirit He had cleansed their hearts."[28] After this meeting the issue was settled. "This chapter [Acts 15] is the Christian's emancipation proclamation."[29] God's power and God's presence were available to every man through faith. To the Early Church, inner purity rather than external evidence was the irreducible evidence of the baptism with the Holy Spirit. In practical experience this inner purity resulting from the baptism with the Holy Spirit is called the experience or state of holiness.

Holiness is the dynamic of spiritual power as well as the basis of spiritual purity.

III. Holiness: The Dynamic of Spiritual Power

The Acts of the Apostles are really the acts of the Holy Spirit. For it was only after the Holy Spirit had submerged the expectant disciples in the experience of Pentecost that the Church emerged as a vital force. In connection with the event called Pentecost it is essential to state three things: the preparation for the Holy Spirit; the presence of the Holy Spirit; the results of the baptism with the Holy Spirit.

A. The Preparation for the Holy Spirit

God can come only to a prepared personality. God can give himself to man only when man gives himself to God. The followers of Christ prepared themselves for the event that would soon revolutionize their lives by acting on a direct promise, by constant prayer, and by unity of purpose.

[27] August Van Ryn, *Acts of the Apostles* (New York: Loizeaux Brothers, 1961), p. 122.

[28] Barclay, *The Acts of the Apostles*, p. 123.

[29] Charles J. Woodbridge, *Standing on the Promises* (Chicago: Moody Press, 1947), p. 93.

1. *Proceeding on a Promise*

The wonder of the resurrection of Christ had transformed the disciples of Christ. For 40 days they reveled in the astounding fact of His victory over death. But now a stark fact confronted the followers of Jesus. Their Redeemer, Counselor, Friend, and Leader was about to leave them to return to His Father. The approaching separation cast a cloud of gloom over them. How could they face the world without Christ? They needed some guarantee, some promise, some life, to sustain them. As one writer has so aptly written, "These promises were not lacking. They winged their way into the consciousness of the disciples with telling force. They spoke peace to their hearts, dispelled their gloom and undergirded them for the struggle ahead."[30] The promises were two in number. The first was a promise of immediate power. The second was a promise of ultimate hope.

a. Promise of power. Jesus had frequently told His disciples that He would leave them, but that He would send the Comforter to them (John 14:26; 15:26; 16:7). As William Barclay points out, the word *Comforter* "comes from the Latin *fortis,* which means *brave;* and the Comforter is the one who fills men with courage and with strength."[31] Jesus again promised that the Holy Spirit would come upon them (Acts 1:8). He also erased forever from their minds any flickering hope of political restoration (Acts 1:6-7). But he promised them a greater, more noble power. As F. F. Bruce writes: "When the Holy Spirit came upon them, Jesus assured them, they would be clothed with heavenly power—that power by which . . . their mighty works were accomplished and their preaching made effective."[32] The disciples now realized that their period of training was over. They were about to enter the arena of spiritual warfare. But first they would be equipped with adequate power, the power of the baptism with the Holy Spirit.

b. Promise of a future return. Jesus had left them. Before the disciples had time to puzzle over their situation, two heavenly messengers appeared, to remind them of their mission. The disciples then hastened the short distance from Olivet to Jerusalem. Jerusa-

[30] *Ibid.,* p. 12.

[31] *The Acts of the Apostles,* p. 2.

[32] *Commentary on the Book of the Acts* (Grand Rapids, Mich.: Wm B. Eerdmans Pub. Co., 1954), p. 38.

lem was preparing for the harvest festival, 50 days after the presentation of the wave-sheaf in the Passover week, described in Lev. 23:15-21. The promise given here was that Christ would return (Acts 1:11). Anxious to carry out the commands of Christ, the disciples "returned to Jerusalem with great joy" (Luke 24:52). The spiritual preparation for the coming of the Holy Spirit had begun. But additional preparation was necessary before the Holy Spirit came to empower the Christians.

2. *Steadfastness in Supplication*

"These all continued with one accord in prayer and supplication" (Acts 1:14). There is no royal road to holiness, for the way is the way of self-emptying and of reverent submission. Christ had taught them the art of prayer (Luke 11:1-13), so the disciples put into practice what they had learned. Remembering that Christ had always prayed as He faced apparently unknown or seemingly difficult situations, the group gave itself to prayer. Prayer was a much more adequate method of preparation than sorrowful reminiscing or hopeful conjecture. Regarding the prolonged period of prayer A. T. Robertson comments: "They 'stuck to' the praying . . . for the promise of the Father till the answer came."[33]

Since the ascension of Christ occurred 40 days after the Resurrection (Acts 1:3), and Pentecost occurred 50 days after the Passover, the time spent in prayer would be between a week and 10 days. The followers of Christ prayed with persistent effort, with unfaltering faith in God's promise and in the specific command of Jesus. They prayed that power should fall upon them with most manifest fullness and unmistakable certainty. Hunger for spiritual power was the main business of that long, protracted prayer meeting, a model prayer meeting for all the future ages of time.

3. *Spiritual Unity*

"And when the day of Pentecost was fully come, they were all with one accord in one place" (Acts 2:1). The followers of Christ met together because they had a common objective. Their physical unity of being in one place pointed to a deeper spiritual unity, which implied "that form of oneness of thought, feeling, and sentiment, on moral and spiritual subjects, a oneness which induces the highest possible forms of moral and spiritual excellence in the individual

[33]*Op. cit.*, III, 14.

and in the social relations of existence. The source of the unity of the one hundred and twenty in the upper room was simple."[34]

They all had faith in the fulfillment of the promise of Christ that the Holy Spirit would come—that something dramatic and supernatural was about to occur. They all felt the need for the coming of the Holy Spirit, for they *had* to have *someone* to fill the void left by the ascension of Christ. They all longed for the coming of the Holy Spirit. The words, the looks, the actions of Christ still haunted them. With the direct support of Christ absent, the followers hungered for a renewing of this vital relationship to the living God. The unity of the disciples "was a united zeal in seeking the blessing."[35] From their common sense of longing and from their united waiting came their unity. Their preparation was complete. God was not long in answering, for God imparts His own nature, His holiness, to those who prepare to receive it.

B. The Presence of the Holy Spirit

"And they were all filled with the Holy Ghost" (Acts 2:4*a*). It was fitting that the new dispensation, realized in the birth of the Church, should begin at Pentecost. Pentecost was a Jewish feast. The name "Pentecost" was given to the Old Testament festival by the Greek-speaking Jews because the holy day occurred 50 days after the offering of the barley sheaf during the Passover feast (Lev. 23:15-21). After the Exile, Pentecost became the traditional time to celebrate the giving of the Law, the birthday of the Torah.

In the Old Testament, the Holy Spirit, in His sanctifying, energizing power, had come on only a few, such as kings, prophets, or leaders called for some special work. Also, under the old dispensation, the indwelling of the Spirit seems to have been transitory. Now, in the New Testament fellowship, it was to be for all people and would be permanent. It is significant that a Person, not a power or influence given by measure, had filled each and every believer.

1. *Symbols of the Spirit*

The scriptural account does not state that there *was* a mighty rushing wind, but rather a sound *resembling* the sound of an exceedingly strong wind, filling the entire house where they were meeting.

[34]Asa Mahan, *The Baptism of the Holy Ghost* (New York: W. C. Palmer, 1876), p. 189.

[35]McLaughlin, *op. cit.*, p. 20.

This represents what was audible to the ear. To the eye there was the appearance of a sheet of flame *similar* to fire. This apparent sheet of flame filled the room, then divided itself, with a part resting on each of them, presumably on the head. In addition to these indications made to the sense of hearing and the sense of sight, the climactic effect was the visible and audible release of energy and response when the people began to speak in languages before unknown to them.

These physical demonstrations of the Holy Spirit's presence were previously unknown in collective human experience. The object of such demonstrations would be to make the event noteworthy in the Church. The gift of the Holy Spirit had been definitely predicted. It was thus vitally important that the fulfillment of this prediction should be recognized and demonstrated by unmistakable signs.

2. *The Meaning of the Symbols*

The symbols used to demonstrate the full and permanent giving and receiving of the Holy Spirit were suited to the nature and the work of the Holy Spirit. The sound of the wind denoted the invisibility, the mysterious operation of the Spirit, as well as the irresistible force and power inherent in the all-pervading presence of the Holy Spirit. The "tongues of fire" are symbols of the refining, purifying, and molding power of the Holy Spirit, as well as energy—the energy that goes with and in spiritual truth presented in word. The speaking in other tongues (languages) was a sign of the universality, the inclusiveness, of the kingdom of God. The speaking in languages would also mean that the Christian faith was to be propagated by word of mouth as well as by example.

It was necessary that the gift of the Holy Spirit should be visible, that the bodily senses might stir up the disciples. As Calvin put it, "Such is our slothfulness to consider the gifts of God, that unless he awake all our senses, his power shall pass away unknown."[36]

3. *Problem of Permanency of Symbols*

It should be noted that these audible, visible demonstrations of the Spirit's presence were special, peculiar and transient, sent in this form at that time for special purposes, and were never designed to illustrate the normal effects of the Spirit's power. Even the gift of tongues, though of longer duration and designed for some other

[36]*Commentary upon the Acts of the Apostles*, I, 75.

uses, apparently did not continue any longer than the generation then living. At first it served to arouse public attention, to bear witness to the divine mission of the apostles, and for a time to aid their access to people using these diverse languages. The demonstration of languages was designed to enlarge their views of the range and scope of their great commission. Thus, Cowles concludes, "it should have have burst the old circumscribing compress of Jewish monopoly and shown them that the gospel was provided, not for Jews only, but for the wide world."[37]

In the light of the teachings of Acts it appears possible to state that the modern phenomenon of speaking in unknown tongues finds only vague and nebulous support. The preponderance of the evidence in Acts is that the speaking in tongues of the Early Church was a speaking in languages designed to meet specific needs in the life and understanding of the times.

C. The Power of the Holy Spirit

1. *The Power of Preaching*

The coming of the Holy Spirit was accompanied by demonstrations of power in the physical area, the area of sense response. Another type of power under the Holy Spirit was revealed in the preaching of Peter. Having received a dramatic spiritual illumination along with a dynamic personal experience, he was enabled to preach a classic and immortal sermon.

"But Peter . . . lifted up his voice, and said unto them . . . hearken to my words" (Acts 2:14). The Holy Spirit came to appeal to the intellect as well as to arouse the sensibilities. With a life throbbing with divine power *(dunamis)* Peter presented a model sermon. He who had been rendered mute and cowardly by the frail finger of a little girl now faced a mob of potential murderers fearlessly, yet persuasively. Peter's Pentecost message stands as a model of homiletical presentation, for it contained and achieved all that a sermon is designed to do.

Peter's sermon was biblical, clear, Christ-centered, courageous, timely, and convincing. But the real power of the sermon was in its content. According to C. H. Dodd, the contents of the sermon contained the basic ideas of all apostolic preaching.[38]

[37]*Op. cit.*, p. 218.

[38]*The Apostolic Preaching and Its Developments* (New York: Harper and Brothers, 1936), pp. 21 ff.

a. First, the age of fulfillment had dawned. Peter declared: "This is that which was spoken by the prophet" (Acts 2:16); "Those things, which God . . . shewed by the mouth of all his prophets . . . he hath so fulfilled" (Acts 3:18). The presence of the Holy Spirit is a great aid in understanding redemptive truth, for "he will guide you into all truth" (John 16:13). Rabbinical exegesis had always associated the coming of the Messiah with outpourings of divine blessing. Peter declared that the Messianic age had dawned.

Peter also stated that the new age had dawned because of the ministry, the death, and the resurrection of Christ. Because of His Davidic descent (Acts 2:29-31), because of His ministry which had been "approved of God among you by miracles and wonders and signs, which God did by him in the midst of you" (Acts 2:22), because of His death and resurrection (Acts 2:24-31), Christ had inaugurated a new age in the history of redemption.

b. Christ was exalted. Peter declared that, by virtue of His resurrection, Jesus had been exalted by the right hand of God. The Holy Spirit in the Church is the sign of Christ's present power and glory. "Being by the right hand of God exalted, and having received of the Father the promise of the Holy Ghost, he hath shed forth this, which ye now see and hear" (Acts 2:33). The relation of the exaltation of the Messiah and the outpouring of the Holy Spirit is supported by Joel 2:28-32. The Messianic age, Peter stated, will shortly reach its consummation in the return of Christ (Acts 3:21). Peter closed his message with an appeal for repentance and a promise of forgiveness and of the Holy Spirit.

2. *Spiritual Illumination*

The structure and the eloquence of Peter's sermon transcends human power. It was an evidence of the presence of the Holy Spirit. But the change in the apostle's understanding is even more significant. In regard to the Resurrection, in particular, the apostles were enlightened. Until Pentecost the apostles were unable to comprehend the idea of the Resurrection. Their conception of the Messiah had been so much at variance with what He proved to be that they could not detect any ray of light from their Scriptures. But after the baptism with the Holy Spirit they understood the doctrine of the Resurrection in the sacred records to the extent that they used the Scriptures to prove it. The Holy Spirit had opened their understanding. However, the greatest power of the Holy Spirit was in the area of spiritual penetration.

3. *A Powerful Spiritual Penetration of the Conscience*

Peter's preaching produced deep conviction. "Now when they heard this, they were pricked in their heart, and said . . . Men and brethren, what shall we do?" (Acts 2:37) According to A. T. Robertson the verb "pricked" used here is the second aorist indicative of *katanusso,* a rare verb meaning "to pierce, to sting sharply, to stun, to smite. Homer used it in describing horses striking the earth with their hoofs."[39] The greatest power of the Holy Spirit is in the area of man's conscience. While the sensibilities are stirred by the infilling of the Holy Spirit, it is apparent that physical demonstration of any kind *may,* but does not of *necessity,* accompany the baptism with the Holy Spirit. Similarly, in the area of intellectual apprehension of truth the Holy Spirit is the divine *Paraclete,* and as such is beneficial for the full enjoyment and the most effective propagation of holiness. But the greatest work of the Holy Spirit is in the area of the sensitivity of the conscience.

The area of spiritual penetration is the *sine qua non* of the baptism with the Holy Spirit, for "when he is come, he will reprove the world of sin, and of righteousness, and of judgment" (John 16:8). Not emotionalism, not intellectualism, but *spiritual penetration,* is the ultimate test of preaching. If preaching makes no difference in one's response to God, if preaching results in no personal inventory, if preaching makes no dent in pride, complacency, immorality, self-centeredness, then it is not the preaching sanctioned by the Holy Spirit. The preaching blessed and owned by the Holy Spirit is the preaching that makes a person love the world less and love God more, that lifts a person to the point of spiritual response where his only question is, "What shall I do?"

The experience of holiness is synonymous with the baptism with the Holy Spirit and with spiritual power. "*The Spirit within is power.* He is the gift of power—power to be, power to do, power to suffer, power to save."[40]

The experience of holiness affords opportunity for physical demonstration, for expressing "the joy of the Lord." However, holiness of the Wesleyan tradition makes the arousement of the sensibilities an incidental rather than in integral aspect of the Spirit's presence, and never makes any physical test to indicate the baptism with the Holy Spirit. Contrary to much external opinion

[39]*Op. cit.,* p. 42.

[40]A. S. Keen, *Pentecostal Papers* (Cincinnati, Ohio: M. W. Knapp, 1896), p. 125.

and to some internal opposition, the Wesleyan concept of holiness does encourage vigorous intellectual response, for of what purpose is the divine Paraclete (Teacher) unless He is given opportunity to enlighten?

The most crucial area of the Holy Spirit's power is in penetrating to the limits of personality, purifying and cleansing it for acceptable worship and service. True holiness interprets physical demonstration properly, it focuses intellectual understanding correctly, and it emphasizes spiritual purity consistently. As such holiness is the foundation of spiritual fellowship.

IV. Holiness: The Dynamic of Spiritual Fellowship

The Primitive Church, while it enjoyed the fellowship of the Holy Spirit and appealed to the openly acknowledged work of the Spirit as evidence of the new Church age, did not reflect upon it.[41] Nor did the early converts embody any clear doctrine of fellowship in its preaching. The concept of fellowship is *lived* rather than *taught* in the Book of Acts. Later Paul added some thoughts on the nature of the fellowship of believers.

However, in both the Acts of the Apostles and in Paul's writings, holiness is the taproot that feeds and sustains the ideal of Christian fellowship. In the Book of the Acts fellowship was indicated by steadfastness in doctrine, consistent acceptance of leadership, congenial social relationships, spontaneous patterns of worship, and an enjoyable self-discipline. These qualities are the trademarks of holiness.

A. Steadfastness in Doctrine

"And they continued stedfastly in the apostles' doctrine" (Acts 2:42*a*). Daniel Steele often said that the Holy Spirit was the great Conservator of orthodoxy.[42] Entire sanctification makes converts steadfast and helps to sustain them in the spiritual life. It is the establishing grace. "This was no loose group of spiritual fanatics, but a clear-cut society, universal in membership, but with firm, definite standards."[43] Repentance, confession, and baptism, evidently with water, but essentially with the Holy Spirit, were necessary.

[41]Dodd, *op. cit.*, p. 59.

[42]*The Gospel of the Comforter*, pp. 325 ff.

[43]E. M. Blaiklock, *The Acts of the Apostles* (Grand Rapids, Mich.: Wm. B. Eerdmans Pub. Co., 1959), p. 61.

B. Acceptance of Leadership

The experience of holiness brings a cooperative spirit. Thus the disciples continued "in the apostles' doctrine and fellowship" (Acts 2:42). Holiness is not opposed to the acceptance of leadership, for the experience of holiness is the unifying experience. The baptism with the Holy Spirit is neither antithetical nor antagonistic to leadership. All that the person in the fellowship of holiness asks is that leadership be exemplary of the doctrine of holiness in practical living and be open advocates of holiness in public presentation. The history of Methodism and of contemporary holiness groups indicates that the experience of holiness not only accepts leadership, but also promotes personal cooperation with leadership to achieve God's purpose.

C. Generous Social Relationships

Holiness produces a social concern. "And all that believed were together, and had all things common; and sold their possessions and goods, and parted them to all men, as every man had *need*" (Acts 2:44-45). Holiness ever since has had profound implications for social relationships.[44] Holiness cannot be exclusive in its disposition nor sectarian in its mission. Holiness cannot be reduced to slogans or clichés, for the principle of holy living, as far as society is concerned, is a basic respect for all personality that is neither sentimental nor frigid. Because all people are by nature creations of God's power and are by grace potential objects of redemption, the life of holiness must always reflect broad social overtones.

The generosity displayed by the Primitive Church was not, as some mistakenly suggest, an attempt at Christian communism, with the giving up of all property to a common fund, but was the donating of all proceeds from the disposal of private property to a common fund, as far as such a fund was needed, *to support the poor.*

D. Spontaneous Patterns of Worship

Joyful worship is a by-product of holiness. "And they, continuing daily with one accord in the temple, and breaking bread from house to house, did eat their meat with gladness" (Acts 2:46). In

[44]The following books present the social impact of holiness groups: Timothy L. Smith, *Revivalism and Social Reform* (New York: Abingdon Press, 1957); J. Wesley Bready, *This Freedom—Whence?* (New York: American Tract Society, 1946); Mary A. Tenney, *Blueprint for a Christian World* (Winona Lake, Ind.: Light and Life Press, 1953).

holiness, worship is not a mournful duty nor is it a monotonous performance. Holiness makes worship vitalizing and strengthening, rather than wearisome and tiring. Holiness echoes the words of the Psalmist: "I was glad when they said unto me, Let us go into the house of the Lord" (Ps. 122:1).

E. Enjoyable Self-discipline

Pentecost brought a happy kind of self-discipline. Thus the Christians "did eat . . . with gladness and singleness of heart, praising God" (Acts 2:46*b*-47*a*). In the classic of self-denial and self-discipline, *The Imitation of Christ*, by Thomas a Kempis, the note of joy is missing. Even in the writings of the devout William Law, holiness often appears to be a burden to be borne rather than an experience to be enjoyed.

Mournful, dyspeptic "holiness" is a poor unifying catalyst. Harsh, gloomy, or critical "holiness" is a hollow imitation of the enjoyable self-discipline which the Primitive Church voluntarily accepted. The Early Church was pure, it was single-minded, it was non-secular—and it was joyful. The world finds it impossible to duplicate joyful self-discipline—and often finds it impossible to resist it.

Holiness satisfies the instinct of mankind for gregarious fellowship. And simply because the source and the power of holy fellowship transcends individual or collective human effort, it produces the noblest and most enriching fellowship. Such fellowship is not turned inward for selfish purposes, but is expressed outwardly in a universal vision. In the final analysis, "all true fellowship among individual believers—and the word implies union of heart and purpose—is the 'fellowship of the Spirit.'"[45]

V. Holiness: The Dynamic of Spiritual Vision

The baptism with the Holy Spirit produces a spiritual vision that is clear and inclusive. Within the Church, in both Roman Catholic and Protestant branches, the groups that have honored the Holy Spirit have had the greatest zeal for the cause of God, have exhibited the highest degree of stewardship, and have fostered the greatest evangelistic endeavor. Spiritual vision, as developed from

[45]Duggan Clark, *The Offices of the Holy Spirit* (Portland, Ore.: Evangel Publishers, 1945), p. 210.

the account of the activities of the Holy Spirit in the Book of the Acts, reflects the following: an articulate witness, an authoritative leadership, a pattern of compassion, a readiness to sacrifice, a workable method of evangelism, and a transcendent task.

A. An Articulate Witness

Pentecost loosens the tongue. "Ye shall be witnesses unto me . . . Then Peter, filled with the Holy Ghost, said unto them" (Acts 1:8; 4:8). The Jewish leaders could not understand the effectiveness of the apostles' preaching. Sir William Ramsey has drawn attention to the power of speech in the Primitive Church.[46] He remarks:

> The Jewish leaders noticed the bold and fluent speech of Peter and John; and yet they observed from their dress and style of utterance that they were not trained scholars . . . and they further took notice of the fact that they were disciples of Jesus; and they gazed with wonder on the man that had been cured at the gate of the temple. These were the facts of the case. The historian's (Luke) point is that there is only one possible inference; and as the Jewish leaders were unwilling to draw that inference, they perforce kept silence not having the wherewithal to dispute the obvious conclusion . . . that these illiterate fishermen had acquired the art and power of effective oratory through their having been disciples of Jesus and through the divine grace and power communicated to them.[47]

Others beside Peter and John were effective and articulate witnesses. Philip, a layman and a Hellenist, had found an opportunity to preach to the Samaritans, with whom the Jews had no dealings (John 4:9). "Peter and John were so impressed with Philip's work and the Holy Spirit's sanction of it that they not only lingered to share in the testimony and speaking of the Word in the city of Samaria, but on their way back to Jerusalem 'even evangelized many of the villages of the Samaritans,' and thus they were led into a blessed ministry."[48] Later Philip, in his angelically directed itinerary, went to the desert of Gaza and was so effective in his witness that a high Ethiopian government official was converted (Acts 8:26-40).

Perhaps the most effective witness in the Apostolic Church was Stephen. "Stephen," writes A. W. F. Blunt, "seems to have

[46] *Op. cit.*, p. 371.
[47] *Ibid.*
[48] Carver, *op. cit.*, p. 85.

brought over with him into Christianity ideas and a point of view which he may have learnt *[sic]* from the more liberal Judaism of the Dispersion."[49] Stephen's ministry notably foreshadowed Paul's in his spiritual interpretation of the law. Orthodox Jewry was quick to see that his teaching involved the supersession of Judaism. Its effectiveness among both Gentiles and Jews was so apparent that the religious leaders felt impelled to silence his voice. But his witness lived on.

B. An Authoritative Leadership

Spirit-filled leadership is often authoritative. "We ought to obey God rather than men" (Acts 5:29*b*). The apostolic authority was revealed in two ways, to those within the group and to those outside the group.

In the incident of Ananias and Sapphira the authority of the apostles was manifest to those within the Church. In the formative days of the Church, some degree of honor was attached to the wealthy who cheerfully sold their estates and donated the proceeds to the funds to help the needy. The desire to gain popular approval under false pretenses was the source of temptation to which Ananias and Sapphira fell. It was especially important to head off this temptation at the outset, or the Christian community would become as corrupt, as full of pride and hypocrisy as the Pharisees whom Jesus had so severely denounced.

Peter had discovered the fraud and charged Ananias with sin (Acts 5:3). The language of the accusation is instructive. Ananias had lied, not to the Church, but to the Holy Ghost enshrined in the Church. Only a drastic type of punishment and authority saved the Church from a possible toleration of evil. When sin is tolerated in the church, holiness has felt the first breath of spiritual death.

One valid test of spiritual leadership is the reaction to those outside the group who condemn, persecute, or criticize. When the disciples were arrested and brought before the Sanhedrin, Peter defined their activities so well that they were dismissed with a stern warning—and a whipping (Acts 5:40). It was a historic moment. "For the first time Christians had suffered in their bodies for their faith and honest preaching."[50] Holiness produces authoritative leadership.

[49]*Op. cit.*, p. 160.
[50]*Ibid.*, p. 73.

C. A Pattern of Compassion

Compassion belongs in the family of holy virtues. "Such as I have give I thee" (Acts 3:6*b*). Holiness is the dynamic of spiritual conquest because it leads to compassion, to an empathic concern for the human race. When the Holy Spirit came on the people at Pentecost they talked, they witnessed, but they did much more. They translated their speeches into acts of Christian compassion.

When Peter and John went into the Temple at three o'clock in the afternoon, they performed the first physical act for those outside the Church. At the gate called "Beautiful" they met a man who had been a lifelong cripple, who had to gain his living the only way a cripple could in that day—by begging. In response to a plea for help Peter performed a miracle of healing that astounded both the man and the bystanders. With the strength restored to his limbs the healed man gave a hilarious demonstration that excited the crowd.

D. A Readiness to Sacrifice

Suffering and sacrifice are often included in a life of holiness. "Which of the prophets have not your fathers persecuted?" (Acts 7:52) First came imprisonment to Peter and John, then arrest and physical beatings. Now the measure of sacrifice was increased as the hand of persecution clamped tighter on the newborn Church. Stephen was haled before the Sanhedrin and after a farce of a trial was dispatched with stones that were not nearly as hard as the hearts of those throwing them. Later the executioner's blade fell on James. A man named Saul of Tarsus organized a campaign to extinguish the Church. But the infant Church was sustained by a power and an experience in the Holy Spirit that made it indifferent to suffering and death.

E. A Workable Method of Evangelism

Pentecost produced a workable plan of evangelism. "And Saul arose from the earth" (Acts 9:8). There are three methods used by churches or by religious groups to win converts, or to make Christians out of non-Christians. These three methods are (1) the sacramental method, (2) the method of education or Christian nurture, and (3) the evangelistic method, or the conversion method.

Volumes have been written regarding the dramatic experience of Paul as he traveled to Damascus. Some regard the experience as illusory, others as an attack of epilepsy, others as sunstroke, others as an experience reserved for rare individuals, but not the common experience of all who become Christians. This we know, that in the mid-course of his mad career, Paul saw Jesus, so clearly, so definitely, that he could only believe and obey. He saw; he heard; he knew; he surrendered; he was a transformed person.

In theory the concept of salvation by *participation in the sacraments* may sound plausible. In practice it results in formalism and institutionalism which are the antithesis to the Christians described in the Acts of the Apostles. In theory the idea of *Christian nurture* may sound feasible. In practice it often ends in rationalism and humanism, which are a denial of the power and the experience of the Early Church. In theory the doctrine of *regeneration* appears attractive. In practice it produces a type of life that is in harmony with biblical teachings and in keeping with man's highest aspirations. Holiness evangelism is the key to spiritual conquest.

F. A Transcendent Task

The task of spreading holiness is unlimited. "Then hath God also to the Gentiles granted repentance unto life" (Acts 11:18*b*). Gradually the immensity of the task of spiritual conquest was realized by the new Church. Slowly the Jewish Christians saw that Christianity was not to be a reformed Judaism, but a supplanter, a new and vital spiritual force that was unique. The task was as broad as the needs of man and as inclusive as perfect love could, and must, be.

Summary

Pentecost marks the beginning of spiritual dynamic out of which came the Christian Church. The cause of the growth of the Church in the Roman Empire as well as the basis for its initial strength was this power resulting from the baptism with the Holy Spirit. This dynamic was demonstrated in spiritual purity, spiritual power, spiritual fellowship, and spiritual vision. The Church was strong because it was made up of Spirit-filled individuals. The strength of the Church determines the character of the Church. "The character of the Christian Church, as a whole," says William Arthur, "must always be ruled by the character of individual Christians; for the Church is but the assembly and aggregate of individuals."[51] The Pentecostal outpouring is thus essential to the Church in all ages, for it is the source of the spiritual dynamic by which the Church is able to sustain itself and to advance its borders.

[51] *The Tongue of Fire* (New York: Harper and Brothers, 1880), p. 196.

CHAPTER XII /

Imperfect Perfection

What happens in the crisis of entire sanctification? Do the holiness churches teach *perfectionism?* Does the experience of holiness suddenly and dramatically elevate a person to the status of sainthood, where the believer has no faults? Do Wesleyans state that it is impossible to sin, or to fall from grace? Do the holiness people believe that they serve God perfectly? To all these questions the answer is that Wesleyan theology includes a paradox or an apparent contradiction—that of imperfect perfection. In presenting this paradox, two aspects of the doctrine of entire sanctification will be dealt with: (1) the place and meaning of *perfection;* (2) what a person may *not* expect in the experience of holiness.

I. The Wesleyan Meaning of Perfection

The term *perfection* is a favorite whipping boy in theology. The use of the term automatically gives rise to pictures of sour, proud, legalistic, self-styled saints who wear their religion like Pharisaical garments. Actually, few people in the holiness churches use the term. In fact, most people would be embarrassed and self-conscious if the term was applied to them. For these people are well aware that holiness is like humility—if one brags about it, it is a certain sign he does not possess it. Thus the term is *never* used in personal witnessing or in spiritual self-evaluation. At least the author, in almost 30 years of association within such a group, has never heard or read of anyone applying the label of *perfection* to his name. Yet the term is one that is used in theological discussion and must be dealt with satisfactorily. For the Wesleyan meaning of the term the explanation first turns to John Wesley, then to some of the later writers in the Wesleyan tradition.

A. Wesley's Idea of Perfection

John Wesley's concept of perfection was a matter of emotional response as well as a matter of technical interpretation. Wesley seemed to vacillate in his emotional regard for the term. But there was never any variation as to what he meant by the term. To understand Wesley's idea of perfection it is necessary to consider both aspects—his emotional response to the term as well as his theoretical explanation of it.

1. *Wesley's Emotional Response*

Wesley's reaction to the use of the term *perfection* might be called both negative and positive. That is, sometimes Wesley wearied of defending the term, while at other times he vigorously supported it.

a. Negative reaction. Wesley became involved in many wordy contests over the term perfection. As Sangster comments, "It provoked the astonishment and anger of his opponents, and it was sometimes pitifully prostituted by his followers."[1] The situation was so bad in 1768 that Wesley almost despaired of using the term. In a letter to his brother Charles in May, 1768, Wesley wrote: "I am at my wits' end with regard to two things—the Church and Christian perfection. Unless both you and I stand in the gap *in good earnest,* the Methodists will drop them both."[2] Exactly a month later he wrote to his brother again in an even more pessimistic vein:

> I think it is high time that you and I at least should come to a point. Shall we go on in asserting perfection against all the world? Or shall we quietly let it drop? We really must do one or the other; and, I apprehend, the sooner the better. . . . I am weary of intestine war, of preachers quoting one of us against the other. At length let us *fix* something for good and all; either the same as formerly or different from it.[3]

Wesley was not fond of the term *perfection.* In a letter to a particularly harsh critic, Wesley bluntly refused to discuss *perfection* by

[1] *Op. cit.,* p. 78.
[2] *Letters,* V, 88.
[3] *Ibid.,* V, 93.

saying: "Of Christian perfection . . . I shall not say anything to you, till you have learned a little heathen honesty."[4] Wesley was well aware of the problems caused by the use of the term perfection. Some of Wesley's critics caricatured the idea, calling Wesley a devil.[5] Some of Wesley's followers cheapened the term by calling themselves angels.[6] The full extent of the problem that the term *perfection* presented to Wesley may be seen from his following statement:

> There is scarce any expression in holy writ, which has given more offense than this. The word *perfect* is what many cannot bear. The very sound of it is an abomination to them; and whosoever *preaches perfection,* (as the phrase is,) that is, asserts that it is attainable in this life, runs great hazard of being accounted by them worse than a heathen man or a publican.[7]

Yet Wesley refused to abandon the term. His theoretical grasp of the content of the word outweighed his emotional reaction to the term.

b. Positive affirmation. Sangster is of the opinion that Wesley used the term *perfection* far more than he realized.[8] The reason is simple: he was convinced it was a scriptural term. In the letter to William Dodd already mentioned, Wesley wrote: "But that it is a *scriptural term* is undeniable. Therefore none ought to object to the use of the *term,* whatever they may do to this or that explication of it."[9] When the wife of General Maitland wrote to him concerning the problems involved in the use of the term perfection, she asked: "Would it not be safer to call it a high state of grace than perfection?"[10] Wesley's reply was as follows: "As to the word, it is scriptural; therefore neither you nor I can in conscience object against it, unless we would send the Holy Ghost to school and teach Him to speak who made the tongue."[11] And, as suggested earlier, it must not be overlooked that Wesley condensed his teachings on the matter of holiness into the now famous tract entitled *A Plain Account of Christian Perfection.* In the opening statement of the *Plain Account,* Wesley stated that his purpose was "to give a plain and distinct account by which I was led, during a course of many years, to em-

[4] *Ibid.,* III, 266.
[5] Sangster, *op. cit.,* p. 79.
[6] Wesley, *Letters,* IV, 192.
[7] *Works,* VI, 1.
[8] *Op. cit.,* p. 78.
[9] *Letters,* III, 168.
[10] *Ibid.,* IV, 212.
[11] *Ibid.*

brace the doctrine of Christian perfection."[12] Thus it is evident that John Wesley, while aware of the problems involved, did accept without reservation the biblical idea of perfection. Wesley was careful, however, to define precisely what he meant by the term.

2. *Perfection as Love*

Wesley used the term perfection interchangeably with holiness, perfect love, and entire sanctification. To him "perfection is only another term for holiness, or the image of God in man."[13] He was careful to teach his preachers the nature of perfection. On Monday, June 25, 1744, the First Conference of Methodist preachers began. The next morning, according to Wesley, "we seriously considered the doctrine of sanctification, or perfection."[14] In response to the question of what was implied in being a perfect Christian, the reply was: "The loving God with all our heart, and mind and soul (Deut. 6:5)."[15] Another definition of perfection expanded this reply somewhat: "Christian perfection is that love of God and our neighbour, which implies deliverance from all sin."[16] Wesley insisted over and over that perfect love was the essence of perfection;[17] that perfection meant "the humble, gentle, patient love of God, and our neighbour, ruling our tempers, words, and actions."[18] The primary aspect of perfection to Wesley was not legalistic or moralistic, but ethical and spiritual. In addition to love, however, perfection included cleansing, or freedom from sin.

3. *Perfection as Cleansing*

Wesley was too practical a thinker to explain perfection only in terms of love. He was well aware that the biblical teaching included inward cleansing as one aspect of sanctification, or perfection. He was also alert to the possibilities of antinomianism when the Christian life is regarded in only abstract terms. So Wesley linked personal cleansing to inner love. In his letter to William Dodd, Wesley wrote: "The *cleansing from all unrighteousness* does not mean justification only . . . it relates chiefly, if not wholly, to sanctification."[19] In his instructions to the 1744 Conference, Wesley presented a series

[12]*Works*, XI, 366.
[13]*Letters*, III, 168.
[14]*Works*, XI, 387.
[15]*Ibid.*
[16]*Ibid.*, p. 393.
[17]*Ibid.*, p. 442.
[18]*Ibid.*, p. 446.
[19]*Letters*, III, 172.

of questions and answers in order to explain the doctrines and practices of the Methodists. One such question and answer referred to "being a perfect Christian:

"Q. Does this imply, that all inward sin is taken away?

"A. Undoubtedly; or how can we be said to be 'saved from all our uncleannesses?' (Ezek. xxxvi.29)"[20]

Wesley thus belonged to the eradication or extinction school of thought. He seems to be vague at this point in writing to Mrs. Maitland: "Whether sin is *suspended* or *extinguished,* I will not dispute."[21] But, as Sangster observes, "When driven to it, he *did* dispute, and came down definitely for extinction."[22] Wesley believed that perfection meant cleansing because he thought it was biblical. Two of his favorite scriptures were Ezek. 36:25 and II Cor. 7:1, both of which stressed the divine act of cleansing. In a letter to Joseph Bolton he wrote:

> And are not the love of God and our neighbour good tempers? And, so far as these reign in the soul, are not the opposite tempers, worldly-mindedness, malice, cruelty, revengefulness, destroyed? Indeed, the unclean spirit, though driven out, may return and enter again; nevertheless he was driven out. I use the word "destroyed" because St. Paul does; "suspended" I cannot find in my Bible.[23]

To Wesley, then, perfection consisted of perfect love and cleansing. Christianity, he said, "implies a destruction of the kingdom of sin and a renewal of the soul in righteousness."[24] Later followers of Wesley accepted his explanation of perfection as love and cleansing.

4. *Perfection—the Christian Standard*

Wesley unceasingly attempted to explain the meaning of perfection. He was aware that it was possible to set the standard of perfection too high. He was also aware that many set the standard of Christian living too low. In his lengthy letter to William Dodd he stated: "If I set the mark too high, I drive men into needless fears: if you set it too low, you drive them into hell-fire."[25] He was careful not to put perfection higher than the Bible did. He constantly taught that the sanctified should grow in grace and he warned against

[20]*Works,* XI, 387.
[21]*Letters,* IV, 213.
[22]*Op. cit.,* p. 82.
[23]*Letters,* V, 203-4.
[24]*Ibid.,* III, 169.
[25]*Ibid.,* p. 168.

pride, enthusiasm (meaning fanaticism), of making void the law, of sins of omission, of desiring anything except God, of schism, and of creating harmful impressions.

Wesley insisted that a Christian did not commit sin even in the justified state. Of course, Wesley defined sin as "a voluntary transgression of a known law." In regard to the idea of sinless perfection, Wesley felt "it is not worthwhile to contend for a term."[26] Again he wrote that "*sinless perfection* is a phrase I never use, lest I should seem to contradict myself."[27] He did admit that a person filled with the love of God is still liable to involuntary transgressions. But he refused to call involuntary transgressions sins, although all involuntary transgressions of a divine law (known or unknown) needed the merits of Christ's sacrifice. In the final paragraphs of his *Plain Account of Christian Perfection,* Wesley suggests the various aspects of perfection as he taught it. From one point of view "it is purity of intention, dedicating all the life to God."[28] In another view "it is the circumcision of the heart from all filthiness, all inward as well as outward pollution."[29] In yet another way "it is the loving God with all our heart, and our neighbour as ourselves."[30] To Wesley there was no difference between these various aspects of perfection. And when dealing with the source of this doctrine, Wesley declared it was not *his* doctrine, but the doctrine of Christ, of St. Paul, of St. James, of St. Peter, and of St. John, and of "every one who preaches the pure and the whole Gospel." Then he adds these words: "I tell you, as plain as I can speak, where and when I found this. I found it in the oracles of God, in the Old and New Testament; when I read them with no other view or desire but to save my own soul."[31] It may be said safely that Christian perfection was the heart of Wesley's thinking and preaching. Later followers of Wesley echoed the teaching that perfection meant purity of intention, cleansing, and perfect love.

B. Perfection in the Wesleyan Tradition

Later adherents of the Wesleyan tradition were as careful as

[26]*Works,* XI, 442.
[27]*Ibid.,* p. 396.
[28]*Ibid.,* XI, 444.
[29]*Ibid.*
[30]*Ibid.*
[31]*Ibid.*

Wesley to define perfection in terms of love, cleansing, and purity of motivation. A random listing of definitions of perfection from Wesleyan writers will reveal this fact.

1. *Definitions of Perfection*

a. It must, therefore, be concluded, that the standard of our attainable Christian perfection, as to the affections, is a love of God so perfect as to "rule the heart," and exclude all rivalry, and a meekness so perfect as to cast out all sinful anger and prevent its return; and that as to good works, the rule is, that we shall be so "perfect in every good work," as to "do the will of God" habitually, fully, and constantly.[32]

b. By Christian perfection, we mean nothing but the cluster and maturity of the graces which compose the Christian character in the Church militant.[33]

c. Christian perfection . . . is nothing more and nothing less, than a heart emptied of all sin and filled with pure love to God and man.[34]

d. The sense in which the entirely sanctified soul is made *perfect,* or *complete,* is in *purity.*[35]

e. Christian or evangelical perfection consists in the conditioning of all our human motivations by the Spirit of holiness to the degree that we are able to love the Lord our God with all our heart, soul, mind, and strength; and our neighbors as ourselves (Mark 12:29-31).[36]

2. *A Qualified Kind of Perfection*

The above statements indicate that Wesley and his followers have never taught and preached an impossible, non-biblical perfection. The opponents and critics of Wesleyanism have often built up a theological straw-man and labeled it Wesleyan perfectionism. But neither Wesley nor his followers taught that absolute perfection was possible in a finite, redeemed believer. The holiness movement has always qualified the term perfection by the word Christian or the term evangelical. Thus Wesleyans have taught that Christian perfection or evangelical perfection was a *relative* perfection. That is, a perfection "modified by the capacity and capabilities of the soul."[37] The words of William B. Pope are relevant at this point: "The term perfection . . . should not be adopted without qualifica-

[32]Watson, *Theological Institutes,* II, 453.

[33]John Fletcher, *The Works of the Rev. John Fletcher* (London: John Mason, 1839), V, 415.

[34]Wiley, *Christian Theology,* II, 511.

[35]Wood, *Purity and Maturity,* p. 26.

[36]Purkiser, *Sanctification and Its Synonyms,* p. 71.

[37]Wood, *Purity and Maturity,* p. 28.

tion; but with its guardian adjectives Christian or Evangelical it is unimpeachable. Christian perfection is relative and probationary and therefore . . . limited."[38]

3. *The Paradox of Perfection*

This, then, is the paradox of perfection. Logically it appears to be a contradiction. Experientially, it is a reality. A Christian may live in a spiritual and ethical state of holiness. The essence of this state of holiness, or perfection, is love to God and man, purity of motivation, and cleansing from inherent sin. But because of finite qualities which still bear the scars of sin, this same believer will *not perfectly* fulfill God's law. Thus "perfection in one respect, and imperfection in another, may consistently meet in the same person; as he may be perfect in one sense, while imperfect in another."[39] The Apostle Paul apparently was aware of the paradox of perfection. In his letter to the Philippians, Paul firmly denied any personal claim to final perfection when he wrote: "Not as though I had already attained, either were already perfect" (Phil. 3:12). Yet almost in the same breath he referred not only to himself, but to others as already perfect: "Let us, as many as be perfect, be thus minded" (Phil. 3:15). J. Paul Taylor has commented that Paul "denied perfection as a winner but professed perfection as a runner and included others in that classification. . . . The perfection of heart here fits us for the perfection of heaven hereafter."[40]

This, then, is the paradox of holiness—imperfect perfection. The paradox of "imperfect perfection" leads directly to another very important aspect of holiness, namely, what entire sanctification does *not* do.

II. What Sanctification Does Not Do

Entire sanctification is an act of divine grace. But the spiritual condition resulting from the act of sanctification is "a perfection accommodated to man's fallen condition: not lowered but accommodated."[41] While the state of holiness, or of Christian perfection, is a valid biblical teaching and experience, there are limitations to

[38]*Christian Theology*, III, 58.

[39]Wood, *Purity and Maturity*, p. 27.

[40]*Holiness the Finished Foundation* (Winona Lake, Ind.: Light and Life Press, 1963), p. 94.

[41]Pope, *Christian Theology*, III, 57.

what the act and the experience will accomplish in the believer. To expect spiritual results beyond the biblical and practical range of possibility is not only misleading, but is damaging. Most writers, theologians, preachers, teachers, administrators, and laymen are agreed that the act of sanctification and the state of holiness do not include the following.

A. It Is Not Adamic Perfection.

Before the Fall, Adam enjoyed direct fellowship with God (Gen. 2:15-17; 3:8). In addition to this direct relationship with God, Adam was perfect in his abilities. His reason was unimpaired, his volitional powers were unhindered, and his affections were untainted. Thus he could rationally discern, he could volitionally choose, he could enjoy what he knew and chose. Also, man's body was perfect, so that it would be a source of right and holy impulses. After the Fall, man's mind became clouded, his will was weakened, his affections perverted, and his body weakened. So man "is no longer able to avoid falling into innumerable mistakes; consequently, he cannot always avoid wrong affections; neither can he always think, speak, and act right. Therefore man, in his present state, can no more attain Adamic than angelic perfection."[42] Adam's perfection pertained to Adam alone.

B. It Is Not Angelic Perfection.

The angels are pure spirits who have evidently passed through a period of probation. Man is a creature of flesh and spirit living in a world of sin, and is in a state of probation. Thus man, redeemed and living in the highest possible spiritual state, cannot attain the perfection of the angels. Since the angels have not fallen from their original perfection, their abilities and faculties are unimpaired. Their knowledge and spiritual light prevent them from making mistakes. So Wesley comments: "It follows, that no man, while in the body, can possibly attain to angelic perfection."[43] Christian perfection is distinct from angelic perfection.

C. It Is Not Resurrection Perfection.

Daniel Steele suggests that there are four kinds of *perfection*

[42]Wesley, *Works*, VI, 412.
[43]*Ibid.*

revealed in the Bible.[44] First and foremost is the *absolute perfection* of God. Since this perfection is infinite, no created being can ever experience a similar perfection. A second type of biblical perfection is the *Edenic,* or *paradisiacal* perfection of Adam and Eve before they sinned. A third type of perfection is the "perfection of the paradise of love" or *evangelical* perfection. The fourth type of perfection is *resurrection* perfection, that of "paradise above." Man stands midway between *Edenic* perfection and *resurrection* perfection, in the experience of *evangelical* perfection. Steele describes man's stance in holiness as follows:

> As we stand midway between the perfect estate of paradise lost and of paradise regained, regretting the one and aspiring to the other, but excluded so long as we are in the flesh, our gracious God, through the mediation of Christ, commissions the Holy Ghost to come down and open the gates of a new paradise of love made perfect, love casting out all fear, love fully shed abroad in our hearts.[45]

The act of entire sanctification is not an act of magic by which man is transported out of his existential situation. But entire sanctification is a divine act which affords power and purity to constantly grow toward the full-orbed perfection following the resurrection. There is a difference between Christian perfection and resurrection perfection.

D. It Is Not the Perfection of Christ.

Christ was unique. He was "the Word . . . made flesh" (John 1:1-14). He was truly human—in fact He was the only *truly* human being since Adam prior to his fall. But there was a difference. His humanity was separate from any act and any memory of sin. He was human, but primarily He was divine. The divine always superintended the human. He was *God* in human form. The sanctified person is "in Christ," which is a state of mystical union with Him. But no human being can ever truly imitate Christ any more than he could imitate God. The sanctified should possess "the spirit of Christ" and manifest the "love of Christ." But beyond this he cannot go. Evangelical perfection is not the perfection of Christ.

E. It Is Not Freedom from Ignorance and Error.

Wesley was clear at the point of the possibility of ignorance

[44] *Milestone Papers,* pp. 27-35.
[45] *Ibid.,* p. 31.

and mistakes in the sanctified life. The following lines from the *Plain Account* refer to the possibility of ignorance and mistakes in the sanctified life:

> Q. Do you affirm, that this perfection excludes all infirmities, ignorance, and mistake?
>
> A. I continually affirm quite the contrary, and have always done so.
>
> Q. But how can every thought, word, and work, be governed by pure love, and the man be subject at the same time to ignorance and mistake?
>
> A. I see no contradiction here: A man may be filled with pure love and still liable to mistake. Indeed, I do not expect to be freed from actual mistakes, till this mortal puts on immortality.[46]

Wesley added that "a mistake in judgment may possibly occasion a mistake in practice."[47] As far as the number of mistakes possible, Wesley declared that "a thousand such instances there may be, even in those who are in the highest state of grace. Yet, where every word and action springs from love, such a mistake is not properly a sin."[48] A summary of the judgment of all Wesley's followers was given at Bristol in August, 1758. It was expressed in these words:

> 1. Every one may mistake as long as he lives.
> 2. A mistake in opinion may occasion a mistake in practice.
> 3. Every such mistake is a transgression of the perfect law.
> 4. Every such mistake, were it not for the blood of the atonement, would expose to eternal damnation.
> 5. It follows, that the most perfect have continual need of the merits of Christ . . . and may say for themselves, as well as for their brethren, "Forgive us our trespasses."[49]

Thus the life of holiness should not engender pride, for the multiplied mistakes of judgment and practice result in a constant need for a Mediator, who gives and sustains spiritual life.

F. It Does Not Free from Infirmities.

Wesley refused to call known sins by the label of infirmities. To those who gave that "soft title to known sins" Wesley gave the

[46] *Works*, XI, 394.
[47] *Ibid.*
[48] *Ibid.*, p. 395.
[49] *Ibid.*

following stern admonition: "It is plain that all you who thus speak, if ye repent not, shall, with your infirmities, go quick into hell!"[50] But Wesley was as quick to point out that not only bodily infirmities, "but all those inward and outward imperfections which are not of a moral nature,"[51] were possible in a life of holiness. Holiness does not eliminate such infirmities as slowness or weakness of understanding, dullness of perception, illogical and confused reasoning, erratic imagination or daydreaming, nor absentmindedness. "These are the infirmities which are found in the best of men, in a larger or smaller proportion. And from these none can hope to be perfectly freed, till the spirit returns to God that gave it."[52] Since infirmities are due to nonethical and non-volitional states or actions, they are present, often painfully so, in the state of holiness.

J. A. Wood wrote that "many who reject the doctrine of Christian perfection confound infirmities and sins. Infirmities may entail regret and humiliation, but not guilt. Sin always produces guilt."[53] Daniel Steele makes a clear distinction between sins and infirmities in his *Milestone Papers*, as follows:

1. Infirmities are failures to keep the *law of perfect* obedience, given to Adam in Eden. This law no man on earth can keep, since sin has impaired the powers of universal humanity. Sins are offenses against the law of love, the law of Christ. . . .
2. Infirmities are an *involuntary* outflow from our imperfect moral organization. Sin is always *voluntary.*
3. Infirmities have their ground in our *physical* nature, and they are aggravated by *intellectual* deficiencies. But sin roots itself in our *moral* nature, springing either from the habitual corruption of our hearts, or from the unresisting perversion of our tempers.
4. Infirmities entail *regret* and *humiliation.* Sin always produces *guilt.*
5. Infirmities in well-instructed souls do not interrupt *communion* with God. Sin cuts the telegraphic communication with heaven.
6. Infirmities, hidden from ourselves, (Psa. xix, 12) are covered by the blood of Christ without a definite act of faith, in the case of the soul vitally united with him . . . Sins demand a *spe-*

[50] *Ibid.,* VI, 4.
[51] *Ibid.,* pp. 4-5.
[52] *Ibid.,* p. 5.
[53] *Perfect Love* (North Attleboro, Mass.: J. A. Wood, Publisher, 1886), p. 66.

cial resort to the blood of sprinkling and an act of reliance on Christ.

7. Infirmities are *without remedy* so long as we are in the body. Sins, by the keeping power of Christ, are avoidable through every hour of our regenerate life.
8. A thousand infirmities are consistent with perfect love, but not one sin.[54]

A person may have many infirmities, and yet be motivated by perfect love. While both infirmites and sins need the atonement, yet only sin in the voluntary or self-aware sense brings guilt and separation from God.

G. It Does Not Change the Personality nor Remove Personality Flaws.

The term "personality," as used here, simply means selfhood. The coming of the Holy Spirit brings about a *revolution* in the personality, but it does not change the basic structure of personality nor does it remove personality flaws and deficiencies.

1. *Sanctification and Personality Structure*

Sanctification refines and purifies the personality, but it does not endow a person with a different temperament. If a person is quiet and reticent before sanctification, he will be the same afterwards—but it will be a purified quietness and reticence. If a person is extroversive and aggressive prior to sanctification, he will retain these qualities. But now these qualities are purified and sensitized by perfect love. If one person tends to be pessimistic and another optimistic before the experience, these tendencies carry over in the sanctified life. Thus the personality expressions of quietness, timidity, boldness, inferiority feelings, aggressiveness, gregariousness, nervousness about public appearances, in fact, all these nonethical and non-spiritual aspects of personality remain in the person. But whatever the personality structure, it is purified so that desirable qualities are purified and are expressed under the motivation of love. Undesirable personality qualities such as stage fright or inferiority feelings are not the result of sin in personal living, and are not eliminated in the act of entire sanctification. But the Holy Spirit does give power, courage, and motivation to overcome unattractive

[54]Pp. 44-47.

or undesirable personality qualities which are not related to sin and guilt.

2. *Sanctification and Personality Crudities*

Even as the act of entire sanctification does not change the basic personality structure, so it does not remove the crudities of personality. The crude and unpolished aspects of personality are the result of environmental and educational factors, or the absence of them. There is no moral or spiritual significance involved when a person uses a double negative when speaking, or when one slurps his soup when eating, or when he applauds at an inappropriate time during a musical concert. As Wesley wrote, perfection does not exclude "slowness of speech, impropriety of language, ungracefulness of pronunciation; to which one might add a thousand nameless defects, either in conversation or behavior."[55]

3. *Sanctification and Personality Development*

While the experience of holiness does not automatically eliminate personality flaws and instantly impart a knowledge of etiquette and of the social graces, it will be the springboard for such development. For the Holy Spirit is most gentle, sensitive, and considerate in all His actions and influences. So crude, inconsiderate, harsh holiness is a contradiction. A Spirit-filled person will anticipate in spontaneous action what he may later learn through formal processes. As Harry Jessop has stated, "A sanctified man, whatever his restrictions, is never a boor. There is no refining influence like the indwelling of the Holy Spirit."[56] Holiness thus should lead to refinement and courtesy.

H. It Does Not Exempt One from Temptation.

Temptation is possible in the highest state of grace. Jesus was sinless, yet He was assailed by temptation at the beginning of His ministry (Matt. 4:1-11; Luke 4:1-13).

1. *Temptation a Persistent Possibility*

Because man's temporal existence is a state of probation, temptation is always a possibility. In fact, in some ways the sanctified person may have more temptations than the unsanctified. Dr. R. T. Williams pointed this out when he said:

[55] *Works*, VI, 5.
[56] *Op. cit.*, p. 65.

> The sanctified person has a great advantage over the unsanctified in the matter of temptation. Not in the number of temptations, as it is possible that Satan will try harder to break down a sanctified life; and too, the sanctified person is opposed and persecuted more by the people, even in some cases apparently good people, than the unsanctified person is.[57]

However, because of the residence of the Holy Spirit, the sanctified man battles only the enemy without and the weaknesses of the flesh, not the alien enemy within, the carnal mind.

2. *Difference Between Temptation and Sin*

It is important to distinguish between sin and temptation. In regard to the difference between temptation and sin, J. A. Wood writes:

> No temptation or evil suggestion to the mind becomes sin till it is cherished or tolerated. Sin consists in yielding to temptation. So long as the soul maintains its integrity so that temptation finds no *sympathy* within, no sin is committed and the soul remains unharmed, no matter how protracted or severe the fiery trial may prove.[58]

R. S. Foster states that temptation is both possible and probable in the life of holiness. Yet such temptation is not sin. For "sin begins whenever the temptation begins to find inward sympathy . . . So long as it is promptly, and with the full and hearty concurrence of the soul, repelled, there is no indication of inward sympathy; there is no sin."[59] Temptation cannot be eliminated, but freedom from sin can be a contemporary experience.

In the area of sin and temptation as related to the life of holiness it is also important to differentiate between certain states of the mind. In this area Thomas Cook remarked:

> It may seem difficult to some to ascertain whether certain states of mind are the result of temptation, or the uprisings of evil in their own nature. . . . An evil thought springs from evil existing in the heart, but a thought about evil is a suggestion flashed upon the mind by what we see or hear, or by the law of association, or by the enemy of souls. Those who are holy and have no evil within, consequently, no evil thoughts; but intruding thoughts and whispers of evil will often need to be resisted. These are an unchangeable condition of probation.[60]

[57]*Temptation: A Neglected Theme* (Kansas City: Nazarene Publishing House, 1920), p. 78.

[58]*Perfect Love*, p. 63.

[59]*Christian Purity* (New York: Hunt and Eaton, 1869), p. 55.

[60]*Op. cit.*, p. 18.

Harry Jessop summarizes the difference between temptation and sin as follows:

> Temptation comes unsolicited and undesired, while sin must have the consent of the will.
>
> Temptation comes with divine permission, but sin brings divine condemnation.
>
> Temptation may have definite beneficial results, but sin is always injurious.[61]

Both from the standpoint of the Scriptures and of practical experience, it is evident that the act of entire sanctification does not *isolate* a person from temptation. The power of God can *insulate* a person from the power of temptation. The person living a life of holiness is less prone to yield to temptation, and *may* have Spirit-generated security to overcome temptation.

I. Sanctification Does Not Remove All Doubts.

The songwriter penned an inspirational line when he said: "All my doubts and fears are gone forever." But it is not realistic. For doubts and fears arise from many sources. It can be safely said that the *majority* of doubts come from sin and unbelief. These doubts assuredly are eliminated in the experience of holiness. But there are doubts that come from honest intellectual struggle. Such doubts are solved by rational understanding as well as by personal affirmation. Other doubts overtake a person as a result of a shocking emergency involving suffering or death. Many people, like Job, are thrown into a confused state by the sudden, overwhelming course of events. Still other doubts are generated by the apparent insincerity or faithlessness on the part of those who are regarded as leaders or examples of Christian piety in the church.

Doubts, like temptation, may *lead* to sin. But doubts, apart from those initiated by sin, may be very real in the sanctified life. However, the sanctified person has a firmer faith, a more dynamic experience, and a more stable experience, so that doubts do not persist. Doubts tend to paralyze spiritual response. Doubts rob one of joy and peace. Thus, while doubts are possible in the life of holiness, they must be overcome. This overcoming power is possible, for God's will is that His people live in a state of grace which is not a perpetual question mark, but a grand affirmation.

[61]*Op. cit.*, p. 123.

J. Holiness Is Not a State of Constant Joy and Ecstasy.

It is neither desirable nor possible to live in a constant state of emotional exhilaration. It would be inconsistent with holiness to rejoice at the death of a friend or to express ecstatic feelings at the scene of a grinding automobile accident. An airplane pilot landing a crowded passenger plane needs to devote all his attention to the process of landing. A surgeon performing a delicate operation on the eye or the brain had better not have a "shouting spell" during the surgery. Jesus was a "man of sorrows" and was "acquainted with grief."

Wesley constantly pointed out that perfect love, or holiness, was more than enjoyable emotional reaction. To Thomas Olivers he wrote: "Barely to feel no sin, or to feel constant peace, joy, and love, will not prove the point."[62] To a Mrs. Bennis he expressed a similar opinion: "A will steadily and uniformly devoted to God is essential to a state of sanctification, but not an uniformity of joy or peace or happy communion with God."[63] In expressing sympathy with a Mrs. Barton, who had lost a child, Wesley again wrote: "Rapturous joy, such as is frequently given in the beginning of justification or of entire sanctification, is a great blessing; but it seldom continues long before it subsides into calm, peaceful love."[64] To be sure, the life of holiness is a life of "righteousness, and peace, and joy in the Holy Ghost" (Rom. 14:17); certainly the fruit of the Spirit is "love, joy, peace" (Gal. 3:22). But to equate this constant undercurrent of joy and peace with a continual feeling of hilarity and ecstasy is misleading.

K. Holiness Does Not Make It Impossible to Backslide or to Sin.

Holiness does not make a person impeccable. Only Christ was impeccable. All other beings in man's history have been liable to temptation and to sin. Holiness makes it less likely that a person will backslide or commit apostasy. Holiness is the great conservator, the effective preservative. But there is no guaranteed security in this life against the possibility of sinning. Regarding the possibility of lapsing into sin, W. T. Purkiser writes: "No person, no power, no *thing* can separate a soul from God. But sin is not a person, power, or thing. It

[62] *Letters*, III, 212.
[63] *Ibid.*, p. 213.
[64] *Ibid.*, II, 226.

is a choice, an act of the will, an attitude of the soul. Sin can and will separate the sinning soul from the grace of God."[65] A person *may* fall from grace and break fellowship and relationship with God. But he *need not* fall, as Jude's prayer indicates:

> *Now unto him that is able to keep you from falling, and to present you faultless before the presence of his glory with exceeding joy, to the only wise God our Saviour, be glory and majesty, dominion and power, both now and ever. Amen* (Jude 24-25).

L. Sanctification Does Not Bestow a Mature Personality.

Entire sanctification is an *act,* which results in a *state,* holiness. The *quality* of holiness is something which does not change, although the *quantity* of holiness constantly increases. To illustrate, the health of a baby enjoying sound physical development would not differ in quality from the health of a 25-year-old man. Both could enjoy perfect health. But the quantity, growth, or strength in the case of the man would be vastly superior to that of the baby. To state it another way, purity should not be confused with *maturity. Purity* is the result of an act of the Holy Spirit. *Maturity* is the result of growth in grace.

To confuse purity and maturity is to confound the whole concept of instantaneous sanctification. In his classic, *Purity and Maturity,* J. A. Wood observes: "Identifying and confounding *maturity* with *purity,* lies at the base of nearly every objection we have seen to instantaneous sanctification."[66] The act of sanctification is not the terminus of a journey, but is the gateway to a highway which offers unlimited possibilites of exploration. J. Paul Taylor has stated that "this experience, though very precious, is not graduation, but rather matriculation in the school of higher learning in the kingdom of God, where heavenly wisdom is learned progressively by those who are perfect in love."[67] Jessop distinguishes between purity and maturity as follows:

> Purity is the entrance into Canaan—maturity is the possession of the land.
>
> Purity is received—maturity is acquired.
>
> Purity is the work of a moment—maturity is the harvest of years.
>
> Purity is always received by faith—maturity is often reached through pain.

[65] *Conflicting Concepts of Holiness,* p. 91.
[66] P. 188.
[67] *Op. cit.,* p. 180.

> Purity has to do with quality—maturity has to do with quantity.
>
> Purity fits the soul for heaven—maturity acquires material for reward.
>
> Purity brings fellowship—maturity develops experience.[68]

Purity and *maturity* are distinct and separate states of spiritual experience. A giggling, gangling teen-ager might be pure in heart, but far from mature in judgment. It is always safe to present the biblical standard of personal purity. It is never safe to insist on any particular level of maturity for all people. Purity is the result of cleansing, while maturity is the result of growth. J. Paul Taylor distinguishes between cleansing and growth, purity and maturity, as follows:

> Cleansing is the subtraction of evil; growth is the addition and multiplication of grace.
>
> Cleansing has to do with quality; growth has to do with quantity.
>
> Cleansing is negative, reducing sin to zero; growth in love is positive.
>
> Cleansing is instantaneous; growth is endless cultivation.
>
> Cleansing is health; growth is the development of the healthy organism.
>
> Cleansing is a finished work; growth is never finished.
>
> Cleansing is by faith; growth is by faith and works.
>
> Cleansing is an act of God; growth results from many acts, human and divine, as we become workers together with God.
>
> Cleansing removes "every weight and the sin which doth so easily beset us"; growth is running the endless race that is set before us.
>
> Cleansing is preparation for heaven; growth provides the capacity for the enjoyment of heaven.[69]

Sanctification does not end spiritual growth. It prepares the soul for the greatest possible growth. Because the carnal opposites of the spiritual graces are removed, because the disease of the soul is cured, because sin has been removed, the soul is now in condition to develop.

M. Sanctification Does Not Make It Impossible to Be Offended.

Some have erroneously taught that this experience produces a kind of calloused condition where it is impossible to be offended,

[68] *Op. cit.*, p. 134.
[69] *Op. cit.*, pp. 180-81.

hurt, wounded, or insulted. The state of holiness, or perfect love, does remove hypersensitive concern for status or recognition. But it does not remove the normal, human sense of justice. Nor does it eliminate natural human sensitivity to fair play. A sanctified person reacts to dictatorial procedures and desires democratic policies. A sanctified person dislikes being exploited as much as does any other self-respecting person.

The difference is in the reaction and in the response. A person in a state of holiness is actually a potential victim of unfairness, exploitation, and dictatorial procedures for the simple reason that he has no weapon with which to oppose such actions, except love and fairness. So often the heart filled with love must bear slights, accept unfairness, face up to being manipulated. The state of holiness does not immunize a person from any normal human sensitivity of soul or spirit.

N. Holiness Does Not Give Perfect Intellectual Powers.

A perfect heart is entirely different from a perfect mind. Because a person has an imperfect mind after he is sanctified he may:

1. Have wandering thoughts while reading the Bible or praying, or while attending church.

2. State something as a fact which is not true. He may *think* it is true, or be convinced that it is right, when in reality it is not factually true or existentially right. But if the *intention* is to be truthful or honest, then no sin has occurred.

3. May have a passing or temporary thought of evil.

4. May misinterpret biblical truth.

On the other side of the intellectual ledger, a person who is in a state of perfect love is not granted automatic knowledge. Thus the sanctified person will, or may:

1. Be forced to study diligently to acquire technical skill or theoretical knowledge.

2. May forget much that he has learned.

3. May have times of "mental lapses," when, under pressure, he is not able to use or to remember things he does know.

What a boon it would be to receive perfect intellectual powers in the experience of holiness. But wait. Soon people would seek the experience to attain the intellectual powers it conveyed. Then pride of intellect would follow, and holiness would be destroyed. So perfect love must stand alone.

O. Holiness Does Not Dehumanize a Person.

All the normal aspects of human experience are present in the experience of holiness. The difference is, these natural human impulses or responses are purified, disciplined, and expressed within the framework of God's law and God's love. Some of the dominant human impulses, along with their relation to perfect love, are listed below.

1. *Desire for Success*

A holy person can desire to succeed. And it is difficult to distinguish between the valid desire for success and the carnal desire for advancement. A person may even camouflage a desire for success beneath institutional concern or under pious professions. A person may promote self-interest under the guise of cooperation and concern. Such actions are carnal. However, there is a valid desire for success that is in harmony with holiness.

2. *Hunger for Fellowship and Acceptance*

Holiness does not make a person a recluse. Nor does it produce an antisocial attitude. The desire for acceptance and for fellowship is often intensified in the sanctified love. But the sanctified person builds friendships and sustains personal relationships on the basis of biblical principles.

3. *Sex Appreciation and Expression*

The sanctified person does not share the sex obsession of the twentieth century. Neither does he mask his sex impulses behind the prudish veneer of the eighteenth century. The sanctified person rejects current barnyard concepts of sexual morality. But he does not adopt the sex habits of the monastery. Holiness accepts sex as a valid aspect of healthy personality. Holiness theology does not apologize for sex nor does it glamorize it.

In the life of holiness, sex can find its highest and healthiest expression. Only perfect love in the heart can perfect love between man and woman. Paul said, "Unto the pure all things are pure" (Titus 1:15). Holiness takes sex from the gutter, adorns it with the blossoms of God's love, and uses it as a means of procreation, of personal self-expression, and of interpersonal appreciation and evaluation within the institution of marriage.

It might be suggested that, while holiness removes rather than creates sexual inhibitions of the harmful kind, it always places sex impulses in the framework of discipline as well as of love. To express sentiment, emotion, or passion apart from discipline is contrary to holiness. Sex is thus restricted to the marital state. For the unmarried, instruction in the place of sex in life may be helpful. But the unmarried, sanctified person is called upon to exert strict discipline upon his discussion of sex, upon his thoughts of sex, and his expressions of sex. A person cannot indulge in heavy petting involving close physical contact without building tensions that eliminate spiritual life. Further, there can be no "pawing and clawing," no indiscriminate caressing of the anatomy, in the unmarried state. And certainly anyone who engages in sexual intercourse outside the marriage relationship has not only lost all vital holiness; this person is unregenerate and backslidden.

4. *Appreciation for and Acquisition of the Finer Things of Life*

A person need not take the vow of poverty when he is sanctified. There is no virtue in poverty, although there are some dangers in wealth, such as pride and rebellion. But, as Wesley found, sanctified people are apt to work harder, to waste less, to be more frugal, than those who are not. Thus they are able to acquire more goods. This acquisition of goods often leads to an appreciation of the finer things, both materially and aesthetically. A person may be sanctified and learn to appreciate fine music, delicate art, skilled workmanship, and comfortable surroundings. The key to holy living is not sacrifice; it is obedience and stewardship. And a person can obey God and express a consistent stewardship regardless of how little, or how much, he has. In fact, the experience of holiness is the key to a life of obedience and of Christian stewardship.

5. *Recreation and Humor*

Holiness does not lessen the emotional and physical need for times of relaxation and recreation. Nor does perfect love cast out humor. Man needs to unbend occasionally, to loosen the strands of tension, to "become a boy again" in free, uninhibited play. Man also needs to appreciate the humor of a situation. A good laugh is good for the digestion, and is often good for the soul. Man can take himself too seriously. Some holiness people resemble a torpedo—grim, relentless, and unswerving. However, a religious torpedo usually ends at the same destination as a military torpedo—an explosion. Sour-faced, gloomy-visaged, frowning holiness is a poor testimony to the inner presence of perfect love. Holiness is dynamic within and radiant without.

Recreation, for the sanctified person, should always be within the boundaries of biblical teachings, within the framework of the church's standards, and within the scope of individual good taste. Humor, for the person in a state of holiness, should always be gentle and inoffensive, clean and non-suggestive, respectful and without recrimination.

P. Holiness Does Not Exempt from Suffering and Death.

The person who witnesses to the experience of heart holiness is not exempt from suffering associated with the disintegration of the mind and body. Normally, a person in a state of holiness will have fewer tensions than the person indulging in sin or the person not living in a state of redemptive deliverance. As a rule the sanctified person will have better health for the simple reason that he abuses his body less and observes the principles of health better.

But man's mind and body are mortal. Thus the mind may lose its balance, the nerves may rebel, and the body may succumb to a disease. So a person in a state of holiness may have a brain tumor, suffer a nervous breakdown, or die a painful, lingering death. Holiness does not produce an elite class of saints who manifest their heavenly citizenship by a display of perpetual youthfulness. Holiness does produce saints who can calmly and realistically face the onslaught of disease and death with a display of divinely imparted grace and glory.

Summary

Such is the paradox of imperfect perfection. The treasury of grace is deposited in earthen vessels. The inner state of perfection may not always find expression in an outer performance of perfection. But the life of holiness can, and should, result in that spiritual perfection which consists of purified intention and maturation. While holiness will always be a kind of imperfect perfection, this is not where the situation must rest. For the experience of holiness does achieve a radical change in the spiritual life.

CHAPTER XIII /

Toward the Stature of Christ

The goal of the Christian is Christlikeness. The Christlikeness called for in the life of holiness is not some sentimental imitation of Christ, nor is it a lifelong groping for some abstract concept of the historical Jesus. The Christlikeness demanded in the profession of holiness is a vital life resulting from the indwelling power and presence of the Holy Spirit.

The life of holiness continues as a process of spiritual growth throughout earthly existence and beyond. There is always "much land ahead to be possessed." This chapter discusses the total process of sanctification, which includes the following: (1) The antecedents of entire sanctification; (2) The crisis of entire sanctification; (3) The results of entire sanctification; (4) Growth in grace.

I. The Antecedents of Entire Sanctification

The term *sanctification* comes from the Latin verb *to make (facio)* and the word *holy (sanctus)*. Thus sanctification, used as a verb, means "to make holy." In this sense it involves all the work of God in human life. According to Harald Lindstrom, Wesley places as much emphasis on development as on crisis, for he writes:

> The idea of a gradual development is a most prominent element in his conception of salvation, and indeed in his thought generally. What happens is that these two elements, the instantaneous and the gradual, are merged, and the order of salvation peculiar to Wesley is the outcome of this mergence. Salvation is seen as a process by which man passes through a series of successive stages, each stage representing a different and higher level.[1]

In his sermon entitled "The Scripture Way of Salvation," appearing in 1765, Wesley stated that the following factors are included in the process of salvation: (1) The presence of prevenient grace; (2) Repentance; (3) Justification or forgiveness by faith; (4) The new birth, or regeneration; (5) A "repentance" following justification; (6) Entire sanctification. The first five aspects of salvation are discussed immediately below, while the sixth is treated briefly in a later section of this chapter.

A. Prevenient Grace

In the broadest sense, the total process of sanctification, or making man holy, is initiated by the operating of prevenient grace in man. Prevenient grace consists of "all the drawings of the Father; the desires after God, which, if we yield to them, increase more and more; all that light wherewith the Son of God 'enlighteneth every one that cometh into the world' . . . all the convictions which his Spirit, from time to time, works in every child of man."[2] In another sermon called "Working Out Our Salvation," Wesley refers to prevenient grace as follows:

> Salvation begins with what is usually termed (and very properly) *preventing grace;* including the first wish to please God, the first dawn of light concerning his will, and the first slight transient conviction of having sinned against him. All these imply some tendency toward life; some degree of salvation; the beginning of a deliverance from a blind unfeeling heart, quite insensible of God and the things of God.[3]

Thus prevenient grace is that grace which "goes before" and prepares the soul for entrance into the initial state of salvation. Wiley defines it as follows: "It is the preparatory grace of the Holy

[1] *Op. cit.,* p. 105.
[2] Wesley, *Works,* VI, 44.
[3] *Ibid.,* p. 509.

Spirit exercised toward man helpless in sin. . . . It may be defined as that manifestation of the divine influence which precedes the full regenerate life."[4] Prevenient grace is the first aspect of salvation in the personal life of the potential convert.

Dr. Wiley summarizes the place of prevenient grace in the process of sanctification as follows:

> 1. Everything which can be called good in man, previous to regeneration, is to be attributed to the work of the Spirit of God. Man himself is totally depraved and not capable of doing any good thing.
> 2. That the state of nature in which man exists previous to regeneration is in some sense a state of grace—preliminary or prevenient grace.
> 3. That in this preliminary period there is a continuity of grace—the Holy Spirit, beginning, advancing and perfecting everything that can be called good in man. The Spirit of God leads the sinner from one step to another, in proportion as He finds response in the heart of the sinner and a disposition of obedience.
> 4. There is a human co-operation with the divine Spirit, the Holy Spirit working with the free will of man, quickening, aiding and directing it in order to secure compliance with the conditions of the covenant by which man may be saved.
> 5. That the grace of God is given to all men in order to bring them to salvation through Jesus Christ, but that this grace so given, may be resisted by the free will of man, so as to be rendered ineffectual.[5]

Prevenient grace is given to man in sufficient degree to enable him to embrace the gospel. Wesley,[6] Watson,[7] and others have felt that the doctrine of prevenient grace is clearly contained in the words of St. Paul: "Work out your own salvation with fear and trembling. For it is God that worketh in you both to will and to do of his good pleasure" (Phil. 2:12-13).

B. Repentance

Prevenient grace is the work of God, through the Holy Spirit, in the heart. The first factor of human cooperation is what Wesley calls "convincing grace," or repentance. Repentance, according to

[4] *Christian Theology*, II, 345-46.
[5] *Ibid.*, p. 352.
[6] *Works*, VI, 506-13.
[7] *Institutes*, II, 377.

Wesley, "brings a larger measure of self-knowledge, and a farther deliverance from the heart of stone."[8]

Wesley presented two aspects of repentance—knowledge of sin and sorrow of heart. In regard to repentance being a knowledge of sin, Wesley wrote:

> Know thyself to be a sinner, and what manner of sinner thou art. Know that corruption of thy inmost nature, whereby thou art very far gone from original righteousness. . . . Know that thou art corrupted in every power, in every faculty of thy soul; that thou art totally corrupted in every one of these, all the foundations being out of course.[9]

To this self-knowledge regarding sin Wesley added the factor of sorrow. In a passage that reveals the nature of sorrow in the sinner Wesley asserted:

> If to this lively conviction of thy inward and outward sins, of thy utter guiltiness and helplessness, there be added suitable affections,—sorrow of heart, for having despised thy own mercies,—remorse, and self-condemnation, having thy mouth stopped, —shame to lift up thine eyes to heaven,—fear of the wrath of God abiding on thee, of his curse hanging over thy head, and of the fiery indignation ready to devour those who forget God and obey not our Lord Jesus Christ,—earnest desire to escape from that indignation, to cease from evil, and learn to do well;—then I say unto thee . . . "Thou art not far from the kingdom of God." One step more and thou shalt enter in. Thou dost "repent." Now, "believe the gospel."[10]

A third factor of repentance was implied in Wesley's emphasis on knowledge of sin and sorrow. This factor was the actual turning away from sin. Thus repentance differs from remorse or regret, self-pity, or human sorrow. In reference to this third element Ralph Earle writes: "Often the term repentance is used today for an emotional display of sorrow. But real repentance goes deeper than that, involving a reversal of one's inner attitude toward life, an abhorrence of his sins and a deliberate turning away from them."[11] Bryan DeMent suggests a definition of repentance which appears to catch the central idea of the word as it is used biblically. He writes:

> The words employed in the Hebrew and Greek place chief emphasis on the will, the change of the mind, or purpose, because

[8]*Works*, VI, 509.
[9]*Ibid.*, V, 82.
[10]*Ibid.*, p. 84.
[11]"Mark," *Evangelical Commentary*, p. 29.

> a complete and sincere turning to God involves both apprehension of the nature of sin and the consciousness of personal guilt (Jer. 25:5; Mk. 1:15; Acts 2:38; II Cor. 7:9-10). . . . The demand for repentance implies free will and individual responsibility.[12]

Wesleyan theology has consistently taught that repentance is a work of the Holy Spirit which precedes regeneration. Repentance leads to saving faith.

C. Saving Faith

Saving faith is the fruit of repentance. Saving faith, for Wesley, was the acceptance of the revelation of God in Christ Jesus. Wesley was quick to point out that faith is more than intellectual assent, for he stated:

> Only beware thou do not deceive thy own soul, with regard to the nature of this faith. It is not, as some have fondly conceived, a bare assent to the truth of the Bible, of the articles of our Creed, or of all that is contained in the Old and New Testament. . . . But it is, over and above this, a sure trust in the mercy of God, through Christ Jesus. It is a confidence in a pardoning God.[13]

Wiley regards faith as "the act of the entire being under the influence of the Holy Spirit."[14] To him saving faith is the highest act of personal life, "an act in which he gathers up his whole being, and in a peculiar sense goes out of himself and appropriates the merit of Christ."[15]

While saving faith is man's sure confidence and trust in God, it does not in itself merit salvation. But faith and work are related. W. B. Pope in his *Higher Catechism of Theology*, expresses the relation of faith and works as follows:

1. Faith is opposed to works as meritorious, and the formula is: *A man is not justified by works of the law, but only through faith in Christ.* Gal. 11:16
2. Faith lives only in its works, and the formula is: *Faith without works is dead.* Jas. 11:26
3. Faith is justified and approved by works and the formula is: *I will shew thee my faith by my works.* Jas. 11:8
4. Faith is perfected in works, and the formula is: *By works was faith made perfect.* Jas. 11:22.[16]

[12]"Repentance," *ERE*, IV, 2599.
[13]*Works*, V, 85.
[14]*Christian Theology*, II, 371.
[15]*Ibid.*
[16]*Op. cit., p. 233.*

Saving faith is the link between repentance and regeneration. Saving faith is a personal act in which prevenient grace becomes regenerating grace.

D. Justification and Regeneration

Justification and regeneration follow saving faith. It is now that salvation in its vital, positive aspects begins. Justification and regeneration are imparted to, or bestowed on, man in a single instant.

Justification is a relative change, dealing with man's standing before God. Justification refers to the pardoning act of God in which a repentant person is freed from the guilt of sin. In justification a new relationship is established, in which man enjoys the favor of God instead of being an object of his wrath. Justification removes condemnation and brings peace. "Therefore being justified by faith, we have peace with God through our Lord Jesus Christ" (Rom. 5:1). According to Wesley, "The plain, scriptural notion of justification is pardon, the forgiveness of sins."[17] Justification, then, refers to man's status before God. As such it is objective and "forensic," belonging to law and legal procedure.

Regeneration is the impartation of spiritual life to the pardoned, believing, repentant person. Wesley distinguishes between justification and regeneration as follows: "The former relating to that great work which God does *for us,* in forgiving our sins; the latter, to the great work which God does *in us,* in renewing our fallen nature."[18] Wesley has been criticized for minimizing the importance of regeneration. However, Wesley considered regeneration to be a fundamental aspect of the Christian life, for he said: "If any doctrines within the whole compass of Christianity may be properly termed fundamental, they are doubtless these two,—the doctrine of justification, and that of the new birth."[19]

Regeneration involves a subjective operation, or work, of the Holy Spirit in man. In this inward change man is given the gift of "eternal life" and is freed from the power of sin. As has been indicated earlier, Wesley called this inward change *initial sanctification* as well as regeneration. Initial sanctification is a state of spiritual life leading to *entire sanctification.*

[17] *Works,* V, 57.
[18] *Ibid.,* VI, 65.
[19] *Ibid.*

II. Entire Sanctification

In summary it may be said that entire sanctification is a climactic part of the total process of becoming holy. Technically, there are three great crises of the process of becoming holy: regeneration, entire sanctification, and glorification. In discussing entire sanctification as a crisis in the total process of becoming holy the following ideas are discussed: (1) the differences between regeneration and entire sanctification; (2) the time element between the two experiences; (3) the crisis of entire sanctification.

A. Differences Between Regeneration and Entire Sanctification

Wesleyan theology has never accepted two categories of Christian living with some being spiritual and others being "more spiritual." To the Wesleyan the ideal and the life of holiness, or the "stature of Christ," have always been the New Testament norm for the Christian. However, Wesleyans have accepted stages of development in the Christian life. Thus it is possible, on biblical grounds as well as on experiential grounds, to state some differences between regeneration and sanctification. These differences are listed below:

1. In regeneration men are saved from sinning, and forgiven every past sin, brought back to the innocency of childhood, and are made new creatures in Christ (II Cor. 5:17; I John 3:7-9); in entire sanctification the positive carnal opposite of each gift and grace of the Spirit is cleansed. This carnal disease is a moral entity, not a physical something. In regeneration the "spiritual Isaac" enters, and in entire sanctification the "carnal Ishmael" is cast out.

2. Justification deals with sin as an act; sanctification deals with sin as a principle.

3. In justification one surrenders in repentance and faith; in entire sanctification one consecrates in obedience and faith.

4. In justification a spiritual nature is imparted; in entire sanctification the carnal nature is destroyed.

5. In justification the "shoots" of sin are destroyed; in entire sanctification the root itself is destroyed.

6. In justification one becomes a branch in the Vine; in entire sanctification the branch is purged to bring forth more fruit (John 15:1-2).

7. In justification one is separated from the world; in entire sanctification "the world" is taken out of the believer—Israel was taken out of Egypt; then Egypt was taken out of them.

8. In justification the "old man" must be suppressed; in entire sanctification the "old man" is destroyed (Rom. 6:6).

9. In justification the Spirit is with the believer; in entire sanctification He is within the believer in His fullness (John 14:17).

10. In justification one becomes a child of God; in entire sanctification the believers are made kings and priests unto God.

11. In justification men are born of the Spirit; in entire sanctification they are baptized with the Spirit (Matt. 3:11).

12. In justification man is restored to the favor of God; in entire sanctification man is restored to the moral image of God.

B. Time Between Regeneration and Sanctification

God, presumably, could save and sanctify a person in one work. However, man is a free moral agent and he cannot be in two places at once, or meet different conditions at one and the same time. Man himself, therefore, necessitates a time element between regeneration and entire sanctification.

1. The length of time is not set by the Bible, but by man himself. Some have more light and some take longer to grasp new truth. Some regenerated people progress easily and naturally into a deeper work. For others the struggle is long and agonizing.

2. The Israelites could have made the journey from the Red Sea to the Promised Land in 11 days. Fear necessitated two years. Disobedience stretched the time to 40 years. The time span between regeneration and entire sanctification depends upon individual response to the call of the Holy Spirit.

3. In the Old Testament the leper was first sprinkled and then re-sprinkled eight days later and declared fully cleansed. Ceremonialism necessitated this eight-day period. However, in the New Testament the cleansing work of the Holy Spirit was not controlled by ceremonialism. Man can be cleansed when he accepts God's power.

4. The disciples of Jesus took from one and one-half to three years to understand and grasp the truth. The delay in the lives of the disciples was probably due to a misunderstanding of the meaning of personal salvation.

5. In Peter's thinking, after Pentecost, the time could be brief (Acts 8:5-8, 14-17). Philip had gone to Samaria and had helped to bring about a revival there. Shortly after the news of the revival

reached Jerusalem, Peter visited Samaria. His first concern was that the people would receive the Holy Spirit.

6. The Jerusalem church thought the time could be short (Acts 15:8-9).

7. Ananias thought Paul could be sanctified at once (Acts 9: 17-19).

8. Paul urged the Thessalonians to become sanctified inside of six months after they were saved (I Thess. 4:3; 5:23-24).

C. The Crisis of Entire Sanctification

Entire sanctification is a crisis experience in man's spiritual pilgrimage. As such it is distinct and is subsequent to regeneration. Since entire sanctification is distinct and separate from regeneration, there are some clearly marked differences between these two landmarks of Christian experience. Entire sanctification is not a mechanical ritual, but is a vital experience. Because it is a vital experience it cannot be reduced to a series of formal steps or activities. Yet there are some general and some detailed directives that may be given, pointing the seeking soul to a practical method of receiving the experience and a workable method of retaining it.

Personal Christian holiness, theoretically and experimentally, is no greater mystery than regeneration. God has not reserved this experience for a select group of elite Christians. The provisions and the possibilities of grace in regard to sanctification are *understandable* to all, *adapted* to all, *needed* by all, and *available* to all. J. A. Wood discussed the conditions and directions to the experience of entire sanctification under general and specific directives. Under general directives are the following:

> Endeavor to obtain a correct and distinct view of the blessing needed. . . .
>
> Come to a firm and decided resolution to seek until you obtain a pure heart. . . .
>
> Humble yourself under the hand of the Almighty. . . .
>
> Make an *entire consecration* of yourself to God—your soul, body, time, talents, influence and *your all*—a complete assignment of *all* to Christ.[20]

In addition to the general directives, the following specific suggestions are presented by Wood:

1. Believe that God has promised it in the Holy Scriptures.

[20] *Perfect Love*, pp. 96-97.

2. Believe what God hath pro
3. Believe that he is able and
4. Believe that he doth it.

If you are earnestly seeking holines
thoroughly by the following interroga

1. Do I see clearly my inbred sin, and co ness?
2. Am I willing, anxious, and resolved to ob
3. Am I willing to give up all to God—self, family, tation, time, talents, everything—to be his, used ed with him, and never withheld or taken from h
4. Do I believe he is able to sanctify me?
5. Do I believe he is willing to sanctify me?
6. Do I believe he has promised to sanctify me?
7. Do I believe that having promised, he is able and willing do it now, on condition of my faith?
8. Do I then, seeing all this, believe that he now will do it—now, this moment?
9. Am I now committing all, and trusting in Christ? If you are, it is done. O that God may aid your trembling faith, and give you purity this moment![21]

III. The Results of Sanctification

The results of the crisis of entire sanctification may be stated in general categories rather than in specific details. Holiness is imparted to man by God. But the impartation of holiness to man by the presence of the Holy Spirit is the result of the harmony of divine grace and human volition. God does not violate human personality either in the offer of holiness or in the impartation of holiness. Thus divine holiness in man is always qualified by certain personal variables in man. Such matters as age, emotional temperament, social environment, education, intellectual capacity, spiritual sensitivity, and the degree of spiritual light all shape the expression of holiness in human personality.

However, despite the variables of human nature, there are some results of entire sanctification that are essential and common to all who experience the fullness of the Holy Spirit. Holiness may, on occasion, find higher expression in some than in others. But the essential results of holiness are at least three in number: (1) the integration of personality; (2) purification of the heart (character);

[21] *Ibid.*, p. 98.

nination of the spiritual perception. Such a division is ad-
ly arbitrary. Yet such a division also makes it possible to
nt a practical discussion of the results of entire sanctification.

Integration of Personality

Personality, as used here, simply refers to individual selfhood. Selfhood is that aspect of the individual person which marks the person as a self-aware, volitional, intelligent, experiencing agent. Biblical thought has consistently regarded the person as a unity, with both material and nonmaterial aspects. Biblical teaching also has consistently presented the human personality as the battleground of opposing tendencies. The entrance of sin resulted in perpetual warfare in the human heart. Thus Cain's punishment was greater than he could bear (Gen. 4:13). Lot ruined his family by weak and selfish choices (Gen. 13:10). Esau bought a life of remorse and jealousy with a bowl of cornmeal mush (Gen. 25:29-34). Samson's mighty muscles were turned to flabbiness by passion (Judg. 16:17). Saul became a tragic suicide because of irrational and uncontrollable jealousy (I Samuel 20). Ephraim was abandoned to idols because of lust (Hos. 4:17). A nation suffered heartbreak and slavery as a result of spiritual blindness (Lam. 1:1-10). The demon-possessed man of Gadara battered his body and bruised his soul because of sin (Luke 8:26-34). Paul describes the spiritual agony of the person who recognizes the right and resolves to do it, only to be frustrated by a civil war within (Romans 7). Biblically, then, sin is presented as a destructive agency within the life of man. When sin is removed, the greatest obstacle to personal integration is removed. Personality flaws not related to sin may yet remain. But with the core of sin removed, the personal selfhood has attained a basic unity that makes possible a consistent personal development.

Among the results of entire sanctification in the area of personality integration are: (1) complete devotement to God; (2) the presence of an all-pervading love; (3) a sense of self-respect and self-worth; (4) a consistent personality which is displayed in all relationships; (5) God-given ability to remain poised and balanced in times of testing and temptation; (6) absence of inner spiritual conflicts; (7) self-acceptance; (8) selfless service. The Holy Spirit works in the human heart to bring about a unity which is expressed by the qualities listed above.

1. *Complete Devotement to God*

The ancient Shema of the Jews presented the ideal of complete surrender to God. In the Book of Deuteronomy the Shema is stated as follows: "And thou shalt love the Lord thy God with all thine heart, and with all thy soul, and with all thy might" (Deut. 6:5). Jesus repeated this command, making it the first and great commandment (Matt. 22:37; Mark 12:30; Luke 10:27). Paul echoes the thought of Moses and Christ when he states that the new life in Christ brings about the crucifixion of the former sinful self (Rom. 6:6; Gal. 2:20; 5:24; 6:14).

Complete surrender to God brings about personal unity. Through the power of the Holy Spirit the sanctified person enters into a unique relationship with God. Even a person cleansed from inner sin needs an object, ideal, or person outside himself to become the center of his living. Otherwise he would be self-centered and would slip into selfish living. But with God as the center of obedience and affection, a unity results in the individual that sustains a condition of healthy, wholesome, spiritual living which is called holiness.

2. *An All-prevailing Presence of Love*

There is sound reasoning behind the use of "perfect love" as a synonym for holiness. This love is both an affection and a principle. As an emotion it is a sense of affinity with God and with man. As an emotion love is joy mingled with confidence. As an emotion love is faith exultant and hope triumphant. As a principle, Christian love is the God-imparted desire to do whatever is possible to help all men realize the will of God for their lives. A. M. Hills describes the effects of perfect love in these words: "A vigorous faith in Jesus ought to be as tuneful as a bird, and as full of joy as a June morning. Let perfect confidence and faith in Christ for a complete salvation rise like a full-orbed sun upon the soul, and now will hope sing in exultation, and every power rejoice in the conscious love of God."[22]

The experience of holiness opens the door into the kingdom of love, as stated by the Apostle Paul: "The love of God is shed abroad in our hearts by the Holy Ghost which is given unto us" (Rom. 5:5). J. Paul Taylor quotes a statement that summarizes the place of love in the sanctified heart:

> There is no despot like love. It will brook no rival, take no denial, effect no compromise. Love cannot be brow-beaten, or

[22]A. M. Hills, *Holiness and Power* (Cincinnati, Ohio: M. W. Knapp, 1897), p. 298.

> bullied, or bribed to abandon its quest. It will wait with a patience that no opposition can wear down, no insolence discourage, no indifference turn sour. Its ingenuity is infinite, its resources inexhaustible, its endurance unending. It will spare itself no pain or tears or blood to gain its beneficent end. It will keep on pursuing the object of its desire with unfaltering foot, with unquenchable ardor, with undying hope.[23]

In I Corinthians 13, Paul presents the life of holiness as the life of love. The way of love is the "more excellent way." The sanctified person thus lives in the atmosphere of I Corinthians 13. The catalogue of graces associated with love in this chapter comprise the activity of God's love in the human heart. The great privilege of the Christian is to enter the sanctuary of love, as described in I Corinthians 13. In external expression it may appear that the sanctified Christian falls short of such a spiritual state. But it is the grand privilege as well as the great obligation of *all* Christians to enter into the courts of holy living, to live in the atmosphere of *love.* According to Paul, love may be presented in the following way:

Love showing patience under pressure is long-suffering.

Love expressed as courtesy in interpersonal relationships is kindness.

Love manifested in goodwill is the absence of envy.

Love is not ostentatious or self-exalting.

Love is not conceited and egotistical.

Love never acts out of character because of wrong motives.

Love is not self-centered and self-seeking.

Love is not roused to a spirit of anger, retaliation, or bitterness.

Love does not harbor resentment and bears no malice.

Love finds no pleasure in the sinful deeds of others.

Love finds joy in honesty and integrity.

Love endures hostility, rejection, or persecution.

Love places the best construction on the motives and actions of others.

Love manifests a spirit of ultimate optimism in spite of discouraging conditions.

Love perseveres until the end.

Love actually never ceases—it will eventually triumph.

Love is the only connecting link with eternity.

[23]*Op. cit.*, p. 168.

3. *A Sense of Self-respect and Self-worth*

Holiness is not a spirit of self-depreciation any more than it is an attitude of self-righteousness or self-exaltation. In the act of sanctification God performs the spiritual work that needs to be done. In one instance God may puncture the egotism of a self-centered, self-assertive, self-seeking Christian. Such a person needs a spiritual surgery to cut away the corruption of selfishness. In another instance God may fill the soul of a self-rejecting, self-depreciating person with divine power and elevate him to the status of self-respect and self-worth. Thus one person is brought *down* while another is raised *up*. In each case he is placed in a position of self-respect and self-worth. Because the motives are pure, because love is the springboard of action, because the intention is service to God and man, self-respect and self-worth are constant aspects of the sanctified state.

The absence of conscious guilt also contributes to the sense of self-worth and self-respect. It is impossible for a Christian to have a sense of guilt and a sense of self-respect at the same time. It is possible, through the power of divine grace, to be free from guilt, which tears the personality asunder. A person may be embarrassed or commit humiliating mistakes. But such episodes are temporary and do not carry the threat to personal unity that conscious guilt does.

4. *Consistent Personality Relationships*

One of the greatest assets to personality integration is a consistent pattern of personal relationships. A sanctified person should be able to manifest poise, balance, and evenness in his interpersonal relationships. This does not mean that a person would not yield to the excitement of the moment. Nor does it mean that a sanctified person would not make emotional pronouncements or strong assertions. Further, it does not mean the elimination of tensions where strong opinions and deep-seated convictions clash.

Holiness, however, does produce a poise and stability in personal responses and personal relationships. Where excitement occurs, where emotional affirmations are made, where tensions rise, such responses should always be contained within the framework of love. Thus there would be no residue of bitterness, antagonism, enmity, or jealousy which affects personal relationships. Since the "root of bitterness," the carnal mind, has been removed, there is the possibility of wholesome personality development, persistently expressed by spiritual poise, spiritual balance, and spiritual control.

5. *Poise and Balance in Testing and Temptation*

A spiritual test is pressure on the soul which does not involve direct sin. In the area of patience, of harassing emergencies, of uncontrollable physical events, of irritating environment, of aggravating circumstances, the indwelling Holy Spirit makes it possible to maintain calmness and to manifest the spirit of Christ. Such poise does not necessarily call for a "shouting spell" when a distressing event occurs, but spiritual balance does make possible an acceptance of the event without rancor, harshness, or uncontrolled outbursts of anger.

A spiritual temptation is a direct inducement to evil. Spiritual temptation may come from any direction. While the sanctified person is subject to all temptations, yet the automatic reaction of the sanctified person is a negative reaction to such temptation. The sanctified person will not deny the realism of temptation. Nor will he evade the weaknesses of his own person in any particular area. But the presence of the Holy Spirit enables a person to look frankly at temptation, to openly acknowledge temptation, and to gloriously overcome temptation. In the state of holiness, temptation becomes a stepping-stone to a stronger spiritual life. The Apostle Paul's words about temptation are appropriate: "There hath no temptation taken you but such as is common to man: but God is faithful, who will not suffer you to be tempted above that ye are able; but will with the temptation also make a way to escape, that ye may be able to bear it" (I Cor. 10:13). The life of holiness is a victorious life. The life of holiness is God's ultimate antidote for temptation. The life of holiness is a life of calmness, of confidence, of poise, of inner strength, of inner control and outer balance.

6. *Absence of Inner Spiritual Conflicts Due to Indwelling Sin*

There is no state of grace that will deliver completely from inner conflicts. But there is a spiritual experience that eliminates all those spiritual conflicts which rise from the presence of sin in the heart of the believer. The greatest spiritual struggles are the result of disobedience. Since surrender to the will of God is a necessary condition for sanctification, this great source of inner conflict is gone. In the sanctified, Spirit-filled life, to know the will of God is to do it. In some areas of personal leadership, God's will may not always be clear. But in the vast area of Christian conduct, ethical principles, and moral mandates, God's will is abundantly clear. In these areas the Christian has no option. He obeys because he loves. He loves because his heart is pure.

With the heart purified by faith, with the Holy Spirit as a constant source of power, the Christian can be freed from tensions produced by the guilt associated with sin. "There is therefore now no condemnation to them which are in Christ Jesus, who walk not after the flesh, but after the Spirit" (Rom. 8:1). Because there is no condemnation, and because the power of sin is broken, the life of holiness is a life of peace and contentment in the Spirit.

During His earthly ministry, Jesus had presented the invitation to rest in these words: "Come unto me, all ye that labour and are heavy laden, and I will give you rest" (Matt. 11:28). The writer of the Hebrew letter states that "there remaineth . . . a rest to the people of God" (Heb 4:9). This writer also indicates that some have entered into this rest (4:10), and he exhorts others to give attention to the importance of entering into the promised rest (4:11). Beverly Carradine describes the rest of the soul in holiness as follows:

> The soul has been stilled and remains still. The spirit of worry is gone. There is a sweet disinclination to fret. An atmosphere of calm pervades the breast and penetrates the life. . . . It certainly would be a novel experience to many Christians to begin and end the day calmly; to wake up in the morning with a sweet serenity of spirit, and to go through each day with a deep, still peace, whose steady flow delights as well as astonishes him. And yet this is the plain promise of God.[24]

God had promised that He would keep those in perfect peace who fixed their minds on Him (Isa. 26:3). This perfect peace is the rest of the spirit in the life of holiness. J. A. Wood states that peace and rest are the result of holiness, and presents an imposing list of the various phases of the rest of the soul. Among them are:

> It is a state of settled and complete satisfaction in God, He being "all in all" to the soul.
>
> It is a state of rest from the former servitude to doubts, fears, and inbred sin.
>
> It is a state of rest in which the tumult of the heart has been hushed into calmness; and fear and discord, and doubt have given place to quietness and assurance.
>
> It is a state of deep and permanent quietude and assurance in respect to all our interests, temporal and eternal.

[24]*Golden Sheaves* (Boston: J. Gill, 1901), p. 81.

> It is a state of sweet rest from all conflict between the will and the conscience.[25]

The *rest* of holiness is thus a vital and persistent force in personality integration.

The experience of holiness is the greatest force in human life toward unity, harmony, and effective personal living. Personal integration is the self unified in love to God and man. Personal integration is the result of divine action, which leads to a sense of self-worth and self-respect. Personal integration is reflected in a consistent pattern of interpersonal relationships based on love. Personal integration is the spiritual potential of facing test and temptation without sinning. Personal integration is a creative soul-rest in which natural abilities may develop without the inhibitions of guilt and condemnation. Personal integration is realistic and wholesome self-acceptance. Personal integration is unpretentious service for God and man. Personal integration is holiness in action.

7. *Sanctification and Self-acceptance*

One of the greatest threats to personality integration is self-rejection. A person may live a life of agonizing self-rejection for many reasons. Some of the reasons for personal self-rejection may be environmental or social. In such cases sanctification will not help greatly, for in these instances self-understanding and personal growth are necessary. Other types of personal self-rejection are the result of personal sin. Only a fool or a fraud can sanction himself if he is a sinner.

The sinner uses a number of ingenious personality gimmicks to make himself acceptable to himself. Such devices as denial, distortion, justification, rationalization, projection, or narcotics and alcohol, are all used to cover up his growing self-rejection. But in the act of entire sanctification a man's soul stands stripped before the ultimate words of self-analysis: "Woe is me! for I am undone; because I am a man of unclean lips, and I dwell in the midst of a people of unclean lips: for mine eyes have seen the King, the Lord of hosts" (Isa. 6:5). Such a vision of God dissolves all personal pretense.

God, however, is in the man-making business. So He does not permit a penitent soul to constantly grovel in the ashes of humiliation and self-rejection. God touched Isaiah with an incandescent

[25] *Perfect Love*, p. 128.

ray of divine glory and said: "Thine iniquity is taken away, and thy sin purged" (Isa. 6:7). God's touch made a difference, for Isaiah now felt qualified for divine service (Isa. 6:8). In subsequent experience Isaiah may have been aware of human shortcomings. But never again did he question his personal experience. Because God had accepted him, Isaiah accepted himself. God's purifying touch leads to self-acceptance. Self-acceptance results in personality integration. Personality integration produces peace, strength, and effectiveness.

8. *Sanctification and Selfless Service*

"No man can serve two masters: for either he will hate the one, and love the other; or else he will hold to the one, and despise the other. Ye cannot serve God and mammon" (Matt. 6:24). The truth of this statement of Jesus is inescapable. It applies to the tyranny of the inner carnal self as well as to domination of an outer ruler. A person cannot serve himself and Christ at the same time. One of the greatest detriments to personal unity is the civil war between selfish concern and selfless service.

In the experience of holiness the carnal self is crucified. As Paul puts it, "I am crucified with Christ: nevertheless I live; yet not I, but Christ liveth in me: and the life which I now live in the flesh I live by the faith of the Son of God, who loved me, and gave himself for me" (Gal. 2:20). With the carnal self crucified, a person can transcend himself and his limitations. Such self-transcendence is a vital aspect of personality integration. When Paul said, "For to me to live is Christ, and to die is gain" (Phil. 1:21), he expressed a vital psychological principle of inner harmony as well as a profound spiritual witness.

The life of holiness is a life of service. For holiness frees one from all the carnal opposites to spiritual growth and power. Thus sanctification, selfless service, and personal harmony are all aspects of the life of holiness.

B. The Purification of Character

There is a difference between the purification of character and the development of character. The Holy Spirit can purify the heart, the ground of character, as indicated by Peter's reference to the Pentecostal experience of the Early Church: "And God, which knoweth the hearts, bare them witness, giving them the Holy Ghost, even as he did unto us; and put no difference between us and them, purifying their hearts by faith" (Acts 15:8-9). The great achievement of the coming of the Holy Spirit is purity of heart, which gives power for service.

But God cannot and does not magically and automatically endow a person with a developed character at the time of entire sanctification. Character is developed as a person makes decisions in life situations. Character is expressed in the manifold activities of daily, routine living, where choices are made constantly. Thus God can purify the heart, or the ground of character. God can give pure motivation and pure intention. But man must utilize, apply, discriminate, and practice in order to develop holy character. The Holy Spirit, in this sense, both fills a person and subjects himself to the person. The Holy Spirit never violates man's volitional powers. The Holy Spirit stands as man's Director, Source of power, Purifier, and Sustainer. Thus man, with and by the presence of the Holy Spirit, can express holiness in character.

In the area of sanctified character the minimum standard of holy character would be: (1) a practical expression of biblical ethics; (2) careful and discriminating conversational patterns; (3) courteousy and respect for personality; (4) modesty and simplicity in personal and social appearances; (5) calm and dedicated individuality; (6) opposition to worldiness and to impurity; (7) affinity for the good, the true, and the beautiful.

1. *A Practical Biblical Ethic*

Sanctification should produce a highly ethical person who practices biblical ethics as naturally as he breathes. Such a practical biblical ethic would include the following:

a. Honesty in business affairs. "Provide things honest [honorable] in the sight of all men" (Rom. 12:17).

b. Truthfulness in speech. "Wherefore putting away lying, speak every man truth with his neighbour: for we are members one of another" (Eph. 4:25). Double-talk, equivocation, and suggestive talk are not a part of holiness.

c. Integrity in personal relationships. "The just man walketh in his integrity: his children are blessed after him" (Prov. 20:7).

d. Conscientiousness in workmanship. "He also that is slothful in his work is brother to him that is a great waster" (Prov. 18:99); "Not slothful in business; fervent in spirit; serving the Lord" (Rom. 12:11).

2. *Careful and Discriminating Conversational Patterns*

Holiness is the best cure for harmful and loose talking. "But speak thou the things which become sound doctrine" (Titus 2:1); "To speak evil of no man, to be no brawler, but gentle, showing all meekness to all men" (Titus 3:2). In his sermon on "The Cure of Evil-Speaking," John Wesley has a sweeping paragraph, which reads as follows:

> Avoid everything in look, gesture, word, and tone of voice, that savours of pride or self-sufficiency. Studiously avoid everything magisterial or dogmatical, everything that looks like arrogance or assuming. Beware of the most distant approach to disdain, overbearing, or contempt. With equal care avoid all appearance of anger; and though you use great plainess of speech, yet let there be no reproach, no railing accusation, no token of any warmth, but that of love. Above all, let there be no shadow of hate or ill-will, no bitterness or sourness of expression; but use the air and language of sweetness as well as gentleness, that all may appear to flow from love in the heart. And yet this sweetness need not hinder your speaking in the most serious and solemn manner.[26]

Wesley's standard of careful and discriminating patterns of conversation may seem extremely high or unpractical. But it should not be forgotten that the experience of holiness is an extremely high and yet thoroughly practical experience. At this point the words of James are appropriate: "If any man offend not in word, the same is a perfect man, and able also to bridle the whole body" (Jas. 3:2). Loose-tongued and irresponsible holiness is a contradiction. Holiness affects the tongue as much as any other part of man's being.

3. *Courtesy and Respect for Personality*

The presence of the Holy Spirit is the greatest refining influence in the world. Holiness will not automatically confer social grace and social ease. Such things are gained in experience. But the experience of holiness should produce a natural and normal sense of courtesy and respect for others. Boorish, aggressive, ill-mannered, uncouth, cocky, overbearing, loud-mouthed, flamboyant holiness is a contradiction and an embarrassment. The Apostle Peter urged the Christian to "be courteous" (I Pet. 3:8).

Holiness considers the rights of others and is kind. Holiness does not ride roughshod over weak or gullible people. Holiness does

[26]*Works*, VI, 117.

not manipulate, exploit, or take advantage of the goodwill of others. Holiness is always decent and in order. Holiness never embarrasses or humiliates another person knowingly. Holiness does not find humor at the expense of another's disability or mistakes. Holiness is the essence of courtesy, the secret of refinement, and the basis for personal appreciation.

4. *Modesty and Simplicity in Personal and Social Appearance*

Modesty and simplicity are the twin graces in the household of the holy. Thus modesty should be a trait of those who profess the experience of holiness. Modesty is essential in speech, in dress, and in personal relationships. Simplicity is needful in all manner of living.

a. Modesty of speech. Modesty in speech is revealed in many ways. Overstatement, exaggeration, self-exaltation, bitterness, cynicism, harshness, and rudeness are all enemies of modesty. Perhaps the greatest threats to modest speech are the dirty joke, the smutty story, the suggestive double-talk, the irreverent reference to God. A person's speech can be salty, fresh, invigorating, fluent, captivating, entertaining, inspiring, informative, and enlightening and still be modest.

b. Modesty of dress. Holiness does not call for prudishness in dress nor for antiquity in fashion. There is no virtue in wearing clothes which are ill-fitting, out-of-date, soiled, and wrinkled. Holiness does not place a premium on sloppiness. But holiness does call for modesty of dress in both men and women. It would be both silly and impossible to legislate the length, size, and color of wearing apparel. It is equally unwise and disastrous to ignore the length, size, and accessories which are in harmony with holiness. Any fashion which causes embarrassment, which over-accentuates the physical, which screams for attention, is out of harmony with holiness. Holiness must draw the line where modesty is threatened or ignored. Modesty of dress indicates good taste as well as vital religion.

It is admitted that legalism and self-righteousness are ever-present possibilities whenever modesty is emphasized. It should be added, however, that indifference to modesty inevitably results in the appearance of fashions which are incompatible with Christian modesty. Antinomianism is as great a threat to faith and life as is legalism. Paul was well aware of the relation between Christian profession and Christian modesty, for he exhorted that dress be modest and sober (I Tim. 2:9).

5. *Vital and Dedicated Individuality*

Holiness does not produce spiritual puppets nor ecclesiastical rubber-stamps. Holiness is creative in its operation within the heart. Holiness frees one from the inhibiting fear of public opinion. Holiness is health and wholeness and openness in one's total response to life. Holiness is freedom to act within the will of God with peace and abandon. Holiness is the power to live according to inner convictions. Holiness is the ability to look at life squarely without apology and without cringing. Holiness is the ability to transcend sin, guilt, condemnation, and temptation, to live in an atmosphere of spiritual vigor and spiritual growth.

6. *Active Opposition to Worldiness*

Worldiness may be defined as anything which reduces one's love for God and increases one's susceptibility to temptation. The character developing in holiness will be tolerant, courteous, and considerate—but it will not condone wrong. The character increasing in grace will participate in any valid activity. But it will not associate with any group or activity that seeks to make sin easy. The person who loves God completely will support any cause that aims to elevate man—but he will not aid or encourage any program that degrades man.

The reaction of the sanctified person to worldliness in any form is automatically negative. As J. A. Wood states it: "The charm of the world has been broken. The pure heart has tastes, motives, consumings, and enjoyments totally dissimilar to the worldling."[27]

In the First Letter of John, the whole concept of worldliness is stated simply and finally: "Love not the world, neither the things that are in the world. If any man love the world, the love of the Father is not in him" (I John 2:15). Holiness prays for the world, works in the world, renders service to the world. But ultimately and finally, the sanctified life is geared to and directed to a different world—the world of God's redemptive love.

7. *Affinity for the Good, the True, and the Beautiful*

The act of sanctification produces a spiritual life that has an affinity for the good, the true, and the beautiful. The affinity for goodness is both conscious and subconscious. Emil Brunner sug-

[27] *Perfect Love*, p. 129.

gests that religion should have some effect below the level of consciousness.[28] W. E. Sangster, however, suggests that some residue of corruption remains in the subconscious.[29] This residue of evil in the subconscious may rise, says Sangster, to the level of consciousness and incite the will to do evil. The person need not sin, however, because as these desires and impulses clamor into consciousness, they are met by "the cooling, cleansing Breath of God and sink away again to carry health and purity to whatever level of our mental life becomes their home."[30]

Leslie R. Marston writes that at this point "Sangster parted company with John Wesley."[31] According to Marston, Sangster's position implied "seriatim cleansings,"[32] which limits the work of the Holy Spirit to those corrupted elements that rise in consciousness. Marston states that the Scriptures adequately deal with man's pride on the levels of both the conscious and the subconscious. The biblical passages suggested by Marston are as follows:

> *For the word of God is living and active, sharper than any two-edged sword, piercing to the division of soul and spirit, of joints and marrow, and discerning the thoughts and intentions of the heart. And before him no creature is hidden, but all are open and laid bare to the eyes of him with whom we have to do* (Heb. 4:12-13, RSV).
>
> *Who can understand ["discern," RSV] his errors? cleanse thou me from secret faults [those that I cannot discern].*
>
> *Keep back thy servant also from presumptuous sins [willful, intentional]; let them not have dominion over me: then shall I be upright [blameless, RSV], and I shall be innocent from the great transgression.*
>
> *Let the words of my mouth, and the meditation of my heart, be acceptable in thy sight, O Lord, my strength, and my redeemer* (Ps. 19: 12-14).

Thus the scriptural provisions cover the sins of which a man is aware, his voluntary and deliberate sins, as well as his hidden thought patterns and his words. For all of these are the outflow of a holy character.

God purifies the character. Out of this purity of character man develops a personal character by his choices. Included in the holy character are practical biblical ethics, Christian sexual morality,

[28] *Romans*, p. 51.

[29] *Op. cit.*, p. 123.

[30] *Ibid.*

[31] Kenneth Geiger, ed., *Further Insights into Holiness* (Kansas City, Missouri: Beacon Hill Press, 1963), p. 306.

[32] *Ibid.*, p. 308.

discriminating conversation patterns, basic courtesy and respect, modesty and simplicity, sanctified individuality, a non-worldly spirit, and a love for all that is pure and good.

C. Illumination of the Spirit

The act of entire sanctification touches every aspect of man. Personal selfhood is integrated around a living presence, the Holy Spirit, and is unified by the dynamic power of love. The ground of character is purified so that holy character is developed in the decisive events of everyday life. Both personal integration and character purification are sustained by spiritual illumination. By spiritual illumination the author means the deepening of a spiritual perception, the broadening of spiritual sensitivity, and the refinement of spiritual appreciation. The spiritual illumination which comes from the crisis of entire sanctification would include the following: (1) Assurance, or the witness of the Holy Spirit; (2) a clearer apprehension of biblical truth; (3) power for service; (4) spiritual courage; (5) sensitivity of conscience; (6) elimination of carnal ambition; (7) potential for growth in grace.

1. *Assurance, or the Witness of the Holy Spirit*

To the question, "But how do you know that you are sanctified, saved from your inbred corruption?" John Wesley answered: "I can know it no otherwise than I know that I am justified. 'Hereby know we that we are of God' in either sense, 'by the Spirit that he hath given us.' We know it by the witness and by the fruit of the Spirit."[33] J. A. Wood calls the witness of the Spirit "a sweet, inward persuasion of the Spirit, that God, for Christ's sake, has either pardoned my sins and regenerated my soul, or that the blood of Jesus Christ has cleansed it from all sin."[34]

John Wesley defined the witness of the Holy Spirit in the following words:

> By the testimony of the Spirit I mean an inward impression on the soul whereby the Spirit of God immediately and directly witnesses to my spirit that I am a child of God; that Jesus Christ hath loved me and given himself for me: that all my sins are blotted out, and I, even I, am reconciled to God.[35]

[33]*Works*, XI, 420.
[34]*Perfect Love*, p. 121.
[35]*Works*, V, 124-25.

To this direct witness of the Spirit, Wesley added the indirect witness. This indirect witness was "the result of reason, or reflection on what we feel in our own souls."[36] Bishop Foster stated that the difference between the Spirit's witness in justification and in entire sanctification is not in the manner or method of witnessing, but as to *what* is witnessed to. The witness "is given in much the same way; it is the same Spirit. Their phenomena are the same, but the testimony itself differs."[37] This witness of the Holy Spirit is simply a humble and grateful assurance that God has done for man what He promised to do.

2. *Clearer Apprehension of Biblical Truth*

Since the Bible is a Book of faith and experience, it is impossible to understand it apart from faith and experience. Paul, in I Corinthians 2, states that the Spirit reveals truth to the believer. Faith leads to holiness. The experience of holiness is the most profound spiritual experience possible to man. As man's faith unfolds and as his experience deepens, his understanding of biblical teaching is heightened. On the Day of Pentecost, Peter was able to more clearly grasp the teachings of the prophet Joel (Acts 2:16-21); he saw the role of Christian redemptive history (Acts 2:22-36); he understood more fully the meaning of personal salvation (Acts 2:38-39). After Pentecost, Stephen developed a perspective which included the entire panorama of salvation (Acts 7). Jesus related man's understanding of redemptive revelation when He said: "If any man will do his will, he shall know of the doctrine" (John 7:17). The crisis of sanctification will not endow one with an automatic knowledge of technical biblical details, but it will do much to help him to understand the sweep of biblical meaning and experience.

3. *Power for Service*

Divine work cannot be done with human power. Spiritual processes depend upon spiritual initiative. After the Resurrection, Christ met with the disciples in a 40-day seminar on theology and personal evangelism. The seminar ended with a commission, a command, and a certification. The commission was: "Go ye therefore, and teach all nations, baptizing them in the name of the Father, and of the Son, and of the Holy Ghost: teaching them to observe all things whatsoever I command you; and, lo, I am with you al-

[36]*Ibid.*, p. 125.
[37]*Op. cit.*, p. 148.

way, even unto the end of the world" (Matt. 28:19-20). The command was to wait in Jerusalem for adequate power (Acts 1:4, 8). The certification was the baptism with the Holy Spirit (Acts 2:4).

The divine power of Pentecost was adequate for the divine work to be done. Three thousand people were converted before Pentecost ended (Acts 2:41). The apostles performed signs and wonders (Acts 2:43). They gained the favor of the people (Acts 2:47). They healed the sick (Acts 3). Pentecost served as a spiritual Niagara which generated power for the Early Church to the extent that they earned the reputation of turning the world upside down (Acts 17:6).

Not only is there a new *power* to witness but a new *drive* to witness. Holiness is the great springboard to evangelism, both personal and group. Pentecostal religion is an aggressive, outgoing religion.

4. *Spiritual Courage*

Courage is the ability to perform dangerous tasks, to support unpopular causes, to live by inner convictions rather than by outer conformity. Courage may be expressed by supporting a theological doctrine, by refusing to be intimidated by political authority, or by acting contrary to popular fashion.

Courage is often required to sustain a theological position or to continue to witness for Christ. When Peter and John were imprisoned and questioned before the religious leaders regarding their activities, the reply of Peter was relevant and pointed: "Be it known unto you all, and to all the people of Israel, that by the name of Jesus Christ of Nazareth, whom ye crucified, whom God raised from the dead, even by him doth this man stand here before you whole" (Acts 4:10). When they were commanded to quit preaching this same intrepid duo sounded this note of courage: "Whether it be right in the sight of God to hearken unto you more than unto God, judge ye" (Acts 4:19).

When Paul was brought to trial before Agrippa, he testified that courage was a part of the spiritual endowment he had received from Christ. The promise of Christ was that He would make Paul a minister: "Delivering thee from the people, and from the Gentiles, unto whom now I send thee" (Acts 26:17). Here is the prophetic paradox—to help people spiritually, one must be freed from fear of them and transcend them. And whether it was Peter or Paul,

Madame Guyon or John Wesley, Francis Asbury or William Booth, the life of holiness has borne the mark of quiet but firm courage.

5. *Sensitivity of Conscience*

Conscience may be defined as "the internal recognition of right and wrong as regards one's actions and motives." Paul speaks of having a conscience "void of offence toward God, and toward men" (Acts 24:16). Paul also stated that the sum total of spiritual living is "charity out of a pure heart, and of a good conscience, and of faith unfeigned" (I Tim. 1:5). Sensitivity of conscience is alertness to possible areas of sin or temptation. Sensitivity of conscience is an awareness of long-range influence as well as of short-range privilege. Sensitivity of conscience allows spiritual freedom, but it also calls for spiritual restraint. Thus Paul said that the person with a strong conscience should avoid doing anything which might cause someone with a weak conscience to fall (I Cor. 8:7).

The sanctified person is thus not an independent meteor flashing across the sky. Rather the sanctified person is a bright star on the ecclesiastical horizon. As such he is always under observation, and cannot act without regard to his impact on others. It was for this reason that Paul made the ringing declaration: "Wherefore, if meat make my brother to offend [stumble], I will eat no flesh while the world standeth, lest I make my brother to offend [stumble]" (I Cor. 8:13). Sensitivity of conscience is thus the constant openness of the soul to the leadership of the Holy Spirit.

6. *Elimination of Carnal Ambition*

A pure heart has one overwhelming desire—to serve God. Thus the state of holiness eliminates all carnal ambition. Holiness does *not* remove the creative powers nor does it cripple productive energy. A sanctified person should be able to perform better, to work harder, to be more dependable, to shoulder more responsibility, to be a more skilled craftsman than he would be if he were not sanctified. There is no conflict between holiness and legitimate ambition.

However, holiness does remove ambition based on selfish motivation. Holiness does eliminate the carnal manipulation of people for selfish purposes. Holiness removes the carnal jockeying for position and the sinful desire for adulation. Holiness dissolves the mask of pretense that covers personal ambition with spiritual activity. Holiness tears away the facade of pious demonstration that conceals self-interest. Holiness refuses to identify spiritual progress with personal promotion. Holiness rebels at buying popularity at the expense of convictions. Holiness recoils from gaining goodwill by flattery or by obeisence.

Holiness is freedom—from sin and from sinful, selfish ambition. Holiness seeks "first the kingdom of God, and his righteousness."

7. *Potential for Growth in Grace*

Holiness is health and wholeness. Holiness is unity and harmony. Holiness is purity and cleanness. Holiness is the absence of the carnal opponents of the spiritual graces. Holiness is spiritual potential unlimited. The focal point of all redemptive activity is in the growth of the holy toward perfection. Paul sums it up in the Ephesian letter as follows:

> *And he gave some, apostles; and some, prophets; and some, evangelists; and some, pastors and teachers;*
>
> *For the perfecting of the saints, for the work of the ministry, for the edifying of the body of Christ:*
>
> *Till we all come in the unity of the faith, and of the knowledge of the Son of God, unto a perfect man, unto the measure of the stature of the fulness of Christ:*
>
> *That we henceforth be no more children, tossed to and fro, and carried about with every wind of doctrine, by the sleight of men, and cunning craftiness, whereby they lie in wait to deceive;*
>
> *But speaking the truth in love, may grow up into him in all things, which is the head, even Christ* (Eph. 4:11-15).

The results of sanctification are significant in human personality. While it is impossible to prescribe every detail of the sanctified life, it is both possible and necessary to state the minimum results which occur in this experience. The results of sanctification are intensely personal, involving the integration of personality, the purification of character, and the illumination of the spiritual life. With the personality unified, the character purified, and the soul illuminated, the Christian is now prepared to grow in grace and to manifest the fruit of the Spirit.

IV. Growth in Grace

Holiness is a dynamic experience rather than a static one. The crisis of entire sanctification does not result in an automatic and irrevocable fixation of character. In a very real sense the Christian must apply himself to spiritual growth. Since the experience is not mechanical, it is impossible to present a concise formula for either receiving it or retaining it. However, there are some general directives or practices which assist the Christian in living a holy life.

A. Retaining the Experience

Writers in the area of holiness theology have suggested the following spiritual practices that help a person retain the experience of holiness. One list comes from the pen of A. M. Hills:

1. Hold on to faith and do not depend upon feeling.
2. Testify to the grace received.
3. Beware of spiritual pride.
4. "Beware," said John Wesley, "of that daughter of pride, enthusiasm [fanaticism]."
5. Welcome all new light.
6. Abstain from doubtful things.
7. Do not wonder at temptations, nor be discouraged by them.
8. Watch.
9. Work.
10. Let love keep guard over your speech and control your life.
11. Guard your thoughts.
12. Associate with holiness people.
13. Read holiness literature.
14. Beware of schism—the separation of yourselves from your brethren.
15. Live moment by moment.[38]

Another list comes from J. A. Wood:

1. You must maintain a continuous, entire consecration—a complete self-abandonment to God.
2. To retain full salvation, you must continue to believe.
3. To retain the witness of the Spirit, and continue in the light of purity, you must confess it.
4. You must live constantly in the spirit of self-denial.
5. You must live in the spirit of watchfulness.
6. You must be faithful to the teachings and drawings of the Holy Spirit.
7. You must read the Holy Scriptures daily.
8. To retain the blessing of perfect love, you must constantly aim at growing in grace.
9. You must live constantly under a sense of the presence of God.
10. You must lead a life of prayer.
11. You must labor faithfully for the salvation of sinners.
12. To retain it, you must oppose sin of every name and kind, without any compromise.[39]

[38]*Holiness and Power,* pp. 345-65.
[39]*Perfect Love,* pp. 227-31.

B. The Means of Christian Growth

The means of Christian growth are both human and divine. Edward F. Walker lists the divine causes of man's sanctification as follows:

First Cause: The Holy Father
Procuring Cause: The Holy Son
Efficient Cause: The Holy Spirit
Determining Cause: The Divine Will
Meritorious Cause: The Sacrifice of Jesus
Instrumental Cause: The Truth of God
Conditional Cause: Faith in Christ[40]

The human means of growing toward the stature of Christ are clearly defined in the Pauline writings:

1. A surrender of the will. All inner resistance to God's will must be shattered. While one will always retain his "self" or his "self-hood," the carnal self, or the self-centered self must die (Rom. 6:6; 12:1; II Cor. 7:1; Gal. 5:24; Eph. 5:26; and I Thess. 5:23).
2. Cleansing of the inner nature (Eph. 5:24-26; II Cor. 7:1).
3. Renewing of the mind (Rom. 12:1-2).
4. Walking in the Spirit (Gal. 5:24-25).
5. Being filled with the Spirit (Eph. 5:18).
6. Discipline of the body (Rom. 12:1).

When the divine and the human cooperate, man grows in holiness.

C. Marks of a Maturing Christian

A fine summary of the marks of the maturing Christian is presented by Hollis F. Abbott in *The Word and the Doctrine.* Abbott's list contains the following features:

1. A mature Christian is one who walks in the Spirit (Rom. 8:4; Gal. 5:16, 25).
2. A mature Christian is one in whom the image of Christ is distinctly seen (Rom. 8:29; II Cor. 3:18).
3. A mature Christian is one who is habitually victorious (II Cor. 2:14-16).
4. A mature Christian is one in whom an ungrieved Spirit is fulfilling His ministry and bearing His fruit in an ever-increasing measure (Eph. 4:30-32; Gal. 5:22-23).
5. A mature Christian has the mind of Christ (Phil. 2:5-8).[41]

[40] *Op. cit.,* pp. 89-90.

[41] "Christian Maturity," *The Word and the Doctrine,* ed. Kenneth E. Geiger (Kansas City: Beacon Hill Press, 1965), pp. 295-97.

Summary

Such is the process of holiness in man. Holiness begins when man responds to the grace of God in true repentance, which is followed by regeneration. Holiness is initiated in regeneration and imparted fully in entire sanctification. But entire sanctification is not the grand climax to Christian growth. It is a landmark, not a monument. The person made holy in a second crisis grows and develops toward Christlikeness. Thus holiness is the Christlikeness that the Holy Spirit can produce in human personality. The experience of holiness is a spiritual pilgrimage that begins in the faint groping of a soul toward God and ends in the blazing glory of God's presence. Holiness lifts man out of sin and points him toward a "topless heaven" where the human personality will develop endlessly.

Bibliography

COMMENTARIES

Alford, Henry. *The Greek Testament.* 4 vols. Cambridge: Deighton, Bell and Co., 1868.

Barclay, William. *The Acts of the Apostles.* "The Daily Study Bible." Philadelphia: The Westminster Press, 1953.

———. *The Letter to the Romans.* "The Daily Study Bible." Philadelphia: The Westminster Press, 1955.

Beacon Bible Commentary. 10 vols. Kansas City: Beacon Hill Press of Kansas City, 1964-69.

Blaiklock, E. M. *The Acts of the Apostles: An Historical Commentary.* Grand Rapids, Mich.: Wm. B. Eerdmans Publishing Co., 1959.

Blunt, A. W. F. *The Acts of the Apostles.* Oxford: The Clarendon Press, 1923.

———. *The Epistle of Paul to the Galatians.* Oxford: The Clarendon Press, 1960.

Bring, Ragnar. *Commentary on Galatians.* Philadelphia: Muhlenberg Press, 1961.

Bruce, F. F. *The Acts of the Apostles.* "The Tyndale Bible Commentaries." Grand Rapids, Mich.: Wm. B. Eerdmans Publishing Co., 1960.

———. *Commentary on the Book of the Acts.* "The Tyndale Bible Commentaries." Grand Rapids, Mich.: Wm. B. Eerdmans Publishing Co., 1955.

Calvin, John. *Commentaries on the Epistles of Paul to the Galatians and Ephesians.* Translated by William Pringle. Edinburgh: T. Constable, 1854.

———. *Commentary upon the Acts of the Apostles.* 2 vols. Edinburgh: Calvin Translation Society, 1844.

Carter, Charles W., and Earle, Ralph. *The Acts of the Apostles.* "The Evangelical Commentary." Grand Rapids, Mich.: Zondervan Publishing House, 1959.

Carver, William Owen. *The Acts of the Apostles.* Nashville: Broadman Press, 1916.

Clarke, Adam. *The New Testament of Our Lord and Savior Jesus Christ.* 6 vols. New York: Methodist Book Concern, n.d.

Cremer, Hermann. *Biblio-Theological Lexicon of New Testament Greek.* Translated by William Urwick. Edinburgh: T. and T. Clark, 1962.

Dale, R. W. *The Epistle to the Ephesians.* London: Hodder and Stoughton, 1938.

Dummelow, J. R., ed. *A Commentary on the Holy Bible.* New York: The Macmillan Company, 1943.

Eadie, John. *Commentary on the Epistle of Paul to the Galatians.* Rev. ed. Grand Rapids, Mich.: Zondervan Publishing House, n.d.

Ellicott, Charles J. *A Critical and Grammatical Commentary on St. Paul's Epistle to the Ephesians.* Andover: Warren F. Draper, 1884.

———. *Commentary on St. Paul's Epistles to the Thessalonians.* Boston: Gould and Lincoln, 1865.

Ellicott, Charles John, ed. *A New Testament Commentay for English Readers.* 3 vols. London: Cassell and Co., 1897.

Erdman, Charles R. *The Epistle of Paul to the Ephesians.* Philadelphia: The Westminster Press, 1931.

Foakes-Jackson, F. J. *The Acts of the Apostles.* New York: Harper and Brothers, 1931.

Godbey, W. B. *Commentary on the New Testament.* Cincinnati, Ohio: M. W. Knapp, 1898.

Henry, Matthew. *Commentary on the Whole Bible.* 6 vols. New York: Fleming H. Revell, n.d.

Koehler, Joh. Ph. *The Epistle of Paul to the Galatians.* Translated by E. E. Sauer. Milwaukee, Wis.: Northwestern Publishing Co., 1957.

Lasker, R. V. G. *The Gospel According to St. Matthew.* London: The Tyndale Press, 1961.

Lenski, R. C. H. *St. Paul's Epistle to the Romans.* Columbus, Ohio: Wartburg Press, 1945.

———. *The Interpretation of St. Paul's Epistles to the Colossians, to the Thessalonians, to Timothy, to Titus, and to Philemon.* Columbus, Ohio: The Wartburg Press, 1956.

———. *The Interpretation of St. Paul's Epistle to the Galatians, to the Ephesians, and to the Philippians.* Minneapolis, Minn.: Augsburg Publishing House, 1961.

Luther, Martin. *Commentary on the Sermon on the Mount.* Translated by Charles A. Hay. Philadelphia: Lutheran Publication Society, 1892.

McLaughlin, G. A. *Commentary on the Acts of the Apostles.* Chicago: The Christian Witness Co., 1915.

M'Neile, Alan Hugh. *The Gospel According to Matthew.* London: Macmillan and Co., 1961.

Meyer, F. B. *Ephesians: A Devotional Commentary.* Fort Washington, Pa.: Christian Literature Crusade, 1953.

Meyer, H. A. W. *The Acts of the Apostles.* New York: Funk and Wagnalls, 1884.

Morris, Leon. *The Epistles of Paul to the Thessalonians.* Grand Rapids, Mich.: Wm. B. Eerdmans Publishing Co., 1956.

———. *The First and Second Epistles to the Thessalonians.* Grand Rapids, Mich.: Wm. B. Eerdmans Publishing Co., 1959.

Morrison, James. *A Practical Commentary on the Gospel According to Mark.* London: Hodder and Stoughton, 1900.

Nicoll, W. Robertson, ed. *The Expositor's Greek New Testament.* Grand Rapids, Mich.: Wm. B. Eerdmans Publishing Co., n.d.

Orchard, Don B., ed. *A Catholic Commentary on Holy Scripture.* New York: Thomas Nelson and Sons, 1953.

Philippi, Friedrich A. *Commentary on St. Paul's Epistle to the Romans.* Edinburgh: T. and T. Clark, 1878.

Rackham, Richard B. *The Acts of the Apostles.* 14th ed. London: Methuen and Company, 1951.

Ricciotti, Giuseppi. *The Acts of the Apostles.* Milwaukee: The Bruce Publishing Co., 1958.

Ridderbas, Herman N. *The Epistles of Paul to the Churches of Galatia.* Grand Rapids, Mich.: Wm. B. Eerdmans Publishing Co., 1953.

Strauss, Lehman. *Galatians and Ephesians.* New York: Loizeaux Brothers, 1957.

Stuart, Moses. *A Commentary on the Epistle to the Hebrews.* Andover, Mass.: Warren F. Draper, 1876.

Synge, F. C. *St. Paul's Epistle to the Ephesians.* London: Society for Promoting Christian Knowledge, 1941.

Tasker, R. V. G. *The Gospel According to St. Matthew.* London: The Tyndale Press, 1961.

Thomas, David. *Acts of the Apostles.* Grand Rapids, Mich.: Baker Book House, 1956.

Van Ryn, August. *Acts of the Apostles.* New York: Loizeaux Brothers, 1961.

Vincent, Marvin R. *Word Studies in the New Testament.* 4 vols. Grand Rapids, Mich.: Wm. B. Eerdmans Publishing Co., 1940.

Walvoord, John F. *The Thessalonian Epistles.* Findlay, Ohio: Dunham Publishing Co., 1955.

Wesley, John. *Explanatory Notes upon the New Testament.* London: Epworth Press, 1941 (reprint).

Westcott, B. F. *The Gospel According to St. John.* London: John Murray, 1896.

Westcott, Brooke Foss. *Saint Paul's Epistle to the Ephesians.* Grand Rapids, Mich.: Wm. B. Eerdmans Publishing Co., n.d.

Whedon, D. D. *Commentary on the Gospels, Matthew-Mark.* New York: Carlton and Porter, 1860.

———. *Commentary on the New Testament, I Corinthians—II Timothy.* New York: Eaton and Mains, 1875.

———, ed. *Commentary on the Old Testament.* 9 vols. New York: Eaton and Mains, 1873-1907.

Wiley, H. Orton. *The Epistle to the Hebrews.* Kansas City: Beacon Hill Press, 1959.

OTHER BOOKS

Abbott-Smith, G. *A Manual Greek Lexicon of the New Testament.* 3rd ed. New York: Charles Scribner's Sons, 1936.

Analytical Greek Lexicon, The. New York: Harper and Brothers, n.d.

Arndt, William F., and Gingrich, Wilbur. *A Greek-English Lexicon of the New Testament.* A translation and adaptation of Walter Bauer's *Griechisch-Deutsches Wörterbuch zu den Schriften des Neuen Testament und der übrigen urchristlicken Literatur.* 4th rev. and augmented ed., 1952. Chicago: University of Chicago Press, 1957.

Arthur, William. *The Tongue of Fire.* New York: Harper and Brothers, 1880.

Assemblies Shorter Catechism, The. Perth, Scotland, 1765.

Aulen, Gustaf. *The Faith of the Christian Church.* Translated by Eric H. Wahlstrom. Philadelphia: The Muhlenberg Press, 1960.

Aumann, Jordan, and Greenstock, David L. *The Meaning of Christian Perfection.* St. Louis: B. Herder and Company, 1956.

Baab, Otto J. *The Theology of the Old Testament.* New York: Abingdon-Cokesbury Press, 1949.

Baker, Eric. *The Neglected Factor.* New York: Abingdon Press, 1963.

Barclay, William. *A New Testament Word Book.* London: SCM Press, 1955.

———. *Flesh and Spirit.* Nashville: Abingdon Press, 1962.

Barth, Karl. *Church Dogmatics.* Edinburgh: T. and T. Clark, 1957-62.

Barton, George A. *The Religion of Israel.* Philadelphia: University of Pennsylvania Press, 1928.

———. *Studies in New Testament Christianity.* Philadelphia: University of Pennsylvania Press, 1928.

Berkouwer, G. C. *Faith and Sanctification.* Grand Rapids, Mich.: Wm. B. Eerdmans Publishing Co., 1952.

Bonhoeffer, Dietrich. *The Cost of Discipleship.* 2nd ed. New York: The Macmillan Co., 1959.

Bowman, John Wick, and Lapp, Roland W. *The Gospel from the Mount.* Philadelphia: The Westminster Press, 1957.

Bowne, Borden Parker. *Studies in Christianity.* Boston: Houghton Mifflin Company, 1909.

Bruce, A. B. *The Training of the Twelve.* New York: Richard R. Smith, 1930.

Brunner, Emil. *Faith, Hope, and Love.* Philadelphia: The Westminster Press, 1956.

———. *The Christian Doctrine of God.* Translated by Olive Wyon. Philadelphia: The Westminster Press, 1950.

Burrows, Millar. *An Outline of Biblical Theology.* Philadelphia: The Westminster Press, 1946.

Burton, Ernest DeWitt, *Syntax of the Moods and Tenses in New Testament Greek.* 3rd ed. Grand Rapids, Mich.: Kregel Publications, 1955.

Carradine, Beverly. *Golden Sheaves.* Boston: J. Gill, 1901.

Carruthers, S. W. *Three Hundred Years of the Westminster Shorter Catechism.* Fredericton, N.B., Can.: University of New Brunswick, 1957.

Cattell, Everett Lewis. *The Spirit of Holiness.* Grand Rapids, Mich.: Wm. B. Eerdmans Publishing Co., 1963.

Chadwick, Samuel. *The Call to Christian Perfection.* Kansas City: Beacon Hill Press, 1943.

Chapman, J. B. *Holiness Triumphant.* Kansas City: Beacon Hill Press, 1946.

Chapman, James B. *The Terminology of Holiness.* Kansas City: Beacon Hill Press, 1947.

Christman, D. Grant. *Evangelistic Comments on the Acts of the Apostles.* Endicott, N.Y.: Eastern Bible Institute, 1923.

Clark, Duggan. *The Offices of the Holy Spirit.* Worcester, England: n.p., 1878.

Clarkson, John F.; Edwards, John H.; Kelly, William J.; and others, ed. and trans. *The Church Teaches.* St. Louis: B. Herder Book Co., 1955.

Cook, Thomas. *New Testament Holiness.* London: Epworth Press, 1902.

Corlett, D. Shelby. *The Meaning of Holiness.* Kansas City: Beacon Hill Press, 1944.

Cowles, Henry. *Luke: General History and Acts of the Apostles.* New York: D. Appleton and Co., 1881.

Cox, Norman W., ed. *Encyclopedia of Southern Baptists.* 2 vols. Nashville: Broadman Press, 1958.

Craig, Clarence Tucker. *The Beginning of Christianity.* New York: Abingdon-Cokesbury Press, 1943.

Curtis, Olin A. *The Christian Faith.* New York: Eaton and Mains, 1905.

Davidson, A. B. *Ezekiel.* Cambridge: Cambridge University Press, 1892.

———. *The Theology of the Old Testament.* New York: Charles Scribner's Sons, 1928.

Davidson, Robert F. *Rudolf Otto's Interpretation of Religion.* Princeton, N.J.: Princeton University Press, 1947.

Davies, D. R. *Secular Illustration or Christian Realism.* London: Latimer House, Ltd., 1942.

Dewar, Lindsay. *The Holy Spirit and Modern Thought.* London: A. R. Mowbray and Co., 1959.

De Wolf, L. Harold. *A Theology of the Living Church.* Rev. ed. New York: Harper and Brothers, 1960.

Dobschütz, Ernst von. *Christian Life in the Primitive Church.* Translated by George Bremmer; edited by W. D. Morrison. New York: G. P. Putnam and Sons, 1904.

Dodd, C. H. *The Apostolic Preaching and Its Developments.* New York: Harper and Brothers, 1936.

Eichrodt, Walter. *Theology of the Old Testament.* Translated by J. A. Baker. 2 vols. Philadelphia: Westminster Press, 1961.

Fairchild, James H. *Elements of Theology.* Oberlin, Ohio: Edward J. Goodrich, 1892.

Ferré, Nels. *The Christian Understanding of God.* New York: Harper and Brothers, 1957.

Finney, Charles G. *Lectures on Systematic Theology.* London: William Legg and Co. 1851.

Fitch, William. *The Beatitudes of Jesus.* Grand Rapids, Mich.: Wm. B. Eerdmans Publishing Co., 1961.

Fletcher, John. *The Works of the Rev. John Fletcher.* London: John Mason, 1839.

Flew, R. N. *The Idea of Perfection in Christian Theology.* London: Oxford University Press, 1934.

Foakes-Jackson, F. J., and Lake, Kirsopp, eds. *The Beginnings of Christianity.* London: Macmillan and Co., 1920-33.

Foster, R. S. *Christian Purity.* New York: Hunt and Eaton, 1869.

Fox, Emmet. *The Sermon on the Mount.* New York: Grosset and Dunlap, 1934.

Frazer, J. G. *The Golden Bough.* 12 vols. London: The Macmillan Company, 1900.

Geiger, Kenneth, ed. *The Word and the Doctrine.* Kansas City: Beacon Hill Press, 1965.

———. *Further Insights into Holiness.* Kansas City: Beacon Hill Press, of Kansas City, 1968.

Girgensohn, Herbert. *Teaching Luther's Catechism.* Translated by John W. Doberstein. Philadelphia: Muhlenberg Press, 1969.

Grant, Frederick C. *An Introduction to New Testament Thought.* New York: Abingdon-Cokesbury Press, 1950.

Greathouse, William M. *The Fullness of the Spirit.* Kansas City: Nazarene Publishing House, 1958.

Hadley, James. *A Greek Grammar for Schools and Colleges.* New York: D. Appleton and Co., 1877.

Harnack, Adolf. *The Acts of the Apostles.* Translated by J. R. Wilkinson. London: Williams and Norgate, 1909.

———. *What Is Christianity?* Translated by Thomas B. Saunders. 2nd ed. rev. New York: G. P. Putnam and Sons, 1903.

Harrison, Everett F.; Bromiley, Geoffrey; and Henry, Carl F. H. *Baker's Dictionary of Theology.* Grand Rapids, Mich.: Baker Book House, 1960.

Henry, Carl F. H., ed. *Basic Christian Doctrines.* New York: Holt, Rinehart and Winston, 1962.

———, ed. *Christian Faith and Modern Theology.* New York: Channel Press, 1964.

Hills, A. M. *Fundamental Christian Theology.* 2 vols. Pasadena, California: C. J. Kinne, 1932.

———. *Holiness and Power.* Cincinnati, Ohio: M. W. Knapp, 1897.

Hodge, A. A., and Hodge, J. A. *Theology of the Shorter Catechism.* New York: A. C. Armstrong and Company, 1888.

Hodge, Charles. *Systematic Theology.* 3 vols. New York: Charles Scribner and Company, 1871-72.

Hodgson, Leonard. *The Doctrine of the Atonement.* New York: Charles Scribner's Sons, 1951.

Horton, Walter M. *Christian Theology, An Ecumenical Approach.* New York: Harper and Brothers, 1955.

———. *Realistic Theology.* New York: Harper and Brothers, 1934.

Hughes, Philip. *The Catholic Faith in Practice.* Wilkes-Barre, Pa.: 1965.

Hunter, A. M. *A Pattern for Life.* Philadelphia: The Westminster Press, 1953.

Jacob, Edmond. *Theology of the Old Testament.* Translated by A. W. Heathcote and Philip J. Allcock. London: Hodder and Stoughton, 1938.

Jacobus, Melancthon W. *A New Standard Bible Dictionary.* New York; Funk and Wagnalls Company, 1936.

Jessop, Harry E. *Foundations of Doctrine.* Kansas City: Nazarene Publishing House, 1940.

Josephus, Flavius. *The Works of Josephus: Comprising the Antiquities of the Jews.* Translated by William Whiston. Hartford, Conn.: The S. S. Scranton Co., 1905.

Keen, A. S. *Pentecostal Papers.* Cincinnati, Ohio: M. W. Knapp, 1896.

King, Peter. *An Inquiry into the Constitution, Discipline, Unity and Worship of the Primitive Church.* New York: G. Lane and P. P. Sanford, 1841.

Kittel, Gerhard. *Bible Key Words,* from *Theologisches Wörterbuch zum Neuen Testament.* Translated by J. R. Coates. 4 vols. New York: Harper and Brothers, 1951.

———. *Theological Dictionary of the New Testament.* Translated by G. W. Bromiley. 5 vols. Grand Rapids, Mich.: Wm. B. Eerdmans Publishing Co., 1964.

Kitts, John, ed. *The Cyclopedia of Biblical Literature.* New York: Hurst and Company, n.d.

Knight, George A. F. *A Christian Theology of the Old Testament.* Richmond, Va.: John Knox Press, 1959.

Knudson, Albert C. *The Religious Teaching of the Old Testament.* New York: The Abingdon Press, 1918.

Köhler, Ludwig. *Old Testament Theology.* Translated by A. S. Todd. Philadelphia: New Westminster Press, 1957.

Kuyper, Abraham. *The Work of the Holy Spirit.* Translated by Henri De Vries. New York: Funk and Wagnalls, 1900.

Lehman, Chester K. *The Holy Spirit and the Holy Life.* Scottdale, Pa.: Herald Press, 1959.

Lindsay, A. D., *The Moral Teaching of Jesus.* New York: Harper and Brothers, 1937.

Lindstrom, Harald. *Wesley and Sanctification.* London: The Epworth Press, 1950.

Lloyd-Jones, D. Martyn. *Studies in the Sermon on the Mount.* 2 vols. Grand Rapids, Mich.: Wm. B. Eerdmans Publishing Co., 1960.

Lowlson, Clifford W. *Moravian and Methodist.* London: The Epworth Press, 1957.

Lowrey, Asbury. *Possibilities of Grace.* Chicago: The Christian Witness Company, 1884.

Lueker, E. L., ed. *Lutheran Cyclopedia.* St. Louis: Concordia Publishing House, 1954.

M'Clintock, John, and Strong, James. *Cyclopedia of Biblical, Theological, and Ecclesiastical Literature.* 10 vols. New York: Harper and Brothers, 1874-81.

Machen, J. Gresham. *New Testament Greek for Beginners.* New York: The Macmillan Co., 1923.

MacKintosh, H. R. *The Doctrine of the Person of Christ.* Edinburgh: T. and T. Clark, 1912.

Mahan, Asa. *The Baptism of the Holy Ghost.* New York: W. C. Palmer, 1876.

Manson, T. W. *The Teaching of Jesus.* Cambridge: The University Press, 1931.

Manual of the Church of the Nazarene. Kansas City: Nazarene Publishing House, 1968.

Miller, Howard V. *The Sin Problem.* Kansas City: Beacon Hill Press, 1947.

Montefiore, C. G. *The Synoptic Gospels.* 2 vols. London: Macmillan and Co., 1924.

Morley, John V. *Voltaire.* London: Macmillan and Co., 1923.

Mosheim, John L. *An Ecclesiastical History, Ancient and Modern.* Translated by Archibald Maclaine. Cincinnati: Applegate and Co., 1858.

Moulton, James H., and Milligan, George. *The Vocabulary of the Greek Testament.* London: Hodder and Stoughton, 1930.

Murray, Andrew. *The Holiest of All.* New York: Fleming H. Revell Co., 1894.

Niebuhr, Reinhold. *The Nature and Destiny of Man.* 2 vols. New York: Charles Scribner's Sons, 1943.

Nielson, John B. *In Christ.* Kansas City: Beacon Hill Press, 1960.

Nunn, H. P. V. *A Short Syntax of New Testament Greek.* Cambridge: The University Press, 1956.

Nygren, Anders. *Agape and Eros.* Translated by Philip S. Watson. Philadelphia: The Westminster Press, 1953.

Oehler, Gustav. *Theology of the Old Testament.* Rev. ed. Grand Rapids, Mich.: Zondervan Publishing House, n.d.

Oesterley, W. O. E., and Robinson, Theodore H. *Hebrew Religion.* New York: The Macmillan Company, 1930.

Otto, Rudolf. *The Idea of the Holy.* Translated by John W. Harvey. New York: Oxford University Press, 1958.

Pache, René. *The Person and Work of the Holy Spirit.* Translated by J. D. Emerson. Chicago: Moody Press, 1954.

Pauck, Wilhelm, ed. *Luther: Lectures on Romans* (The Library of Christian Classics). Philadelphia: The Westminster Press, 1964.

Paxson, Ruth. *Called unto Holiness.* London: Marshall, Morgan and Scott, 1936.

———. *The Wealth, Walk and Warfare of the Christian.* Westwood, N.J.: Fleming H. Revell Co., 1939.

Payne, J. Barton. *The Theology of the Old Testament.* Grand Rapids, Mich.: Zondervan Publishing House, 1962.

Pierson, Arthur T. *Forward Movements of the Last Half Century.* New York: Funk and Wagnalls, 1900.

———. *The Heart of the Gospel.* London: Passmore and Alabaster, 1892.

Pope, William Burt. *A Compendium of Christian Theology.* 3 vols. New York: Phillips and Hunt, 1881.

Purkiser, W. T. *Conflicting Concepts of Holiness.* Kansas City: Beacon Hill Press, 1953.

———. *Sanctification and Its Synonyms.* Kansas City: Beacon Hill Press, 1961.

Ralston, Thomas N. *Elements of Divinity.* New York: Abingdon-Cokesbury Press, 1924.

Rayle, Robert C. *Scriptural Holiness.* New York: Comet Press Books, 1958.

Renan, Ernst. *The History of the Origin of Christianity.* London: Mattueson and Co., 1890.

Richardson, Alan, *An Introduction to the Theology of the New Testament.* New York: Harper and Row, 1958.

Robertson, A. T. *A Grammar of the Greek New Testament in the Light of Historical Research.* 4th ed. Nashville: The Broadman Press, 1923.

Ruth, C. W. *Entire Sanctification.* Chicago: The Christian Witness Co., 1903.

Ryle, J. C. *Holiness.* Westwood, N.J.: Fleming H. Revell Co., n.d.

Sangster, W. E. *The Path to Perfection.* New York: Abingdon-Cokesbury, 1943.

Schechter, Solomon. *Some Aspects of Rabbinic Theology.* New York: The Macmillan Co., 1910.

Scott, E. F. *The Spirit in the New Testament.* London: Hodder and Stoughton, 1923.

Scott, E. K. *The Kingdom of God.* New York: The Macmillan Co., 1931.

Smith, C. Ryder. *Bible Doctrine of Man.* London: Epworth Press, 1954.

Smith, George D., ed. *The Teaching of the Catholic Church.* London: Burns and Oates, 1952.

Smith, W. Robertson. *Religion of the Semites.* London: Adamond Charles Black, 1907.

Snaith, Norman H. *The Distinctive Ideas of the Old Testament.* London: The Epworth Press, 1950.

Sockman, Ralph W. *The Higher Happiness.* New York: Abingdon-Cokesbury Press, 1950.

Stagg, Frank. *The Book of Acts.* Nashville: Broadman Press, 1955.

———. *New Testament Theology.* Nashville: Broadman Press, 1962.

Steele, Daniel. *The Gospel of the Comforter.* Boston: The Christian Witness Co., 1904.

———. *Milestone Papers.* New York: Phillips and Hunt, 1878.

———. Steele's Answers. Edited by E. L. Kletzing. Chicago: The Christian Witness Co., 1912.

Stevens, George Barker. *The Theology of the New Testament.* New York: Charles Scribner's Sons, 1936.

Stevensen, Herbert F. *Keswick's Authentic Voice.* Grand Rapids, Mich.: Zondervan Publishing House, 1959.

Strong, A. H. *Systematic Theology.* 3 vols. Philadelphia: Griffith and Roland Press, 1907.

Taylor, J. Paul. *Holiness, the Finished Foundation.* Winona Lake, Ind.: Light and Life Press, 1963.

Taylor, Richard S. *A Right Conception of Sin.* Kansas City: Nazarene Publishing House, 1939.

Telford, John, ed. *The Letters of the Rev. John Wesley.* 8 vols. London: The Epworth Press, 1931.

Temple, William. *Basic Conviction.* New York: Harper and Brothers, 1936.

———. *Readings in St. John's Gospel.* London: Macmillan and Co., 1959.

Tennant, F. R. *The Concept of Sin.* Cambridge: University Press, 1912.

Thayer, Joseph H. *A Greek-English Lexicon of the New Testament.* New York: American Book Co., 1886.

Thelan, Mary. *Man as Sinner.* New York: King's Crown Press, 1946.

Tillich, Paul. *Biblical Religion and the Search for Ultimate Reality.* Chicago: University of Chicago Press, 1955.

———. *The Protestant Era.* Chicago: University of Chicago Press, 1948.

———. *Systematic Theology.* 3 vols. Chicago: University of Chicago Press, 1957.

Toynbee, Arnold. *Christianity Among the Religions of the World.* New York: Charles Scribner's Sons, 1957.

Tozer, A. W. *The Knowledge of the Holy.* New York: Harper and Brothers, 1961.

Trench, Richard C. *Synonyms of the New Testament.* Grand Rapids, Mich.: Wm. B. Eerdmans Publishing Co., 1958.

Turner, George Allen. *The More Excellent Way.* Winona Lake, Ind.: Light and Life Press, 1952.

———. *The Vision Which Transforms.* Kansas City: Beacon Hill Press, 1964.

Upham, T. C. *Principles of the Interior or Hidden Life.* 8th ed. New York: Harper and Brothers, 1859.

Von Rad, Gerhard. *Old Testament Theology.* Translated by D. M. G. Stalker. New York: Harper and Brothers, 1962.

Vriezen, T. C. *An Outline of Old Testament Theology.* Newton, Mass.: Charles T. Branford Co., 1960.

Walvoord, John W. *Doctrine of the Holy Spirit.* 3rd ed. Findlay, Ohio: Dunham Publishing Co., 1958.

Watson, Richard. *Theological Institutes.* 30th ed. 2 vols. New York: Phillips and Hunt, 1865.

Webb, C. C. J. *God and Personality.* London: George Allen and Unwin, Ltd., 1918.

Weidmer, Revere F. *Biblical Theology of the Old Testament.* Minneapolis: Augustana Book Co., n.d.

Wells, Donald A. *God, Man, and the Thinker.* New York: Random House, 1962.

Wenger, John Christian, ed. *The Complete Writings of Menno Simons.* Scottdale, Pa.: The Herald Press, 1956.

———. *Glimpses of Mennonite History and Doctrine.* Scottdale, Pa.: The Herald Press, 1949.

Wernlick, John R. *Count Zinzendorf.* New York: Abingdon Press, 1957.

Wesley, John. *The Works of John Wesley.* 14 vols. Kansas City: Nazarene Publishing House, n.d. (From the authorized edition published by the Wesleyan Conference office in London, England, in 1872.)

Wiley, H. Orton. *Christian Theology.* 3 vols. Kansas City: Beacon Hill Press, 1940-52.

Wiley, H. Orton, and Culbertson, Paul T. *Introduction to Christian Theology.* Kansas City: Beacon Hill Press, 1949.

Williams, R. T. *Temptation: A Neglected Theme.* Kansas City: Nazarene Publishing House, 1920.

Winchester, Olive M., and Price, Ross E. *Crisis Experience in the Greek New Testament.* Kansas City: Beacon Hill Press, 1953.

Winer, G. B. *A Treatise on the Grammar of New Testament Greek.* Edinburgh: T. and T. Clark, 1870.

Wood, John A. *Mistakes Respecting Christian Holiness.* Chicago: The Christian Witness Co., 1905.

———. *Perfect Love.* North Attleboro, Mass.: J. A. Wood, Publisher, 1886.

———. *Purity and Maturity.* Chicago: The Christian Witness Co., 1913.

Woodbridge, Charles J. *Standing on the Promises.* Chicago: Moody Press, 1947.

Wright, G. Ernest, and Fuller, Reginald H. *The Book of the Acts of God.* London: Gerald Duckworth and Co., 1960.

Wuest, Kenneth S. *Treasures from the Greek New Testament.* Grand Rapids, Mich.: Wm. B. Eerdmans Publishing Co., 1941.

Scripture Index